PINTER AT 70

CASEBOOKS ON MODERN DRAMATISTS
Kimball King, General Editor

PINTER AT 70
A Casebook

edited by
Lois Gordon

ROUTLEDGE
NEW YORK and LONDON

Published in 2001 by
Routledge
29 West 35th Street
New York, NY 10001

Published in Great Britain by
Routledge
11 New Fetter Lane
London EC4P 4EE

Routledge is an imprint of the Taylor & Francis Group.
Copyright © 2001 by Routledge

Printed in the United States of America on acid-free paper.

10 9 8 7 6 5 4 3 2 1

Library of Congress Cataloging-in-Publication Data

Pinter at 70 : a casebook / edited by Lois Gordon.
     p. cm. -- (Casebooks on modern dramatists ; v. 30)
     Rev. ed. of: Harold Pinter / edited by Lois Gordon.
     Includes bibliographical references and index.
     ISBN 0-415-93630-6 (alk. paper)
     1. Pinter, Harold, 1930---Criticism and interpretation. I. Title: Pinter at seventy. II.
Gordon, Lois G. III. Harold Pinter. IV. Series.

PR6066.I53 Z6664 2001
822'.914--dc21

                                                                        2001018094

CONTENTS

GENERAL EDITOR'S NOTE

Harold Pinter may well be the most respected writer for the stage in the world today. Some consider Samuel Beckett a greater artist, but Pinter is still a relatively young man and is at the peak of his powers. Beckett read all of Pinter's scripts and made suggestions on them, and the latter considers Beckett his master. Yet Pinter, more than anyone else in this century, has changed our expectations for stage language and has made more traditional treatments of stage space, action, and language seem ridiculous and pretentious. He is an enigma to critics. Some consider him an absurdist (the Beckett influence), others an existentialist, and some the ultimate naturalist. Pinter is a genuine theater person. He has been an actor, writer, and director and is almost totally involved in the world of the stage. Perhaps it is the tension between Pinter's use of the absurdist tradition, with its baffling non sequiturs and purposeless activities, and his naturalistic use of language, dialect, and precise, believable detail that gives Pinter his unique hold on drama. His earliest play, *The Room*, was performed in 1957, but it was *The Homecoming*, ten years later, that brought Pinter worldwide recognition. The proliferation of scholarship concerning his playwriting in the past decade is unequaled. He may not be as brilliant as Stoppard, as entertaining as the Shaffers, or as startling as Bond. Yet he is the "Shakespeare" of his age, the central figure in the New Wave.

Professor Lois Gordon edited the hardback volume *Harold Pinter: A Casebook*, and she has re-edited it for this paperback version. Gordon is the perfect choice for editor because she was the first American to write a book-length study of Harold Pinter's works in 1969. In the summer of 2000 Pinter turned seventy years old. A special conference was held in London to honor this event. A high point of the conference was Pinter's reading aloud all of the voices of his new play, *Celebration* (2000). Professor Gordon has added four new essays to the volume, including a summary of Pinter's achievement and original essays by Ann C. Hall, Mel Gussow, and Michael Billington. It is appropriate that a Pinter festival held in New York City in July 2001 should be so closely followed by this up-to-date critical volume.

Kimball King

PREFACE TO THE SECOND EDITION

I've always been aware that my characters tend to use words not to express what they think or feel but to disguise what they think or feel, to mask their actual intentions, so that words are acting as a masquerade, a veil, a web, or used as weapons to undermine or to terrorise. . . . In the world in which we live, words are as often employed to distort or to deceive or to manipulate as they are to convey actual and direct meaning. So that a substantial body of our language is essentially corrupt. It has become a language of lies. . . . When words are used with a fearless and rigorous respect for their real meaning, the users tend to be rewarded with persecution, torture and death.

--Pinter (1995)

This volume is being updated on the occasion of Harold Pinter's seventieth birthday. Widely acknowledged as one of the great dramatists of our age, Pinter is also one of our most politically active artists, and, in many ways, his life and work parallel one another. As a "citizen of the world," he has long publically protested injustices around the globe. When he engages his creative muse, a similar impulse emerges. The abuse of power, he would seem to be saying, in any of its manifestations--in personal relationships or in matters of state--is all too prevalent and all too devastating.

Perhaps predictably, as Pinter's work is increasingly performed throughout the world gathering new accolades for its author, and the "citizen" continues to remonstrate against oppression, the man is subject to the extremes of idolatry and criticism. "I have the feeling," he has said, "that lots of people have wanted to punch me in the face for a very long time." The one-time "Bollinger Bolshevik" pickets outside 10 Downing Street or in front of the House of Commons and the next day finds himself misquoted on the front pages of the London press. His brilliant work, needless to say, continues to invite serious, laudatory commentary. On occasion, a newswriter is also inspired to a turn of wit; one began an article: "Harold Pinter, a legendary figure only slightly less glamorous than Dietrich, but with a voice as deep and rich . . ." It should come as no surprise to anyone who has followed the Pinter legend to hear that while the citizen is irrepressibly vocal in his public protests, the man is private and modest. He is known to his family and friends as a person of uncommon loyalty, generosity, and kindness.

The beautiful Antonia Fraser has said of her husband that in all the years she has known him he has never told a lie. This is an astonishing remark, but one that is entirely credible, since the power of most of Pinter's plays, as well as his political life, originates from the consequences of the spoken lie. The truth of a speaker's feelings, in the plays, always lies in the unspoken words and in what has come to be known as the "Pinter pauses"-- in both the well-disguised violence that underlies and sustains the banal chatter and the paralysis of imminent victimization. Pinter's audiences feel this underlying menace and the personal disintegration it may effect. Internalizing his dialogue, they respond viscerally to his work at the same time they find it difficult to articulate exactly what the play has meant, since the threat to personal stability has been clothed in banalities and lies. Although the plays have specific settings, through his unique use of language Pinter addresses violence as a universal reality. His concern is the survival or destruction of the species.

Pinter insists that his early plays were political. He says of *The Birthday Party*, for example, written a dozen years after the Holocaust: "[It] is certainly shaped by persecution. . . . Where do these two messsengers come from? It always surprised me then, the fact that people seemed to have forgotten the Gestapo had been knocking on people's doors not too long ago. And people have been knocking on people's doors for centuries in fact." The degree to which the early works are political, together with the development of Pinter's "style," continue to offer lively subjects for scholarly discourse.

Pinter's most recent plays--*Moonlight*, *Ashes to Ashes*, and *Celebration*--may be read in these terms, although they suggest a new direction in his writing. They are, without doubt, among his finest work. Although he returns to familiar themes within even more complex structures, *Moonlight* and *Ashes to Ashes* have an emotional intensity and substantive accessibility that is new to the Pinter canon. Once again the works illustrate the power of language to distort and control, the persistence of the past in the present, the pride and insecurity that isolate human beings from one another, and the roles as victim or victimizer that characterize most human relationships--as though this alternative were inevitable in the human experience. The wildly funny *Celebration* is a satire of contemporary manners, and its target is the sleaziness and self-indulgence of the nouveau-riche. The play is set in "the best and most expensive restaurant in the whole of Europe," with exchanges such as the following: "I want you to be rich so that you can buy me houses and panties and I'll know that you really love me." Despite its serious overtones regarding the enormous power of these insufferably arrogant and basically insecure people, the play has moments of wonderful, delectable farce: "You don't have to be English to enjoy sex. You don't have to speak English to enjoy sex. Lots of people enjoy sex without being English. I've known one or two Belgian people, for example, who love sex and they don't speak a word of English."

Moonlight and *Ashes to Ashes* mingle Pinter's uncanny verbal wit with the most serious of subjects--death and war. His puns and comic play with words remind us of the managable, at times, ridiculous side of life: he juxtaposes "masturbation," "approbation," "blasphemy," "gluttony," and "buggery" in a way that defies explanation, as he plays with "Tooting Common" [for Tutankhamen] and sets up an amusing confusion over the names Buckminster, Bigsby, Belcher, and Bellamy. His black comedy, however, particularly in *Moonlight*, evokes the depths of despair, as a dying man, the paragon of a civil servant, expatiates on the virtues of the system, as well as his role in it: "I inspired them to put their shoulders to the wheel and their noses to the grindstone and to keep faith at all costs with the structure which after all ensured the ordered government of all our lives, which took perfect care of us, which held us to its bosom, as it were."

In *Moonlight*, Andy, in his fifties, is dying. Despite the fact that he is "coarse, crude, vacuous, puerile, obscene, and brutal to a degree," he was, as one of his sons puts it, "an innocent bystander to his own nausea." One senses that he was a decent fellow in his youth. Life, with its dominant irrationalities, has brought him to this point; Andy is no better or worse than anyone else. Andy's fear of dying is moving in the extreme: although a bully as an adult, he returns to the illusions of childhood: "Why am I dying, anyway? I've never harmed a soul. You don't die if you're good. You die if you're bad." He also says: "What would have been the point of going through all these enervating charades in the first place? There must be a loophole. The trouble is, I can't find it." On the one hand, Pinter arouses unconditional compassion toward this most terrifying, universal situation: "Am I dying? . . . I don't know. I don't know how it feels." He allows Andy to ask Hamlet's question about the "undiscovered country" in more mundane language (with a final grim, comic twist), without surrendering the power of the question: "The big question is, will I cross it ["the horizon"] as I die or after I'm dead? Or perhaps I won't cross it at all. Perhaps I'll just stay stuck in the middle. . . ." On the other hand, rejecting sentimentality, Pinter exposes the reality of Andy's life--the hostility and tenderness that, even now, connect him and his wife. Most poignantly, he reveals the complex ambivalence that exists between two sons and these parents.

The pace is rapid as the play moves from character to character, subject to subject, and mood to mood. Andy cries: "I don't believe it's going to be pitch black for ever," and we are obliged to listen to the details of both his, and his wife's, marital infidelities. Similarly, as the couple exchange affection and insults, we witness their sons' enactment of their own guilt-ridden, retaliative acts of harsh communication.

Moonlight portrays a disconnected family, with each person in need but incapable of relating. The power of the play, however, derives from each one's interaction with a fifth character, a deceased daughter, Bridget, who embodies the play's moral core--the power of regenerative love. As she walks in and out of darkness in her own stage space and is visited by each of the characters, she is like the moonlight, a supernatural entity, and she has crossed, we are told, "fierce landscapes" of "thorns" and "barbed wire." From her vantage point--the isolated realm in which she dwells--she understands the extremes of suffering, from the crucifixion and Holocaust to the present. She has also died. Like moonlight, her actual time in this world has been brief, and she has crossed into the darkness and mysterious unknown that so frightens her father. Her intention in the play, announced in her first speech, is to watch over her parents and to give them peace. She accomplishes this at the end as she hears her father's last words and in the darkness goes home, where the moon is still bright, "the house, the glades, the lane . . . all bathed in moonlight," although the interior is dark. Child and parent are united in the peaceful interim of death.

Until the end, Bridget seems to be the eternal life force that is squandered or misunderstood by the living. As she comes to suggest resurrection after death--and is realized as a character on stage--she is Wordsworth's child. Andy intuits the cycle of life and rebirth, of how "the child is father of the man," when he speaks of imagined grandchildren, and Bel comforts him with: "Oh, the really little ones I think do know something about death, they know more about death than we do. We've forgotten death but they haven't. . . . [The] very young remember the moment before their life began." That Pinter wrote the play shortly after his mother died is of interest, for the play *Moonlight,* like the natural phenomenon after which it is named, reaches to the unknowable. *Moonlight* is Pinter's exquisite poem on death and transcendence, with death a "terrible beauty"--exalting in its universal mystery, terror, and promise of peace.

One of Pinter's remarks describes *Ashes to Ashes*: "The dead are still looking at us, steadily, waiting for us to acknowledge our own part in their murder." The play begins with a woman telling her lover or husband about a former lover and the erotic appeal of his physical violence. In vintage Pinter dialogue, the woman explains her sexual arousal. Excited by his "Kiss my fist," as he gripped her neck, she would kiss the palm of his fist and hand and respond: "Put your hand round my throat," after which her "body went back, slowly but truly."

As she first speaks of this lover, she betrays no indication of the significance of her remarks. She says he was a travel agent who ran a factory and, like a Pied Piper, led people into the sea. But her tale eventually reveals, to her as well as the audience, the horror of its actualization-- of warfare and genocide, of screaming mothers hiding babies in their shawls, being herded on to trains, and wailing as their children are wrenched from them. As the woman initially represses the truth of her lover's activities, Pinter sardonically targets any distortions or minimalization of the cruelties of war, particularly the reality of mass murder. She speaks, for example, of visiting her lover's "factory," and says, "But it wasn't the usual kind of factory. . . . They were all wearing [skull?] caps. . . . They would follow him over a cliff and into the sea, if he asked them, he said." Again, dispelling any revisionist notion about the culture of the concentration camps, like that of Auschwitz, where music accompanied prisoners to the gas chambers, Pinter's character says: They would "sing in a chorus, as long as he led them. They were in fact very musical." But the woman's denial disintegrates, as she proceeds to recall other details, like the lack of facilities in these factories, and she gets closer to the historical truth. In an ironically lyrical passage, Pinter evokes the brutal reality of the Holocaust, from arrest to the ovens. She says:

> I saw a whole crowd of people walking through the woods, on their way to the sea, in the direction of the sea. They seemed to be very cold, they were wearing coats, although it was such a beautiful day. A beautiful, warm, Dorset day. They were carrying bags. There were . . . guides . . . ushering them, guiding them along. . . . And I saw all these people walk into the sea. The tide covered them slowly. Their bags bobbed about in the waves.

As the woman recalls the barbarity of war, the Second World War becomes all wars--"As the siren faded away in my ears I knew it was becoming louder and louder for somebody else"--and she shares both the vanquishers' responsibility and the victims' despair. At the end, instead of responding to "Kiss my fist," she becomes one of the mothers whose child has been wrenched from her. She--and we, Pinter seems to be saying--must bear the guilt and endure the terror of past, present, and potential violence. From this may come moral courage.

Hopefully, there will be another edition of this book, for Pinter continues with extraordinary energy as a playwright, director, screenwriter, actor, and political activist. And lest we overlook the man's sense of humor and congeniality in his daily life, an anecdote might be in order. When acting in one of his own plays, Pinter asked that a dressing room be set aside for visiting friends, including thirsty cricket buddies; he dubbed the room "Harry's Bar." Just as his friends shared his good cheer, we now, on the occasion of this milestone birthday, longtime Pinter devotees and theater-lovers of the world, also raise a cup in celebration and convey to him our best wishes.

The first of the new essays in this volume is by Kimball King, professor of English at the University of

North Carolina. He is the author of *Sam Shepard: A Casebook* and *Hollywood on Stage: Playwrights Evaluate the Culture Industry*, as well as a full-length study of Tennessee Williams's *Orpheus Descending* and a volume on the plays and films of Woody Allen. King has also published numerous essays on a wide variety of contemporary dramatists. He is not only co-editor of the *Southern Literary Journal* and on the editorial board of the *Pinter Review*, but he is also General Editor of Routledge's Casebook on Modern Dramatists series and its Studies in Modern Drama series.

King begins "Harold Pinter's Achievement and Modern Drama" with general comments on Pinter's accomplishment. "Pinter has brought a form of natural speech to the stage that has surpassed the most ambitious attempts of his predecessors," King writes, after stating that Pinter has had a "guiding role in virtually all important aspects of contemporary drama" and changed our expectations forever, with the result that "language, action, and meaning of all performance art" has come to be "inevitably measured" against his work. King focuses on Pinter's extraordinary use of natural speech and the variety of ways he manipulates it for any number of different purposes. Pinter's use of irony, to King, is his "most radical yet enduring contribution to the stage."

In turning to the patterns of Pinter scholarship, King describes how, in each decade, the critical apparatus has been different and certain works have received more attention than others. Both of these conclusions become immediately comprehensible to the reader by way of two sets of charts that conclude the essay. For example, Pinter's three most frequently discussed works first appeared thirty-five to forty years ago: *The Homecoming*, *The Caretaker*, and *The Birthday Party*; *The Lover* is among the last in receiving critical attention.

The charts are starting points for King's discussion of the relationship between the critical approaches and the sociocultural milieu of each period. For example, he speculates that psychological criticism, which peaked in the

1980s, was dramatically reduced in the 1990s, perhaps, he suggests, because this was a time of "divisions within the psychiatric profession itself over the value of insight therapy vs. biomedical solutions to personal problems." He offers comparable explanations for the rise or decline of many other types of criticism, and his survey includes Pinter's relationship to the "Theatre of the Absurd," his literary influences, the linguistic analyses of his plays via such thinkers as Wittgenstein, Jameson, Foucault, Kristeva, and Lacan; women's roles; and, of course, the most popular subject for Pinter scholars, his language and the nature of his subtexts.

King then suggests fertile areas for future investigation. He indicates, for example, specific plays that deserve more scrutiny; the need for psychological analysis in the more recent works; and additional work on women's issues, the poetry, and Pinter's influence on other writers such as Churchill, Shepard, and Mamet. King is especially concerned that future researchers attend to the novel *The Dwarfs:* "Almost all of Pinter is there in that early novel," he writes, "but almost no one writes about it."

Mel Gussow, who has known Harold Pinter for thirty years, is the author of *Conversations with Pinter*, *Conversations with Stoppard*, *Conversations with and about Beckett*, *Theatre on the Edge: New Visions, New Voices* and the biography *Edward Albee: A Singular Journey.* For his work as a drama critic for *The New York Times*, he was a winner of the George Jean Nathan Award for Dramatic Criticism. He is now a cultural writer for the *Times.*

Gussow's essay, "Acting Pinter," is about Pinter--the dramatist, film-script writer, and director--as an actor. Gussow writes: "There is a close connection between Pinter's writing and acting, both in the kind of roles he has chosen to do and in his approach to performance." Gussow surveys Pinter's acting career--from his earliest experience in Anew McMaster's traveling repertory company to his more recent roles in his own plays (such as *The Hothouse*), his screenplays (including *Turtle Diary*), as well as his work in other writers' films, like Patricia Rozema's

Mansfield Park, and his readings (or, in fact, one-man performances) of his own work, when he takes on all the roles of his play. If, as a dramatist, Gussow continues, Pinter demonstrates the way words empower the speaker and can be manipulated into weapons, Pinter the actor instinctively understands how to dominate others and threaten violence.

Gussow covers a wide range of subjects that relate to Pinter as an actor--from his absolute respect for the written word and his invariable stage fright to his preference for playing villains, which he has done since his earliest work with McMaster, taking on, for example, the role of Iago, or more recently, the character of Roote, the brutal, crazy tyrant in his own *The Hothouse.*

Gussow raises and answers such questions as, "Does Pinter the playwright or Pinter the director watch Pinter the actor?" and "Why is Pinter such a superb actor of his own work?" He also shares a number of Pinter's comments, pertinent to Pinter in any of his professional capacities, such as: "I suppose Shakespeare's dominated my life the way he's dominated many people's lives. We don't recover from Shakespeare." Gussow concludes with a discussion of Pinter's splendid performance in the film *Mansfield Park.*

Ann C. Hall, the current president of the Pinter Society, organized the June 2000 International Pinter in London Conference, which drew participants from ten countries--in honor of Pinter's seventieth birthday. In addition to numerous articles on drama, she has published *A Kind of Alaska: Women in the Plays of O'Neill, Pinter, and Shepard* and edited *Delights, Dilemmas, and Desires: Essays on Women and the Media.* She serves as chair of the English Division at Ohio Dominican College.

Hall approaches *Moonlight* and *Ashes to Ashes* in terms of storytelling as a means of defining reality or establishing authority in personal relationships. In *Moonlight*, the characters live within realities of their own or inherited linguistic constructs. The dying Andy, clinging to his role as an authoritarian father, faces the last moments of his life in rage and in uncertain fantasies of an afterlife and remaining grandchildren. His sons, Hall continues, face their own despair, due to "their own impotence," with a variety of tales. They "toy with language, alter reality through fantasy, and create comic narratives to pass the time." Similarly, the daughter, Bridget, is held in thrall by the notion of family connection. At the end, a victim of her own fantasy, she is abandoned by her parents. Bel, Andy's wife, would seem to be the only figure in this "patriarchal society," who understands the power of language and identity.

If storytelling is not "entirely comforting" in *Moonlight*, in *Ashes to Ashes* it provides "the key to personal and social freedom." As Rebecca tells of her former sadomasochistic love relationship to her present lover/listener, he becomes so caught up in her tale that he becomes her present-day abuser. In this play, which Hall views as a metadrama about "patriarchal power," authority becomes synomymous with verbal control. Rebecca's present-day lover asserts power over her by identifying with the abuser/torturer/lover in her narrative (as a listener identifies with the central figure in an unravelling story). The power play between the two continues until Rebecca regains final control of the narrative, "a story of her own victimhood or victimization of millions of women throughout the centuries."

Michael Billington has been drama critic of *The Guardian* since 1971. He also broadcasts frequently on the arts, teaches London theater courses to students from the University of Pennsylvania and Boston University, and is the author of several books. They include studies of Tom Stoppard and Alan Ayckbourn, the authorized biography of Peggy Ashcroft and *The Life and Work of Harold Pinter*, which depended upon close collaboration with the subject and which gave him rare access to Pinter's friends and colleagues.

Billington discusses *Celebration*, both "the funniest play Pinter has written in years" and a quasi-political play. *Celebration* brings two groups of London's "nerdy nouveau-riche" into a restaurant that functions as a paradisal retreat, at which they can indulge their most essential appetites--of food and sex--in reality or in recollection. One character, for example, "was once a plump young secretary who existed in a state of seemingly permanent sexual arousal. 'Sometimes,' she remembered, 'I could hardly walk from one cabinet to another I was so excited.'" However, as Billington continues, beneath their trashy conviviality, vulgar materialism, and coarse revelations lies their contemptible indifference to the pain and suffering in the outside world. As he puts it: "Materialistic individualism breeds moral vacancy and . . . there is an umbilical connection between male chauvinism and political brutality."

Billington is fascinated by Pinter's young waiter, as he eavesdrops on the diners and drifts into the past with recollections of his grandfather. This element of recollection of things past, for Billington, is the key to *Celebration*, as it is, he believes, to all of Pinter's work. In the early plays, the real or fantasied past buttressed the present; by *Old Times*, a reinvented past was created to meet the needs of the present. In *Ashes to Ashes*, a simple figure embraces "the collective memory" of the terrible persecutions of the twentieth century. In *Celebration*, memory is "largely a form of sexual twitch: a recollection of who had whom and when." In fact, as the plot unfolds, after Lambert at Table One realizes that he had sex with Suki, at Table Two, the two groups come together in conversation for the remainder of the evening and share their common vulgarity. Sex is crass and loveless before, within, and outside marriage.

For the staff, and in counterpoint to the diners, the past is "variously rose-tinted, rebarbative, fantastic, and spellboundingly real." Yet the young waiter stands apart from the owner and his maitresse d'hotel, who pamper and flatter their clients. His comic and grandiose memories of his grandfather are an implied repudiation of the lack of culture and altruism in the modern world. Later, his realistic recollections represent elements of love, natural beauty, and mystery, which "rebuke . . . the hollow rituals of the guests." At the end of the essay Billington weaves a Freudian dimension into his discussion.

INTRODUCTION TO
THE FIRST EDITION

Lois Gordon

When I began soliciting essays for this casebook, I had no idea that such a distinguished group of scholars and authors would rally to the project. I was aware of the abundance of work already published on Pinter and the growing body of scholarship in preparation. I assumed that my proposed group of essayists would be too busy pursing other projects or that, in many cases, their earlier work was already excerpted for reprint. Garland, furthermore, had indicated a preference for new material. When virtually everyone to whom I wrote expressed interest in preparing a new essay--and others even contacted me to contribute--I was delighted.

The compliment implied in this, of course, goes to Mr. Pinter, both for the stimulus his work continues to provide and the homage he has earned in the world of letters. Among those who expressed enthusiasm for the project was the late Raymond Carver, who, in fact, planned to write an essay. During his last illness, Carver had the kindness to write me, and he virtually apologized for being unable to contribute. Knowing of Pinter's enormous regard for Samuel Beckett, I had also written to Beckett. He too had the kindness to reply that to his "great regret, [he was] in no condition to accept."

Pinter, who has only recently called himself a "citizen of the world," has, I think, always had a vital concern for people and their survival in any variety of social, professional, or political situation. Although this was not the overt subject matter of his earliest plays, it permeates their deepest levels of meaning and is perhaps at

xxiii

xxiv   *Lois Gordon*

least partially responsible for the kind of admiration he receives. I don't pretend to know the man, apart from some brief correspondence and few meetings over the years, but I have always been struck by his lack of pretension and obvious interest in the welfare of others.

I wrote one of the early Pinter monographs, and on a subsequent visit to London in 1970, I met Pinter. Then, as now, he was down to earth, open, charitable, and modest. He was deeply concerned about the Vietnam War and American opinion regarding the war. He asked numerous questions about American education--what our students were reading and writing about. He was also very willing to discuss his current interests and projects. He had just been filming *The Go-Between*, and he discussed his pleasure in working with the gifted Joseph Losey. He spoke with great empathy about the rigors to which a difficult location had subjected their talented actors. He told me that he had begun L. P. Hartley's novel late one night when he was at home alone and was unable to put it down; it had moved him deeply. Although he was not disposed to discuss the "meaning" of his plays--he spoke instead of how they dictated themselves to him--he was very kind about my work. We talked at some length of my career and family. I mention these details, only because the "menace" and emotional remove often associated with Pinter's characters have at times been projected onto the man.

The last time I spoke with Pinter, in November 1988, both before and after his reading/performance of *One for the Road* at Fairleigh Dickinson University, he was again eager to discuss his political activities and current film and stage projects. He described how it felt to act Goldberg again (in the 1987 BBC production of *The Birthday Party*) and was very proud of his recent collection of 100 poems by 100 poets; he mentioned some that I "should have a look at." Once more, he seemed interested in my new projects and asked about our American students; we also talked in the most general of terms about the 1980s social and cultural scene. His deepest concern, without a doubt, was for the people living under brutal dictatorial regimes and the efforts necessary to acknowledge and hopefully ameliorate their circumstances. Later, at dinner with Lady Antonia, her daughter Natasha, and my colleague Gene Barnett, the conversation was relaxed as we spoke for several hours on any number of subjects, ranging from the economic "mess" in England to healthy eating habits and the Pinters' different work habits. As this goes to press, I am deeply touched by a note Pinter wrote me in response to one I sent him following Beckett's death.

Indeed, Pinter's relationship to Beckett has been the subject of considerable discussion--particularly in the light of Pinter's habit of sending Beckett most of his new work for commentary. Despite the different circumstances under which Beckett knew James Joyce, Pinter may indeed have revered Beckett in the same way Beckett revered Joyce. Matters of personal, political, and literary styles aside, Beckett and Pinter clearly share one trait: an absolute commitment to the purity of the word. With their common starting point "I speak, therefore I am," dramatic "action" becomes a function of the most subtle modifications of sound, gesture, silence, and intonation--in addition to word choice, rhythmical patterns, and the most minute details of stage setting, all of which contribute to the complexity of mood and perspective. Traditional action, motivation, climax, and denouement--and time and space--have been replaced by the open-ended richness of meaning inherent in the play of words, the infinite textures and colorations that develop within complex linguistic designs. This is theater that touches the boundaries of music and dance.

But the word--and most recently the political power of language--has always been Pinter's subject. As he himself defined language many years ago, it is the "stratagem" that "cover[s] nakedness"; his plays have always been "stratagems" that "uncover nakedness." Towards this end, for Pinter (as for Beckett), minute attention to details of presentation also becomes vital. Pinter's visit to Fairleigh Dickinson illustrates this.

Unlike the many other important writers who had appeared for our Literary Society, Pinter was specifically concerned about our auditorium--so much so that he arranged to arrive two hours early to examine the "stage," the design of the seating, the acoustics and the lighting. In fact, our auditorium must be one of the least likely "theaters" in the country--an enormous and bright white lecture hall in our dental school. Pinter initially peeked in, stood on the stage, and then climbed the stairs to the top of the room, walked to the end of each of the uppermost rows, returned to the stage, tested the equipment for echoes, made sure that his few stage props were correct, measured the height of the chair on stage in relationship to the table (at which he would be sitting)--this was all done at record speed--may have noted my mounting anxiety, smiled reassuringly, and said that everything was fine. His performance, two hours later, mesmerized the audience and transformed the barren hall (chemical smells and all) into the landscape of his imagination. Like his predecessors in the great dramatic tradition, Pinter integrates the multiple perspectives of director, actor, and author.

Whether, or how, Pinter's work thus far is divisible thematically and stylistically is a subject of current critical interest. For a time, it was common parlance to speak of (1) the signature "Pinteresque" (the room, a menacing intruder, and the subsequent disintegration of character, as in *The Room* or *The Homecoming*), (2) the more lyrical reflections on time and memory (*Silence, Landscape*), and (3) the recent, overtly political works (*One for the Road, Mountain Language*). When I first wrote on Pinter, I questioned the term "absurd" and rejected philosophical commentary or symbolic interpretation of "menace" as the key to the plays. Instead, I spoke of the Pinter pattern as one in which the routine banalities of everyday life (in carefully assigned word games) were disrupted by the appearance of an often benign intruder. This figure, I thought, acted as a screen onto which Pinter's emotionally precarious figures projected their "true nakedness" of self--their inner menace, so to speak--and this was reflected in the disintegration of their word games.

Pinter criticism has come very far since then. Although subsequent work continued to focus on the nature of the intruders, the more substantial scholarship has demonstrated how plot and characterization occur at the level of language. A great deal of the present research follows these lines of linguistic and semiotic investigation, with the ideas of Wittgenstein, Jakobson, Barthes, and Lacan, among many others, the starting point for analysis. Important thematic studies on subjects like gender, class, sexuality, love, loneliness, identity, and time, also continue, along with work on genre. A growing body of scholarship, however, is reevaluating the early plays in terms of Pinter's more recent political activities, just as other investigations are reevaluating issues of language, time, space, and specific themes, as these have "evolved" throughout his career. Pinter's life as an actor, screenwriter, and poet--and his transformations of fiction or drama into film--have also been of growing critical interest.

Most of these concerns are represented in the essays which follow, and all but two were written for this volume. As the new decade gets under way, with Pinter's sixtieth birthday on October 10, 1990, there will be film and play revivals, along with birthday celebrations, throughout the world. Numerous other books will undoubtedly also be timed to mark the occasion. I am enormously grateful to Garland Publishing and particularly to Kimball King for inviting me to edit this casebook. It brings together a collection of essays by a group of highly thoughtful writers-- all of whom were asked if they would care to write their most recent thoughts regarding Pinter's work. As it turns out, their essays celebrate one of the most distinguished writers of this century.

Martin Esslin, who teachers Drama at Stanford University, is one of the most revered of contemporary drama critics. Author of *Pinter, the Playwright*, *Brecht--A Choice of Evils*, *Artaud*, and *The Field of Drama*, and head of the BBC Radio Drama from 1963-1977, his *The Theatre of the Absurd* (1961) virtually defined the midcentury avant-garde and introduced Harold Pinter to a generation of students, scholars, and theatergoers. Focusing on the "poetic" stage image, Esslin also introduced many of the new stylists in terms of their polyphonic and poetic constructs, which, as he put it, originated from "a free flow of the imagination and the release of . . . subconscious fantasies" which then assumed "a prophetic content."

It is understandable that Pinter's 1958 letter to Peter Wood (which Pinter shared with Esslin in 1980) describing the unconscious "engendering image" should be of great interest to Esslin. Written to Wood when he was directing the first *The Birthday Party*, the letter clarifies Pinter's creative process. It also helps account for the seemingly "infinite," open-ended interpretations of his work. Indeed, although Esslin makes absolutely no claim to this, Pinter's remarks verify Esslin's earliest speculations some thirty years ago about the "poetic image."

Wood had asked Pinter if he would expand Stanley's lines to better enable the audience to understand his predicament--i.e., why he was staying at Meg's sleazy house and why two sinister figures were after him. As Esslin writes, the key to the letter, and to Pinter's method of writing, lay in Pinter's acknowledged *incapability* of further defining Stanley's character *because of Stanley's incapability of understanding his situation.* As Pinter had put it: "Stanley *cannot* perceive his only valid justification--which is he is what he is--therefore he certainly can never be articulate about it."

Esslin then reminds us that Pinter's methodology has always been inspirational ("The thing germinated and bred itself," wrote Pinter); his responsibility has been to the *consistency* of the dramatic image ("I followed the clues. . . . I interfered with them only on the technical level"). Pinter's skill in subsequently fleshing out the characters, Esslin continues, developed from his repertory acting experience in the realistic, well-made drawing room and mystery plays of the 1950s. It was his sensitivity to the techniques of these plays, along with the intuitions he derived from Joyce, Beckett and Kafka, that contributed to his unique signature.

Pinter's letter to Wood, concludes Esslin, is "brilliant" and "remarkable," for in saying he could not analyze his dramatic image (i.e., Stanley), Pinter produced an analytical commentary on his own creative process.

Ruby Cohn, the preeminent Samuel Beckett scholar, is professor of Comparative Drama at the University of California, Davis. Her many books include *Samuel Beckett: The Comic Gamut, Just Play, Back to Beckett*, and *From Desire to Godot*, as well as *Modern Shakespeare Offshoots, Dialogue in American Drama, Currents in Contemporary Drama*, and *New American Dramatists 1960-1990*. She has also been publishing on Pinter since the early 1960s. In "The Economy of Betrayal," she brings to her subject, once again, a remarkable ear for the nuances of language. Typically, she writes, Pinter "caresses and teases the language; he rides roughshod over it or rolls single words on a sensuous tongue. From menace to mannerism, from brand name to braggart warrior, this pacifist writer commands a linguistic arsenal for his Lorenzian stage skirmishes."

As she surveys repeated lexical and rhythmic techniques in Pinter's early "polyvalenced" work, she adds a new dimension to the so-called "Pinteresque," traditionally associated only with "the unverifiable and the disjunctive." She will later discuss Pinter's "economizing" of these linguistic elements in *Betrayal*.

Until *Betrayal*, as she illustrates, Pinter's work was marked by specific kinds of puns, verbal duels, and the intrusion of technical, sexual, geographical, class (or even Latinate) jargon or clichés--all of which functioned for their speakers as weapons of gaining control. Pinter also used subtle rhyme, alliteration, repetition of words or phrases, noticeably lengthened monologues or dialogues--and even units of silence (indicated through periods, commas, three dots, silences, or pauses)--as instruments of power play.

Although Cohn agrees that *Betrayal* departs from the earlier "Pinteresque" (the past is "verified" and indeed illustrated in its nine scenes; the "intruder" is no longer menacing), of special interest to her is Pinter's new shaping of lexical and rhythmic patterns. Cohn asserts that Pinter actually dramatizes his complex subject of "betrayal" (in emotional and institutional terms) by "economizing" on his usual linguistic instruments--using fewer dialogues and briefer monologues and less frequent sound play, alliteration, rhyme, jargon, and cliché. Although the pauses remain, an "economics of emotional expression" works even through his more measured use of three dots and silences. Ultimately, Pinter creates a comedy of manners which, through its economy of language, also "indicts such manners as a betrayal of a richer, more instinctual life." In a sense, *Betrayal* is Pinter's betrayal of his earlier technique in the service of a new subject.

Austin Quigley is chairman of the English Department at the University of Virginia and the author of *The Pinter Problem, The Modern Stage and Other Worlds*, and a variety of articles on modern drama and literary theory. In "Time for Change in *No Man's Land*," he responds to those critics who find *No Man's Land* puzzling and abstract, who argue that it lacks a coherent theme and dramatic resolution because of its continuous disruption of character and plot evolution and odd treatment of time. Quigley, in an extremely subtle examination of image, anecdote, dialogue, and character interaction, proposes a structure beneath the play's careful manipulations of discontinuity and fragmentation: "There is an insistence upon emerging but suspended narrative lines, upon fragmentary episodes that suggest more than they can ever confirm, upon moments of shared significance whose potential value remains potential but nevertheless remains."

As Quigley suggests, Pinter's interruption of dialogue and character interaction--like his "invoked" rather than "displayed" imagery and continually "arrested" actions--reinforces a larger view regarding the two central aged characters. By also establishing both local and global time, the play, both structurally and thematically, suggests the simultaneity of human possibility and limitation, the latent and limited potential for change and fixedness in all of human experience. Quigley cites, as one of many examples, the well-described but never produced photo album, and how the sequence epitomizes, in a sense, the variety of time zones Hirst (and Spooner) inhabit. A collection of seemingly frozen images, the photos, as Hirst can only imagine them, display the many possibilities of what was or seemed to have been in his youth, together with an entire separate body of associations evoked through adult recollection, rationalization, and anticipation. Like old age, the photos are an aggregate of "intriguing but discontinuous moments."

Quigley rejects the play as a nihilistic vision of old age. Pinter's suspended resolutions--in dialogue, anecdote, image, character interaction, and plotting--with everything occurring in a context (and often counterpoint) of local and global indefiniteness--reinforces Hirst's and Spooner's identities as examples of thwarted potential. Nevertheless, their repeated return to past events with a nostalgia that "continuity might eventually conquer discontinuity" gives the play a unique poignancy and power. As Quigley observes, even in their final, complex and ambiguous remarks, when they again put the past on trial, they reveal a redeeming awareness that life forever consists of potential hope, engagement, recovery, *and* doubt, distance, and failure.

David Lodge is both a celebrated novelist (his most recent fiction is *Nice Work*) and the author of numerous critical works, including *The Language of Fiction*, *The Modes of Modern Writing*, and *Working with Structuralism*. Professor of English at the University of Birmingham, he has long been concerned with what makes a text a work of art--his focus in "*Last to Go:* A Structuralist Reading."

Lodge takes Pinter's 55-line review sketch, first performed in 1959, as a microcosm of his dramatic universe. He illustrates how the poetic techniques within the well-defined dramatic structure convey, in condensed form, the central themes of Pinter's work: life versus death (or presence versus absence), as manifest in speech versus silence (and pause).

Lodge begins with concepts from Malinowski and Jakobson, as well as Deirdre Burton's applied linguistic approach to the play, and then applies his own structural poetics. First, he discusses the initial mutually and simultaneously phatic conversations of the two lonely old men at their coffee stall. Instead of facing their own solitariness, they "desperately keep a conversation going," although they really have little to communicate. Lodge illustrates their recycling of trivial information, primarily about the sale of the last evening newspaper, and how this functions to maintain a kind of human contact.

He then proceeds to show how within Pinter's artful "narrative . . . process," banal repetitions take on a variety of poetic techniques, and poetic discourse operates in an "aesthetic [dramatic] frame,"--noting, for example, the symmetries and echoes in "*about ten/about then; sold my last/sold your last; "'Evening News' it was"/"'Evening News' was it?"* In addition, when a new phrase or topic (like the man named "George") enters the conversation, the tacit rules that have operated thus far disintegrate, and questions and answers become "genuinely referential." In fact, it is at such moments that elements of confrontation and challenge provide dramatic tension, and the conversation of the two men risks termination. As the play returns to rhythms and questions of the earlier dialogue, each utterance takes on multi-levels of accrued meaning, "for the meanings [the play] generates for its own sake-- that is, for meanings it generates independent of any real context." Ultimately, even the title transforms--referring first to a conversation about the last newspaper sold or even the last man to go home, and finally suggesting the ontological issues of time, place, and being. Which man will be the last to occupy the coffee bar, the last to speak, the last to remain alive?

President of the Samuel Beckett Society, Linda Ben-Zvi is the author of *Samuel Beckett* and numerous essays on Beckett, Pinter, James Joyce, and language and literature.   Professor of English at Colorado State University, she has also edited *Women in Beckett: Performance and Critical Perspectives* and is completing a biography of the American playwright Susan Glaspell. Here, in "*Monologue*: The Play of Words," she examines Pinter's subtle manipulations of language and grammar.

Monologue, a television play with little critical attention thus far, portrays a man alone on stage, as he speaks to an imagined friend about their friendship and the woman they both desired.   Like a minimalist painting or sculpture, Ben-Zvi begins, *Monologue* is the pure embodiment of Pinter's dramatic interests: "a catalogue, pared to its essentials of the major preoccupations in all Pinter's plays: the loss of love, the isolation experienced in maturity, the desire for male bonding, and the slippages caused by the vagaries of memory and the imprecision of language."   Anticipating *Betrayal* by six years, it also reveals how the significant connections that may exist between men are necessarily threatened by the presence of a woman.

Ben-Zvi takes the reader step-by-step through the play, illustrating, for example, how the use of stative, rather than modal, verbs reinforces *Monologue*'s image of the paralyzed self in an equally deadened contemporary world. She carefully points out how transformations to conditional or present verb tenses indicate potential change and self-knowledge.   She does the same with juxtapositions of contemporary and older vernacular or clichéd expressions and demonstrates how these reinforce the play's central images of alienation and paralysis--all measured against a past time of potential vitality.   She is, throughout, sensitive to the meanings conveyed through grammatical inversions and slippages in meaning, and as she measures these from section to section, she suggests that at the conclusion, the tentativeness of human connection drawn thus far turns at last to potential self-revelation.   In the absence of cliché, modals or conditional verbs, Pinter finally evokes in his speaker a poignant sense of "the intimacy and love between men [which] shapes so many of [his] plays."

George E. Wellwarth, professor of Theatre and Comparative Literature at the State University of New York at Binghamton, is the author of *The Theatre of Protest and Paradox*, *Spanish Underground Drama*, and *Modern Drama and the Death of God*, as well as co-founder and co-editor of *Modern International Drama*. He begins his lively essay with the provocative "One of the few advantages of growing older is that one becomes wiser; and one of the few disadvantages of becoming wiser is that one is forced to look back in embarrassment and regret on the intellectual indiscretions of one's past. Especially if one has published them." As such, the author of *The Theatre of Protest and Paradox* writes "a revisionist approach" to *The Dumb Waiter*, *The Collection*, *The Lover*, and *The Homecoming*--although he begins with a few swipes at Pinter's "romanticizing critics."

"The time has come," he writes, "to recognize the fact that Pinter is the only critic who has made any sense of Pinter." And he looks at the same letter (1958) to Peter Wood that Martin Esslin discusses in his essay in order to underscore Pinter's (and his) contention that "The play is itself." Wellwarth takes this to mean that Pinter's plays are "situation pieces that encapsulate an atmosphere or mood," not plays of ideas or philosophical works; in fact, he continues, they are obscured by symbolic and philosophical interpretation. Instead, Wellwarth insists, they should be approached as works of "amorphous meanings and atmosphere," as dramatic provocations of a "mood, often vague in its specifics but emotionally pervasive." He discusses *The Dumb Waiter*, *The Collection*, and *The Homecoming* in these terms.

The Lover, which he considers to be Pinter's "masterpiece," is unusual in its "straightforward psychological observation" and "celebration of life." In its lovers'/spouses' role-playing with each another, it portrays a richness of identity in personal and existential terms. "To live as many lives as possible," Wellwarth writes, "no matter how temporarily, how spuriously, how self-deludingly, is to enrich the basic life we live." Richard and Sarah live "their real life, but they play variations on it and give these variations equal stature with their real, outward life while they are living them." In addition, "these variations are their own creations so that in their fantasies they are--momentarily--the gods of their own destiny."

Katherine H. Burkman has been largely responsible for the International Pinter Festival at Ohio State University in honor of Pinter's sixtieth birthday. A professor of English at Ohio State, Burkman has published several books and numerous articles that focus on ritual in modern drama, including *The Dramatic World of Harold Pinter: Its Basis in Ritual, The Arrival of Godot: Ritual Patterns in Modern Drama*, and the collection of essays which she edited, *Myth and Ritual in the Plays of Samuel Beckett*. In her essay for this volume, Burkman discusses the displacement of "realistic" time and space in *Family Voices, A Kind of Alaska*, and *Victoria Station*--the "trio" of plays collected in *Other Places*. Her thesis is that Pinter has created in these plays landscapes of "frankly interior spaces." *Other Places*, she writes, is actually "a kind of three act exploration of the quest for self in the modern world." In each play, Pinter handles "the falseness of attempts at realistic orientation" through a series of ironies: in each, as well, the true location of self in interior space is hampered by issues of "domination."

Treating each play as an integral part of a tripart pattern, Burkman begins by noting how in most productions of *Family Voices*, the parents' and son's voices are presented as though they were virtually disembodied--as though defining themselves psychologically, rather than physically. In focusing on a young man who has left home and who is now writing his mother, she suggests, Pinter actually creates a protagonist suspended in space. His unmailed letters function as projections of old family fears, so that at least on one level, time is circular and his distance from home only physical. But additional complications with a potentially new family lead him to other menacing situations. Ultimately, the boy "remains unaware of his lost condition," and like the other voices in the play, remains suspended in a void. His "sense of absence from home" remains his "sense of absence from self."

For Deborah, the twenty-nine-year victim of sleeping sickness in *A Kind of Alaska*, the return to health initially signals a profound disorientation both spatially and temporally. But Deborah's ultimate "relocation" involves retaining the self she nurtured in her "retreat," her illness. Burkman suggests that Deborah experiences the fragmentation of the modern condition, as she also accepts herself as a woman in a patriarchal society; she is able, unlike the boy in *Family Voices*, to undergo a reorientation--a "rebirth"--into self. In *Victoria Station*, the "protagonist is doubled," as Pinter initially establishes the "immobilization" of both a cabbie and his dispatcher. Although the taxi "Driver" must deal with his "Controller," who would presumably help him "relocate" himself, both figures drop the markers of traditional time and begin a reorientation toward inner time and space. As Burkman writes, *Victoria Station* provides "a kind of third act in *Other Places*" that "leads the audience" to a "more hopeful stance."

Currently Endowed Professor of Humanities at Kentucky State University, Steven H. Gale has published several books on Pinter, including *Butter's Going Up: A Critical Analysis of Harold Pinter's Work*, *Harold Pinter: An Annotated Bibliography*, *Harold Pinter: Critical Approaches*, and *Harold Pinter: Critical Essays*. His other books include studies of S. J. Perelman and the *Encyclopedia of American Humorists*. Gale is also co-editor of *The Pinter Review* and president of the *Harold Pinter Society*.

Pinter had said that *The Guest*, his film version of *The Caretaker*, "hit the relationship of the brothers more clearly than . . . the play." Although Gale is clearly interested in this relationship, his essay is even more comprehensive, as it indicates how Pinter's skillful understanding of the film medium permitted him to successfully translate one highly effective art form into another. Gale lists the potential dangers of transforming drama into film. Stage dialogue, for example, often becomes wooden or choppy, because the normal preponderance of words on stage appear static or disjointed in film. Too, since dramas occur within confined stage space, which allows for the development of "intellectual and psychological themes," the same space limitations on film often seem confining. An entirely different medium, film instead relies on varied visual images for emotional effects.

Gale examines the first thirty-four seconds of *The Guest* in order to illustrate how Mick's "somewhat menacing" behavior in his parked car establishes the tone and themes of the subsequent narrative. He also discusses how this opening sequence actually parallels the thematic cluster of the original 1960 production of *The Caretaker.* He then goes on to question whether the film "further elucidates the meaning gleaned from the drama," and, furthermore, if "the information gathered from this extraneous source (the film)" is "valid in interpreting the play." Or, he asks, are the play and film separate entities "that perforce must stand on their own?" These questions, as one of his endnotes explains, raise issues that will be examined in his forthcoming book on Pinter's films.

Susan Hollis Merritt is presently a visiting scholar in the Departments of English and Theater Arts at Cornell University. The author of the forthcoming *Pinter in Play: Critical Strategies and Plays of Harold Pinter* (Duke University Press), she has written numerous essays and reviews about modern drama and its critics and is the bibliography editor of *The Pinter Review.* In "Pinter and Politics," Merritt sets out to examine the question of Pinter's commitment to political drama from his earliest work through the recent *One for the Road*, *Precisely*, and *Mountain Language.* Her focus is essentially twofold. On the one hand, she reviews what Pinter has himself said about his active interest in politics since *the Hothouse* and the clearcut political implications of early plays like *The Birthday Party.* That is to say, although his work during the first twenty years of his career was only "metaphoric," in terms of power and domination, its (latent) political content was undeniable. Merritt then reviews the complexities of categorization within the vast and varied body of scholarship on this subject, reminding us that "judgments are contingent on the perspectives of the critics, on their particular politics or ideologies."

Analyzing the critic--that is, analyzing his or her perspective in terms of his or her background and ultimate bias--is Merritt's specialty, for she has written an extensive survey of Pinter criticism in which she evaluates a broad spectrum of scholarly approaches in terms of each critic's personal history: her book is about the (Pinter) critic as writer as much as it is about Pinter as dramatist. In the essay included here, a section from her *Pinter in Play*, she examines the problems of virtually any discussion of Pinter as a "political" writer (either in current, retroactive, or metaphoric terms), of placing him, for example, within the conventional Left/Right spectrum, of classifying him as a "political," as opposed to "social," dramatist, of calling him the author of "political drama," rather than "political theatre," or of labeling him a "bourgeois dramatist." Finally, her essay includes a brief discussion of Pinter's political activities and his more recent screen adaptations of "sociopolitically" relevant subjects.

Ewald Mengel is associate professor of English Literature at the Otto-Friedrich University of Bamberg, West Germany. He has published books on Pinter (*Harold Pinters Dramen in Spiegel der soziologischen Rollentheorie*), the English historical novel, and Charles Dickens, as well as several articles in English and German on Pinter, Arden, Mortimer, the English historical novel, Dickens, Tennyson, and Sterne. Since 1988, he has held the prestigious Heisenberg grant.

Although Mengel focuses on *Other Places* here, his essay in many ways surveys Pinter's stylistic development, at least in his treatment of "lyrical themes in dramatic form." Mengel considers the trilogy of *Other Places* as a variation of major themes in works like *Landscape* and *Silence*--the isolation of the individual in modern mass society. Mengel interprets each of the three plays in great detail. He discusses *A Kind of Alaska* in relationship to Oliver Sacks' *Awakenings* and illustrates how Pinter takes Sacks' three stages of clinical awakening and condenses the pathology that would occur over weeks and months into a few minutes of dramatic action. Deviation from clinical findings, he argues, contribute to the play's "mythic" quality. The final complexity of Deborah's "rebirth" suggests a basic conflict between the authenticity of self available either in the subjective, psychological world or in the objective, empirical one.

Mengel's focus in *Victoria Station* is the unverifiability of the conversation between the controller and driver and the indefiniteness and ambivalence of their reality. He discusses the "chiastic dramatic structure," the reversal of roles of mother and son, in *Family Voices*. Mengel argues that *Family Voices* goes even further than the first two plays, which transpose dramatic process to audience response, and actually creates a new form of dramatic monologue. It is "a drama of mind" that elucidates "mental processes" which the audience, rather than the characters, understand. Among Pinter's most recent tendencies of the past ten years, he concludes, are his rejection of the techniques of mystification for a surplus of information within reversed chronology (*Betrayal, A Kind of Alaska, Family Voices*) and a shift "of focus from the mimetic towards the receptional pole of . . . dramaturgy."

Frances Gillen is Dana Foundation Professor of English and Director of the Honors Program at the University of Tampa. He is also founder and co-editor of *The Pinter Review* and the author of numerous articles on dramatists such as Pinter, Anthony Shaffer, Williams, Miller, and Stoppard, and modern novelists such as Woolf, Forster, McCarthy, James, and Heller.

In "'To Lay Bare': Pinter, Shakespeare, and *The Dwarfs*," Gillen demonstrates how discussions of *King Lear, Macbeth, Othello,* and *Hamlet* in Pinter's early novel, *The Dwarfs,* prefigure terms and concepts applicable to Pinter's later stage figures. Pinter's characters, he asserts, like Shakespeare's, all deal with ambiguous, nonverifiable signs, "the interpretation of which leads them to act outside their territorial limits upon an essentially private vision which cannot be justified by a more objective, social reality of which they nevertheless remain a part." In *The Birthday Party, The Caretaker,* and *The Homecoming,* among others, Pinter's characters act out of a certain degree of *hubris* which "pushes them blindly" beyond their safe territorial limits until they "collide with a greater force which their blindness had momentarily led them to deny."

Gillen's reading, while not ignoring the menace or external force often associated with early Pinter, emphasizes the power of the characters' interior worlds and suggests that to some extent, like Shakespeare's tragic heroes, they are responsible for their fate. In addition, the fact that they remain a part "of an objective machine," despite their illusions, "helps define the limits of theatricality and language in creating and negotiating reality." Some of Pinter's most telling moments, Gillen concludes, occur "when language collides with what it can no longer shape nor negotiate."

The book concludes with three informal essays, one a student's initial response to *The Dumb Waiter*; the second, an account of Pinter's appearance in New York in October 1989, when he recited *One for the Road* and was "interviewed" by Mel Gussow; and the third, a selection of photos borrowed from the actress Pauline Flanagan, who joined Anew McMaster's repertory company in Ireland at about the same time as Pinter.

"Mind-Less Men: Pinter's Dumb Waiters" is an essay that Robert Gordon, a sophomore at Harvard College, wrote for a modern drama course during his senior year in high school. Gordon ponders the selfhood of conventional dramatic protagonists--in Cartesian terms, as well as in those of the more recent philosopher Gilbert Ryle. He considers how the absence or barely residual presence of the Cartesian "windowless chamber," which has traditionally defined the "morally aware" protagonist, typifies Pinter's characters and is critical in distinguishing Ben from Gus. After a close reading of specific sequences, Gordon assesses what he calls Pinter's post-modern morality play, wherein what he calls the "post-ghost" man who "believes he has a consciousness must die."

Although he read no secondary sources for this assignment, Gordon also discusses Pinter's puns, the ironic allusions to the Biblical Abraham-Isaac sacrifice, and the more important issue of how word choice seems to have replaced moral choice. In the end, he finds Pinter's vision of human nature in which the "morally aware mind" is "banished" to be "at least as horrifying to our sensibility" as any in Western literature. At Harvard, Gordon is book review editor of the *Harvard Political Review* and a contributor to *Forum* and *Perspective* magazines.

Pauline Flanagan, who says: "The classics and repertory theater have remained my first love," has performed in all the major American repertory companies. Among her many credits, she has acted in some thirty of Shakespeare's plays, as well as a wide variety of classic and contemporary theater on and off Broadway--all of which she attributes to her early training in the McMaster company.

Born in Sligo, Flanagan came to the United States in the mid-fifties, where she first acted Shakespeare at Antioch College. One of her earliest roles in New York was Molly Bloom, opposite Zero Mostel, in Burgess Meredith's *Ulysses in Nighttown*, which subsequently traveled to London, Paris, Amsterdam, and The Hague. She also appeared with Zoe Caldwell and Dame Judith Anderson in *Medea* (and was cited for the Critics Circle Award), and with Claire Bloom in *The Innocents* (directed by Pinter). Her other Broadway shows have included *The Father*, *Under Milkwood*, *The Complaisant Lover*, *Steaming*, and *Corpse*. She acted in the Lincoln Center productions of *The Plough and the Stars*, *Antigone*, and *The Crucible*. Her repertory experience includes the Seattle (where she spent five years as leading lady), the Goodman, Arena, Houston Alley, and Guthrie (where she won the Judos award for *The Entertainer*). She has also done extensive work in stock and on television.

Flanagan remarks that whenever she sees Pinter and her other friends from the McMaster company, they all speak of the years with "Mac" as a "golden" time (Pinter's word). Flanagan's brother was a camera buff, so she collected an extraordinary record of the company both on and off stage. Portraits of Pinter as Horatio, Iago, Bassanio, and Lord Windermere, among others, appear below, as well as informal shots of the company relaxing and traveling; I have placed these alongside Flanagan's reminiscences and citations from Pinter's *Mac*.

CHRONOLOGY

1930   Harold Pinter is born in Hackney, London's East End, on October 10, the only child of Frances Mann and Hyman (Jack) Pinter, a hard-working tailor. "I lived in a brick house on Thistlewaite Road, . . . a working-class area, [of] some big, run-down Victorian houses, . . . a soap factory with a terrible smell, and a lot of railway yards, [and] shops" (*New Yorker*). Although this is an area with a large Jewish population, an ultra-right movement is headed by Sir Oswald Mosley, who, in 1932, forms the British Union of Fascists and becomes a supporter of Mussolini and Hitler.

1939-1942   "I was evacuated to the country . . . with twenty-four other boys" to a John Nash Gothic castle. Despite Cornwall's "desolate beauty," Pinter is "morose" and "very homesick" *(Observer)*. He is later moved closer to London, this time with his mother. It "was really frightening. The whole thing was very disturbing, to be a child, evacuated, . . . coming back to London, bombs, rockets, evacuated again. . . . It was all very unreal. . . ." (Kroll). "The sense of the Gestapo was very strong in England" (*Listener*). "Jewish families had a great respect for education. I was reading Joyce and Kafka and Dostoevski and writing . . . from about twelve" (Kroll).

xliii

1942-48　　Pinter attends Hackney Downs Grammar School. One of his masters recalls: "I had two brilliant boys. John Bloom [the former washing machine millionaire] and Harold Pinter. . . . Neither did a stroke of work" (*Observer*). Pinter comes under the influence of Cambridge-educated Joseph Brearley. He pursues his love of reading: "I had a pretty vigorous time with them all [Eliot, Dostoevski, Hemingway, Sartre, Joyce]. I used to discuss them at length with my friends" (Gross). "[When I was sixteen,] there were four or five of us. We went round in a gang. We stuck together and led our own lives. We went in for sports, we talked about literature, philosophy, girls" (Schifres). Pinter plays football and cricket, although "my main ability was sprinting" (*New Yorker*) and sets a school record. He writes poetry after the style of Dylan Thomas.

1942-48　　Traveling the ten-minute walk from his house to school, "I got into quite a few fights. . . . If you looked remotely like a Jew you might be in trouble. . . . I went to a Jewish club . . . and there were quite a lot of people often waiting with broken milk bottles" (Bensky). "There was a good deal of violence there, in those days" (*New Yorker*). "[Anti-semitism] took a brutal form, . . . but also one learnt how to avoid the fights by various means--by words, in fact" (*Listener*). Earlier on, of course, there was the frequent street bombing. "There were times when I would open our back door and find our garden in flames. Our house never burned, but we had to evacuate several times" (*New Yorker*).

1946   Pinter writes "James Joyce" for the school
        magazine, discussing the "screen of the
        subconscious mind" in *Ulysses*; he writes of
        Finnegans Wake: "Here we are in a dream
        world, having as its main axis, the River
        Liffey [where] all the rivers of the world
        meet. . . . At length the whole dream world
        falls asleep, and the words become drowsy
        and sleepy, and slowly the words subside
        into softness, softly drifting, and the work
        ends where it begins, in the middle of a
        sentence" (*Hackney Downs School
        Magazine*, 160, p. 32).

1947   Pinter participates in the Hackney Downs
        Literary and Debating Society, first
        opposing the proposition "That a United
        States of Europe would be the Only Means
        of Preventing War"; then he argues for the
        proposition "That War is Inevitable." His
        first acting role is a "word-perfect, full-
        voiced" Macbeth. He is also appointed
        prefect in Hammond House and debates
        "Realism and Post-realism in the French
        Cinema."

1948   Pinter receives the school cricket and
        football awards; he debates that "Film is
        More Promising in its Future as an Art Form
        than the Theatre." The school magazine
        reports that his Romeo was excellent "where
        strong action reinforce[d] words, as when he
        flung himself on the floor of the Friar's cell
        in passionate histrionic abandon." About
        pursuing an acting career, "contrary to what
        one might think, my parents were delighted"
        (Schifres). He has, in any case, considered
        Oxford or Cambridge but lacks the
        prerequisite Latin for matriculation.

1948   Pinter enrolls at the Royal Academy of
        Dramatic Arts on a London County Council
        Grant. He plays in *The Merry Wives of
        Windsor* and *The Barretts of Wimpole
        Street.* "I was a very unsophisticated young
        man, and they all seemed to be very
        sophisticated" (Crist). Pinter leaves the
        school, feigns a nervous breakdown and
        wanders around London. Having retained
        the L.C.C. grant during this time, he "went
        in and spoke [to the Principal] . . . on the
        verge of tears. [He] was a very nice man,
        I'm sorry I deceived him" (Gross).

1948   Pinter becomes a conscientious objector and
        appears at two trials; he is fined thirty
        pounds. That he "certainly" would have
        accepted National Service in 1939 is beyond
        question: "The feelings I had about
        National Service in 1948 wouldn't have
        applied in the war. I never said [I was] a
        pacifist. I simply said: 'I'm not going to
        subscribe to the Cold War'" (*Listener*).

1949   Pinter writes *Kullus* and other poems and
        short stories in monologue and dialogue
        forms.

1950   Pinter's first publications "New Year in the
        Midlands" and "Chandeliers and Shadows"
        appear in *Poetry London* under the
        Portuguese form of his name (Harold) Pinta.
        He also gets his first professional acting
        engagement on BBC radio, in "Focus on
        Football Pools" and "Focus on Libraries,"
        and works on *The Dwarfs.*

1951   Pinter acts the role of Abergevenny in *Henry
        VIII*, on the BBC's Third Programme and

enrolls at the Central School of Speech and Drama.

1951-53   Pinter answers an ad in the *Stage* for Anew McMaster's repertory company in Ireland. After a tryout at Willesden Junction, he begins to tour and performs classic theater (Sophocles, Shakespeare), comedies, and mysteries (Oscar Wilde, Agatha Christie). He continues his writing, including a chronicle of his youth in London.

1952   Pinter writes, in "The Anaesthetist's Pin": "At that incision sound/The lout is at the throat/And the dislocated word/Becomes articulate."

1953   Pinter joins Donald Wolfit's classical repertory company. Wolfit is an actor he idolized as a boy ("I saw [Lear] six times. I couldn't stop seeing it" [Gross]), and meets Vivien Merchant; both play in *As You Like It.*

1954-57   Continuing to tour in provincial repertory companies, like the Huddersfield, Richmond, Whitby, Colchester, and Palmer's Green, Pinter plays a large variety of roles and adopts the stage name David Baron. He also takes on odd jobs like bouncer at the Astoria dance hall on Charing Cross Road and waiter at the National Liberal Club, as well as other jobs as doorman, dishwasher, snow-shoveler, door to door salesman, and streethawker.

1956   Pinter meets up with Vivien Merchant again, at Bournemouth, and appears with her in *Witness for the Prosecution* and *Jane Eyre.*

They marry in 1956. He acts no less than twenty-five roles in the year, including romantic leading man, sophisticated author, farcical husband, psychotic, killer, whodunit detective, and antisocial rebel.

1957   Pinter attends a party in London and observes two men seated in a small room, one speaking continuously as he butters the other's bread. The latter, who wears a cap, is a silent lorry driver. "This image would never leave me" (Kroll).

1957   While touring in the Torquay company, his childhood friend Henry Woolf, now at Bristol University, asks him to write a play. Pinter completes *The Room* in four afternoons, and it is staged in a converted squash court at Bristol. Pinter also writes *The Dumb Waiter.* During this touring period, he acts in such diverse plays as *Doctor in the House, Hay Fever, All My Sons, Look Back in Anger, Separate Tables, Bell, Book and Candle, Love from a Stranger, Mornings at Seven,* and *Spider's Web.* Accommodations are often inadequate; at one hotel, there was "an obscene household-- . . . filth . . . tea strainers . . . infantility. . . . I was in those digs, and this woman [became] Meg [of *The Birthday Party*]. . . . There was a fellow staying there . . . on the coast" (Bensky).

1958   Daniel Pinter is born. Independent producer Michael Codron buys the option on *The Birthday Party* for 50 pounds. Pinter understudies for N. F. Simpson's *A Resounding Tinkle* at the Royal Court as *The Birthday Party* opens in Cambridge and then

Oxford; when the play is later produced in London at the Lyric Hammersmith, it closes after one week, having earned a total of £206, 11s, 8d. Harold Hobson defends it in the next Sunday *Times*. Pinter begins *The Hothouse* and *Something in Common* (still unperformed).

1959   *The Dumb Waiter* is premiered in Germany. *The Black and White* and *Trouble in the Works*, review sketches for *One to Another*, are produced by Michael Codron at the Lyric Hammersmith; four sketches--*Special Offer*, *Getting Acquainted, Last to Go*, and *Request Stop*--are included in *Pieces of Eight*. A *Slight Ache*, commissioned in 1958 for the BBC Third Programme, is broadcast with Vivien Merchant and Maurice Denham and later televised. Pinter writes *The Caretaker* and *A Night Out.*

1960   Pinter directs the London production of *The Room* and *The Dumb Waiter*, starring Vivien Merchant and Henry Woolf, at the Hampstead Theatre Club and acts the role of Deeley in a broadcast and television version of *A Night Out*; he also plays Goldberg in a Cheltenham production of *The Birthday Party*, which is also staged at the Actors' Workshop in San Francisco and on television. His first commercial success, *The Caretaker* opens at the Arts Theatre Club and then moves to the West End (with Alan Bates, Peter Woodthorpe, and Donald Pleasence). It wins the *Evening Standard* award. *The Dumb Waiter* is staged in London and Madison, Wisconsin; Pinter writes the radio version of his autobiographical novel, *The Dwarfs*, which is then broadcast (with Pinter directing). *Night School* is both broadcast and televised.

1961   *A Slight Ache* is adapted for the stage and produced at the Arts Theatre Club. Pinter plays Mick in the final four weeks of *The Caretaker* in London; it closes after 425 performances. *A Night Out* is staged in Dublin and London. *The Collection* is televised, and *The Caretaker* opens in New York at the Lyceum, with Robert Shaw replacing Peter Woodthorpe; it wins the Page One Award of the Newspaper Guild of New York.

1962   Pinter directs, with Peter Hall, *The Collection* at the Aldwych, thus beginning his association with the Royal Shakespeare Company. *The Dumb Waiter* and *The Collection* are produced in New York. Pinter reads *The Examination* on BBC radio and writes the screenplays of *The Guest* (from *The Caretaker*) and *The Servant*, based on Robin Maugham's novel. He also writes *The Lover.*

1963   Pinter writes the short story "Tea Party," as well as an original filmscript *The Compartment* (for *Project I*, with Samuel Beckett and Eugene Ionesco). *The Lover* and *The Dwarfs* are staged at the Arts Theatre Club (with Pinter codirecting). *The Lover*, produced on television with Vivien Merchant, wins the Italia Prize and British TV Producers and Directors Award. *The Guest* wins the Edinburgh Festival Certificate of Merit, the Berlin Film Festival Silver Bear, and the Screenwriters Guild Award. *The Servant* is released (with Pinter

in a small role).   Pinter also writes the
screenplay of *The Pumpkin Eater*, based on
Penelope Mortimer's novel.

1964   Pinter writes *The Homecoming* and directs
the Royal Shakespeare production of *The
Birthday Party.   A Slight Ache* (with *The
Room*) and *The Lover* are all staged in New
York; *The Dumb Waiter* is televised.   Pinter
writes five new sketches and reads a prose
version of *Tea Party* on BBC radio.   He
wins the New York Film Critics and British
Screenwriters Guild awards for *The Servant*,
which is also entered in the Venice Film
Festival.   He moves into an 1820 five-story
Nash house in Regent's Park that overlooks
the boating lake.

1965   *The Homecoming*, in its pre-London tour, is
presented   by   the   Royal   Shakespeare
Company   at   the   New   Theatre,   Cardiff
Wales, and then the Aldwych--with Ian
Holm, Vivien Merchant, Michael Bryant,
Paul   Rogers,   Terence   Rigby,   and   John
Normington.   *The Room* and *Tea Party* are
televised; the latter is broadcast to eleven
countries.   Pinter wins the British Film
Academy Award for *The Pumpkin Eater.*
He acts the role of Garcia in Sartre's *No Exit*
for BBC television.

1966   Pinter is awarded the Order of the British
Empire.   *A Slight Ache* and *The Caretaker*
are   televised.   He   writes   *The   Quiller
Memorandum* from Adam Hall's novel *The
Berlin Memorandum.*

1967   *The Birthday Party* is produced in New
York   at   the   Booth   Theater.   *The*

Homecoming also opens in New York at the Music Box with the Royal Shakespeare Company; it wins an Antoinette Perry (Tony) Award, the Whitbread Anglo-American Theater Award, and New York Drama Critics Circle Award. Pinter also writes the screenplay *Accident* from Nicholas Mosley's novel and appears in one scene; the film wins the Cannes Jury Prize and is called one of the ten best of the year by the National Board of Reviewers. Pinter directs Robert Shaw's *The Man in the Glass Booth* in London. *The Basement* is produced on BBC television, with Pinter in the lead. Pinter is voted one of England's ten best-dressed men.

1968   *Landscape*, after being censored for stage production because it includes a four-letter word, is broadcast on the BBC with Peggy Ashcroft and Eric Porter. Pinter directs *The Man in the Glass Booth* in New York. His *Tea Party* and *The Basement* are also staged in New York. *Pendragon* is banned from the stage. Pinter writes the screenplay of *The Birthday Party.*

1969   *Silence* and *Landscape* are staged at the Aldwych; Pinter directs the *Innocents*, by William Archibald, at the Morosco, in New York. He plays Lenny in the Watford production of *The Homecoming* and takes the voice of two cartoon characters in "NBC Experiment in TV: Pinter People" (also with Donald Pleasence). *Night* is presented in *Mixed Doubles* at the Comedy Theatre. Pinter writes the screenplay *The Go-Between* from L. P. Hartley's novel. Pinter also writes the screenplay of *The Homecoming.*

1970 Pinter writes *Old Times. Silence* and *Landscape* are staged in New York. *Tea Party* is produced in London. Pinter acts in the film *The Rise and Rise of Michael Rimmer* and directs *Exiles* (James Joyce) at the Mermaid. He wins the Hamburg Shakespeare Prize (where he makes the frequently quoted remark that his plays are about "the weasel under the cocktail table"). He also wins an Hon. D. Litt. from the University of Reading. He is elected an Honorary Fellow in the Modern Language Association.

1971 *Old Times* is staged in London and New York. Pinter directs Simon Gray's *Butley* in Oxford and London. He earns the Hon. D. Litt. from Birmingham University, the Writers Guild Award, the Cannes Film Festival Golden Palm (for *The Go-Between*), and another BAFTA award. He writes *Langrishe, Go Down* from Aidan Higgins' novel.

1972 Pinter writes *Monologue* for television and is commissioned by Joseph Losey to write the screenplay of Proust's *À la recherche du temps perdu.*

1973 Pinter directs his first film, his screenplay of *Butley*, and wins the Austrian State Prize for European Literature. *Monologue* is televised, and the American Film Theater films *The Homecoming.* He publicly states his position against U.S. support of the overthrow of Allende in Chile.

1973   Pinter is appointed by Peter Hall as an
            Associate Director of the National Theatre,
            London.

1974   Pinter writes *No Man's Land* and the
            screenplay of *The Last Tycoon*. He also
            directs John Hopkin's *Next of Kin*, at the
            National. He earns honorary doctorates
            from Glasgow and East Anglia universities.

1975   Pinter directs Simon Gray's *Otherwise
            Engaged* in Oxford and London and acts in
            the BBC radio production of *Monologue*.
            No Man's Land is staged at the Old Vic with
            Ralph Richardson and John Gielgud. Vivien
            Merchant begins divorce proceedings
            against Pinter.

1976   Pinter directs Noel Coward's *Blithe Spirit* in
            London and William Archibald's *The
            Innocents* in New York. *No Man's Land*
            opens in New York. Pinter directs *Butley* on
            television and acts in *Rogue Male*, as well as
            in the radio production of Samuel Beckett's
            Rough for Radio.

1977   Pinter directs Simon Gray's *Otherwise
            Engaged* in New York. He acts in *Two
            Plays* by Vaclav Havel.

1978   *Betrayal* is produced at the National; Pinter
            revises *The Collection* for television;
            Langrishe, Go Down is adapted for
            television (Pinter acts in it). He also directs
            Simon Gray's *The Rear Column* at the
            Globe; *No Man's Land* is televised.

1979   *Betrayal* wins the SWET Award. Pinter
            directs Simon Gray's *Close of Play* at the

National. He earns the Hon. D. Litt. from Stirling University.

1980   Pinter and Vivien Merchant divorce. Pinter marries writer Lady Antonia Fraser. He directs *The Hothouse* at the Hampstead and wins the Pirandello Prize. *Betrayal* opens in New York. Pinter wins a second New York Drama Critics Award. Pinter donates the proceeds from his birthday celebration at the National to Vaclav Havel.

1981   Pinter directs Simon Gray's *Quartermaine's Terms* and Robert East's *Incident at Tulsa Hill*. He writes the screenplays *The French Lieutenant's Woman* and *Betrayal*. *The Hothouse* is televised, and *Family Voices* is broadcast in London and produced in Cambridge, Massachusetts, and London. He shares the third annual Commonwealth Award for Distinguished Service in Dramatic Arts with Tennessee Williams.

1982   *Other Places* (*Victoria Station*, *A Kind of Alaska*, *Family Voices*) is produced in London; *Family Voices* wins the Giles Cooper Award. Pinter also wins the David De Donatello Prize and earns the Hon. D. Litt. from Brown University. At Brown, *The Hothouse* is premiered (U.S.) by the Trinity Square Repertory company. *The French Lieutenant's Woman* receives an Academy Award nomination for best film. Pinter and Lady Antonia organize an International PEN event for imprisoned writers.

1983   Pinter directs Jean Giraudoux's *The Trojan War Will Not Take Place* at the National.

He also becomes director at United British Artists and wins the British Theatre Association Award. The sketch *Precisely*, in *The Big One*, is produced in London; *Betrayal* is filmed.

1984   Pinter revises *Other Places* (now substituting *One for the Road* for *Family Voices*) for the London production, which he directs; it opens in New York at the Manhattan Theatre Club. The receipts from the Dublin production are donated to famine relief in Ethiopia. Pinter directs Simon Gray's *The Common Pursuit* at the Lyric Hammersmith and earns the Elmer Holmes Bobst Award in Arts and Letters from New York University.

1985   On behalf of PEN, Pinter travels with Arthur Miller for five days to Turkey to express their solidarity with dissident writers. They appear before the Istanbul Journalists' Association with a petition signed by 2,330 writers, scientists, and churchmen demanding international respect for human rights. Pinter also writes the screenplay *Turtle Diary* and directs Tennessee Williams' *Sweet Bird of Youth*; *One for the Road* is televised. He wins another British Theatre Association Award and plays Deeley in a London production of *Old Times* with Liv Ullmann. Pinter becomes an honorary fellow of the American Academy of Arts and Sciences, as well as of Queen Mary College, London.

1986   Pinter and Lady Antonia host the anti-Thatcherite seminars at their home ("the June 20th Society"), with John Mortimer,

Margaret Drabble, Salman Rushdie, and others. The "Bollinger Bolsheviks" are ridiculed by the likes of Peregrine Worsthorne (*Spectator*) and the Liberal Paul Bailey (*Independent*). Pinter directs Donald Freed's *Circe and Bravo* at Wyndham's and earns an Hon. D. Litt. at Hull University. Lifeline Theater, in Chicago, presents "Ten Pinter Plays." In Richmond, Edward de Souza does a one-man "Players and Other Pinter Pieces." Pinter tours the U.S. with Liv Ullmann in *Old Times*.

1987   Pinter begins the screenplay *The Handmaid's Tale* from Margaret Atwood's novel and wins the Literary Lions Award at the New York Public Library. He acts Goldberg in the BBC *The Birthday Party*. He and Lady Antonia, Ken Follett, and George Galloway release 1800 black balloons in Grosvenor Square, outside the U.S. Embassy, in protest against U.S. involvement in the Contra war. Pinter founds the Arts for Nicaragua Fund.

1988   *Mountain Language*, described in the London press as "agit-prop," is televised, and Pinter directs the London production at the National. He writes the screenplay *The Heat of the Day* from Elizabeth Bowen's novel. He and Lady Antonia continue to host the June 20th Society, with David Hare, John Mortimer, Margaret Drabble, Michael Holroyd, and Germaine Greer, among others. Pinter speaks out increasingly on human rights, British censorship and anti-homosexuality policies, and U.S. involvement in Central America. He delivers a lecture to the European

Conference on City-linking Nicaragua in Amsterdam. Pinter also writes screenplays of Fred Uhlmann's novel *Reunion* and Ian McEwan's *The Comfort of Strangers.*

1989   *Mountain Language* opens in New York. Pinter writes the filmscript of Conrad's *Victory* and begins working on Kafka's *The Trial.* He films *Reunion* with Jerry Schatzberg: "When you look at the photos of 1932, of the early days of Nazism in Germany, it is the blue eyes, the shining smiles, that are so extraordinarily vivid, and it is the conviction and apparent innocence, which are so alarming" (*Film Comment*).

1990   Pinter delivers a speech by Salman Rushdie (in hiding), at the Institute of Contemporary Arts in London. He organizes the April 1 celebration in honor of Samuel Beckett at the National Theatre. *The Dwarfs* is published. On the occasion of his sixtieth birthday, the BBC sponsors a lengthy tribute that includes a broadcast of *Betrayal*, in which Pinter plays the role of Robert. *The Birthday Party* is revived. The screenplays *The Handmaid's Tale* and *The Comfort of Strangers* are released; Pinter writes some scenes for the screenplay of Kazuo Ishiguro's *The Remains of the Day. The Heat of the Day* airs on television. Pinter directs Jane Stanton Hitchcock's *Vanilla.* He is awarded a D.Litt. at the University of Sussex. Pinter speaks out against numerous injustices, including Israel's treatment of the Palestinians and the sabotage and terror caused by the U.S. against the Sandanistas. He speaks on television about language, a "permanent masquerade."

1991   *The New World Order* is staged with Ariel
        Dorfman's *Death and the Maiden* at the
        Royal Court. *Party Time* is introduced at the
        Pinter Festival: An International Meeting, at
        Ohio State University, Columbus, Ohio. It
        debuts (with Pinter directing) in London
        with *Mountain Language.* Peter Hall directs
        The Homecoming at the Comedy Theatre;
        the play is also revived in New York.
        Donald Pleasence, 71, returns to play Davies
        in *The Caretaker. The Caretaker* has several
        New York revivals. Pinter speaks out against
        Israel's politics in the occupied territories, as
        well as its arrest of Mordecai Vanunu,
        accused of exposing Israel's nuclear
        resources; the Turks' treatment of the Kurds;
        Thatcher's right-wing policies--for example,
        her government's plan to deport Iraqi and
        Palestinian nationals and the arrest of Abbas
        Cheblak; and U.S. policy in Nicaragua and
        the Gulf War, with its "battle carnage on a
        scale . . . [with] some of this century's
        most horrifying military engagements"
        (Billington). His poem "American
        Football," about America's obscene politics,
        is rejected by numerous newspapers because
        of its "obscene language."

1992   Pinter acts the role of Hirst in the revival of
        No Man's Land. Party Time is televised with
        the 1991 Almeida cast. "Pinter Review: A
        Revival of Five Short Pieces by Harold
        Pinter" is mounted. *The Caretaker* is
        revived in New York. Pinter begins
        Moonlight. It started with "an image of a
        man in bed, dying, and his wife was in the
        room. . . . I am pretty sure that the line
        'Where are they?' [meaning his sons] was
        central to the whole. It was a question of

children who weren't there" (Gussow). He receives the insignia of Grand Officer, the Chilean Order of Merit for his "support for the Chilean people in their fight to recover democracy." The June 20th Society disbands.

1993   *Moonlight*, Pinter's first full-length play in fifteen years, is staged at the Almeida, then transferred to the Comedy Theatre. *No Man's Land* is revived, with Pinter acting in the production. *The Trial* is released. Pinter directs David Mamet's *Oleanna*. He donates sixty boxes of manuscripts to the British Museum.

1994   The Gate Theatre in Dublin holds a Pinter Festival; six plays are presented over three weeks: *The Dumb Waiter* and *Betrayal*; *One for the Road* and *Old Times*; and *Landscape* (directed by Pinter) and *Moonlight*. *No Man's Land* is revived at the Roundabout Theater in New York; *The Caretaker* is also revived in New York. *The Birthday Party*, *The Caretaker*, *A Kind of Alaska*, and *Landscape* (with Pinter directing) are revived in London. Pinter begins a screenplay for *Lolita*. He reads *Mountain Language* at the Cardiff Festival of Literature and donates the proceeds to Amnesty International and the PEN Writers in Prison Committee. He continues writing and speaking out against the brutalities caused by "democratic" powers, their "funding of mass murders" (Knowles).

1995   Pinter wins the David Cohn British Literature prize of £30,000 for lifetime achievement. He is awarded an honorary doctorate at the

University of Sofia, in Bulgaria, and delivers "A War on Words" speech. At the Chichester Festival Theatre, he directs Ronald Harwood's *Taking Sides* and plays Roote in *The Hothouse*; *The Hothouse* moves to Bath and then to the West End. *Moonlight* opens in New York at the Roundabout Theatre. *Old Times* is revived. Pinter continues to protest global brutalities and persecution in the name of democracy. He signs a petition on behalf of U.S. former Black Panther and writer Abu-Jamal and joins a PEN group at the Nigerian Embassy to protest the treatment of Ogoni writer Saro-Wiwa, later hanged. "Murder is the most brutal form of censorship" (Billington).

1996   *Ashes to Ashes*, which Pinter writes in ten days and in four drafts, is staged at the Royal Court. Pinter comments: "*Ashes to Ashes* is about torturers and victims. The woman in this two-character play is haunted. And so am I. . . . I'm haunted by barbaric acts around me" (Ross). *The Homecoming* is revived. A Kurdish group in London presents *Mountain Language*. *The Collection* and David Mamet's *Sexual Perversity in Chicago* are mounted in New York. Pinter directs Reginald Rose's *Twelve Angry Men* and acts in Hugh Whitemore's teleplay *Breaking the Code*. Pinter wins the Laurence Olivier "Special Award" for his "outstanding contribution to the theater." His portrait, by Justin Mortimer, is hung in the National Portrait Gallery.

1997   Pinter receives the Molière d'Honneur for lifetime achievement; the *Sunday Times* awards Pinter the Award for Literary

Excellence. At the Gate Theatre in Dublin, a second Pinter Festival includes *Ashes to Ashes*, *No Man's Land*, *A Kind of Alaska*, and *The Collection* (with Pinter playing Harry). Pinter directs *Ashes to Ashes* in Palermo. Pinter plays Sam Ross in the film *Mojo*. The National Film Theatre hosts a retrospective of Pinter's films. *The Collection*, included in a program called "Begot," is revived in London. Pinter directs Simon Gray's *Life Support*. He writes *My Dark House*, a film adaptation of Karen Blixen's (Isak Dinesen's) story "The Dreaming Child." He continues to publicly denounce nations like the United States and Britain for the barbaric conditions in East Timor, Latin America, Turkey, and Central America. His demands for the repeal of the Police Bill, authorizing phone bugging, is covered on the first page of the *Telegraph*. He, and other writers, read their own and other banned work at the South Bank Center.

1998   A number of revivals include *A Kind of Alaska*, *Collection*, and *The Lover; The Collection* (in which Pinter acts), *Betrayal*, and *The Homecoming*. *The Lover* is also staged in London with Strindberg's *The Stronger*. *The Dumb Waiter* is revived in New York. *The Dwarfs* is selected for the 1998 National Student Drama Festival, sponsored by the *Sunday Times*. Pinter and Antonia Fraser join antiwar protesters at the House of Commons denouncing U.S. sanctions on Iraq, saying the policy is killing children. Pinter continues to speak out on a number of issues, including the Kurds' lack of free transportation across borders and the

West's immoral sale of arms to Turkey. He again expresses his disillusion with New Labour and with Tony Blair's collusion with America's corrupt power politicians; he speaks against the curtailment of civil liberties in Britain (Knowles). He reads in London from *A Bright Shining Hill* by imprisoned Mumia Abu-Jamal.

1999   Pinter is made a Companion of Literature by the Royal Society of Literature. He also receives an honorary D.Litt. from the University of London. Queen Mary and Westfield College opens the Harold Pinter Drama Studio. *Ashes to Ashes* opens in New York at the Gramercy. *The Homecoming*, *The Birthday Party*, and *Betrayal* are revived in London. *A Kind of Alaska*, *The Lover*, and *The Hothouse* are revived in New York. Pinter plays Sir Edmund Bertram in the film adaptation of Jane Austen's *Mansfield Park*. He directs Simon Gray's *The Late Middle Classes*. In May, Pinter joins Noam Chomsky, Alan Clark, and Germaine Greer in opposition to the U.S.-NATO bombings of Serbia. He protests against Pinochet's extradition to Spain. He says: "I've been told so often that I live in a free country, I'm damn well going to be free. . . . I'm going to retain my independence of mind and spirit, and I think that's what is obligatory upon all of us" (O'Toole).

2000   Pinter receives the Lifetime Achievement award from the Critics' Circle and the Brianza Poetry Prize (Italy). He also receives a D.Litt. from Aristotle University, Thessaloniki, Greece. *Celebration* and *The Room*, directed by Pinter, are staged in London. *The Dwarfs* is revived. Tim Roth invites Pinter to write a screen version of Shakespeare's *King Lear*. Pinter's screenplay of *À la recherche du temps perdu* is performed at the National Theatre; Pinter has adapted it to the stage. When eleven Kurds rehearse *Mountain Language* with the weapons called for in the play--and they use plastic guns--their illegal arrest (after which they are forbidden to speak their native language) results in Scotland Yard's agreement to pay the Kurds £55,000 in compensation. Pinter says: "The line between fiction and reality sometimes becomes very blurred" (O'Toole). David Mamet directs Pinter and Sir John Gielgud (shortly before his death) in Beckett's *Catastrophe*, planned for the Beckett Film Project, to include all of Beckett's works. The Pinter Society hosts an elaborate three-day celebration of meetings and performances for Pinter's seventieth birthday in London; another of many birthday celebrations is organized by PEN. In addition to a major London revival of *The Caretaker*, with Michael Gambon, *Betrayal* returns to New York. Plans are made for a major Pinter retrospective at New York's Lincoln Center in 2001.

INTERVIEWS CITED

"*Caretaker's* Caretaker," *Time*, 10 November 1961, 76.

Lawrence Bensky, "Harold Pinter: An Interview," *Paris Review* 10 (fall 1966): 13-37.

Alain Schifres, "Harold Pinter: Caretaker of Britain's New Theater," *Réalités* 193 (December 1966): n.p.

"Two People in a Room: Playwriting," *New Yorker*, 25 February 1967, 34-36.

Judith Crist, "A Mystery: Pinter on Pinter," *Look*, 24 December 1968, 77-78.

"Master of Silence," *Observer*, 27 April, 1975, 11.

Jack Kroll, "The Puzzle of Pinter," *Newsweek*, 29 November 1976, 75-78, 81.

Miriam Gross, "Pinter on Pinter," *Observer*, 5 October 1980, 25, 27.

"Radical Departures, Harold Pinter and Anna Ford," *Listener*, 27 December 1988, 4-6.

Mel, Gussow, *Conversations with Pinter*, New York: Grove, 1994, 98.

Ronald Knowles, *The Pinter Review: Collected Essays 1995 and 1996:* 167; *The Pinter Review: Collected Essays 1997 and 1998:* 183.

Michael Billington, *The Life and Work of Harold Pinter*, London: Faber and Faber, 1996: 327-30, 373.

Mireia Aragay, "Writing, Politics, and *Ashes to Ashes:* An Interview with Harold Pinter," *The Pinter Review: Collected Essays 1995 and 1996* (1997): 10.

Lillian Ross, "The Things that Haunt Harold Pinter," *New Yorker* 1 (February 1999): 22-32.

Fintan O'Toole, "Our Own Jacobean," *New York Review of Books.* 7 (October 1999): 28-32.

PINTER AT 70

CREATIVE PROCESS AND MEANING--
SOME REMARKS OF PINTER'S
"LETTER TO PETER WOOD"

Martin Esslin

In its 1981 summer issue, the *Kenyon Review* published a letter that Harold Pinter had written twenty-three years earlier to Peter Wood, the director of the original production of *The Birthday Party*.

I was, at that time, acting as drama editor of the recently revived *Kenyon Review* and had asked Pinter whether he had any hitherto unpublished material that would enhance the prestige of the once so influential quarterly. He replied to me, on 17 December 1980, that he had, in digging through his papers, discovered this letter he had written, adding: "It seems to me a very young man's letter, but I suppose the interest might lie in that."

This letter, dated 30 March 1958, is a remarkable document and of wider interest than merely providing insights into Pinter's ideas at that time. It has a bearing on broader aspects of our understanding of the creative process in dramatic writing in general.

The context of this letter, written on the eve of the start of rehearsals for the first production of *The Birthday Party*, Pinter's first full-length play, is clear: Peter Wood, an established and highly regarded director in the English theatre, had asked Pinter to give Stanley, the leading character in the play, some lines that would help the audience to understand his situation and motivations in withdrawing into the sleazy seaside boarding house where he is being sought out by the two sinister messengers of some ill-defined evil power. This Pinter categorically refused to do:

> To put such words as we discussed into Stanley's mouth would be an inexcusable imposition and falsity on my part. Stanley *cannot* perceive his only valid justification--which is he is what he is--therefore he certainly can never be articulate about it. He knows only to attempt to justify himself by dream, by pretence and by bluff, through fright. If he had cottoned on to the fact that he need only admit to himself what he actually is and is not--then Goldberg and McCann would not have paid their visit, or if they had, the same course of events would have been by no means assured. Stanley would have been another man. The play would have been another play.

So, here as in so many other situations, the author stands by what he has written. He wrote this play and no other. In my wide experience with dramatists over a lifetime's work with them, that is a familiar and expected reaction. An attack on what they have constructed, thought out and devised is perceived by them as an attack against their intelligence and their skill.

There are, of course, wide differences in the mentality and working processes of playwrights. At one end of the spectrum are those for whom the act of writing is mainly an intellectual process, to be planned and worked out by strict reasoning. At the other end of the spectrum are those who rely on the subconscious processes of "inspiration." There are many different gradations between these extremes. In Pinter's case, as in that of many others, often the very best playwrights, the text is not primarily a product of planned and conscious reasoning. Pinter describes how the play developed from a first image of the kitchen and the characters he saw in that kitchen:

The thing germinated and bred itself. It proceeded according to its own logic. What did I do? I followed the indications, I kept a sharp eye on the clues I found myself dropping. The writing arranged itself with no trouble into dramatic terms. The characters sounded in my ears--it was apparent to me what one would say and what would be the other's response, at any given point. It was apparent to me what they would not, could not, ever, say, whatever one might wish. I interfered with them only on the technical level. My task was not to damage their consistency at any time-- through any external notion of my own.

There could hardly be a more graphic description of the process of "inspiration," so widely referred to by poets throughout the ages--and Pinter is a poet, make no mistake about that. Not only is this a process by which the "Muse" dictates the words to the hand that holds the pen; in the case of a dramatic poet it is the characters themselves who speak in their own voice. The key word Pinter uses here is "consistency." The consistency of each character, his remaining true to his own personality and mode of utterance, must not be damaged.

When the thing was well cooked I began to form certain conclusions. The point is, however, that by that time the play was now in its own world. It was determined by its own original engendering image. . . . When I began to think *analytically* about it (as far as I can manage to do that, which isn't very far) I did so by keeping in step with what was being suggested, by judging the whole caper through an accurate assessment of the happenings described. . . .

Yet, and here we come to the mystery and paradox at the very core of the creative process, while the writer feels that the text develops spontaneously under his pen, that the words are being dictated to him by his "Muse" or by his characters, he is yet deeply aware of the fact that this is *his* text, his own, most personal utterance. The somnambulist may not choose where and how he is to walk, yet there can be no doubt about the fact that it is he who is doing the walking, that, in the case of the dramatic poet, it is *his* "Muse" who is dictating to him, that these are most profoundly *his* characters who are uttering their words.

> None of what I have said means that I disclaim responsibility for my characters. On the contrary. I am responsible both for them and to them. The play dictated itself but I confess that I wrote it--with intent, maliciously, purposefully, in command of its growth. Does this appear to contradict all that I said earlier? Splendid. You may suggest that this command was not strict enough and not lucid enough but who supposes I am striving for lucidity?

Here Pinter puts his finger on the basic dividing line between expository, discursive writing, on the one hand, and creative writing on the other. The play does not represent a process of thought. It was, as Pinter clearly states, "determined by its own original *image*" (my emphasis). An image does not have to be lucid, or logical, although, in the case of a play, it must have the consistency of the world that image represents and the consistency also of the characters who people that world. It is that basic image--which was the starting point of the process which, by the very fact that it so obsessed the author that he felt compelled to embark on the process of seeing it develop under his own hands--that makes it and the work that grew from it so profoundly his own. The creative process here can thus be seen as an act of surrender to the power of one's own obsession with an image and its implications.

Of course, there has also to be present in the individual who surrenders to this impulse the technical ability, the know-how and sense of form to translate the image into a viable dramatic structure. Yet these technical skills must have become instinctive, and almost automatic, so that they do not interfere with the free flow of the inspiration. The analogy here is that of someone who has to learn to drive by consciously learning all the moves involved in the skill of driving, but once he has internalised these skills, no longer has to think each time he uses the gear lever or the gas pedal; he is conscious merely of where he wants to go. In the same way a ballet dancer, once she has learned all the steps and has internalised the rhythms and moves, can concentrate on the emotions the ballet requires her to express.

It is no coincidence that Pinter started to produce plays of the quality of *The Birthday Party* after having spent many years as a repertory actor who, by having to rehearse and perform a different play every week, had to internalise all the techniques of playwriting--the techniques, in this case, of the then current middle-brow drawing room comedy or detective play, from Agatha Christie to Rattigan, from Frank Vosper to J. B. Priestley, that dominated the English provincial repertory theatres in the fifties.

It is the confluence of the obsessive image that springs from the very depths of the writer's subconscious with the technical skills that have become second nature to him that creates the curious quality of Pinter's plays. By taste and inclination, Pinter is a poet deeply influenced by Joyce, Beckett, and Kafka. But Pinter's technical formation came from the well-made, middle-brow play-- with one set, few characters, a realistic milieu, carefully contrived exits and entrances, and dialogue stemming from the tradition of English high-comedy timing (that traditionally most valued skill of English actors) developed to the highest pitch of skill by Wilde and Coward.

Works produced by this type of creative process, based on obsessive inspiration and fashioned by instinctive stage-craft, are like, for example, the political parables of Brecht, constructed with the premeditated intention of putting over a political or philosophical meaning. The author himself must approach their ultimate meaning with the same unprejudiced objectivity with which any other critic embarks on the interpretive process. In his letter to Peter Wood, Pinter tentatively arrives at just such an interpretation:

> We've agreed: the hierarchy, the Establishment, the arbiters, the socioreligious monsters arrive to affect censure and alteration upon a member of the club who has discarded responsibility (that word again) towards himself and others. (What is your opinion, by the way, of the act of suicide?) He does possess, however, for my money, a certain fibre--he fights for his life. It doesn't last long, this fight. His core being a quagmire of delusion, his mind a tenuous fusebox, he collapses under the weight of their accusation--an accusation compounded of the shitstained strictures of centuries of "tradition."

Note that this interpretation is unspecific: there is no definition of the kind of establishment, the kind of tradition, the kind of non-conformity involved. This is wholly in tune with the concept of the "image" as against that of the logical "concept" or the specifically factual element in discursive thought. It is the lack of definition of the image which gives it its generality, its universality. It represents a mood, an atmosphere, a generalised attitude to a universally present experience which lifts it above the mere topicality of specific political or religious or cultural polemics. As Pinter himself has it here:

> Meaning begins in the words, in the action, continues in your head and ends nowhere. There is no end to meaning. Meaning which is resolved, parcelled, labelled and ready for export is dead, impertinent--and meaningless.

Pinter here displays, brilliantly, that negative capability of which Keats speaks in a famous letter: "when a man is capable of being in uncertainties, mysteries, doubt, without any irritable reaching after fact and reason." It is precisely this very infinite openness of meaning that constitutes the essence of a piece of poetic imagery like *The Birthday Party*. Pinter shares this refusal of self-interpretation with his admitted models Joyce, Beckett, and Kafka. "Everything to do with the play is in the play" he tells Peter Wood, in the same spirit in which Beckett told Alan Schneider, in a famous letter, dated 29 December 1959, that

> my work is a matter of fundamental sounds (no joke intended) made as fully as possible. If people want to have headaches among the overtones, let them. And provide their own aspirin. Hamm as stated, Clov as stated, together as stated, nec tecum nec sine te, in such a place and in such a world, that's all I can manage, more than I could.

It is remarkable how closely Pinter's attitude in his letter to Peter Wood, written nine months before Beckett's letter to *his* director, parallels that of the older playwright.

Yet what must be stressed here is that while the writer himself refuses to become a commentator on his own work, simply because his own intention is as obscure to him as to anyone else, and because everything that the play has to say must be in the play itself, the hermeneutic process is by no means discouraged by the author; on the contrary, both Beckett and Pinter stress the openness of their work to interpretation. Beckett positively invites the interpreters to acquire headaches among the overtones, and Pinter considers the infinite recession of possible meanings as a positive asset of a work like his.

Once the creative process has produced the text, the umbilical cord that binds it to its author is broken; the work exists by and for itself, apart from the author. The author can contemplate it as something wholly outside himself. As Pinter tells Peter Wood, "the play exists now apart from me, you or anybody." Hence the author no longer possesses any greater right to interpret the text than anyone else. The work is there and anyone who encounters it must make of it what he can. The author cannot provide the reader or spectator with a *mode d'emploi*, "directions for use."   In that sense the post-structuralist view of the autonomy of the text is here recognised by Pinter himself. Does that mean, then, that any interpretation is as good as any other? Yes and no.

The meaning of the text--or in a theatrical performance, the meaning of the whole infinitely more complex structure of the semiotic systems--emerges from the whole hierarchy of semantic levels, of signifiers of different orders of precision.   There is the level of the language itself: when corn flakes are mentioned, all those familiar with the product will have a very clear picture of what is involved.   Similarly the clothes Stanley wears will be, to all those familiar with sartorial habits of English people around 1960, clear and unmistakable signs of his slovenliness and lack of interest in being well dressed. Hence on a basic level of analysis, acquaintance with the English language of the period (the meaning of the vocable "corn flakes") might be important for someone interpreting the text at a different period of history when, perhaps, these commodities are no longer produced.   The same applies to the clothes mentioned or presented and a multitude of other elements.   They make up, as it were, the material infrastructure of the image.

In more conventional drama the same might be said of the motivations and psychological problems faced by the characters.   In plays like *The Birthday Party* that level of factual infrastructure is not provided.   It is this which makes the image more mysterious, more open to a very much wider range of interpretation.

Even in the most conventional play, however, the ultimate "meaning" of the experience that the individual spectator has gone through remains wide open: for the experience will resonate in the mind and memory of the spectator over a longer period: even the most conventional bedroom farce or detective play has a multitude of moral and social implications: did the bedroom farce advocate or condemn adultery? Was the murderer or the victim the ultimately guilty party? What ethical implications, what human dilemmas did the action open up? Peter Wood's demand for clarification sprang from his treating Pinter's play on that level. He wanted motivations that would narrow down an infinity of hermeneutic possibilities. Pinter's reply sprang from his conviction that he had not written a play of that type, that, in fact, he had created an open image of much wider implications.

In a way, Peter Wood was right; in the event, the audience was so baffled by the piece that it ran for only a week and puzzled even most of the professional critics, because the play transcended the then established conventions of genre. Beckett and Ionesco had not yet consolidated the new convention of the Theatre of the Absurd. Pinter was well aware of the fact that *The Birthday Party* was difficult to classify under the then prevailing categories of genre and subgenre. He closed his letter with the remark:

> The play is a comedy because the whole state of affairs is absurd and inglorious. It is, however, as you know, a very serious piece of work.
>
> A simple matter don't you think.

Pinter's letter is a remarkable document, precisely because he expresses his refusal to be analytical in the most brilliantly argued analytical style, because he expresses his determination not to over-explain himself, or rather not to allow his leading character to explain himself in contradiction to his own nature, in a most lucidly argued explanatory discourse. It is this extreme self-awareness about where to draw the line in exploring his own self-awareness and thus to respect and maintain the subconscious sources of his deeper creativity that is the hallmark of a major intelligence and a major artist.

In 1980, when he found this letter in rummaging through old papers, Pinter remarked that he found it a very young man's utterance. He certainly must, in the thirty years since he wrote to Peter Wood, have acquired a very much larger store of experience in how to handle his own creative process. A considerable distance has been traversed between *The Room, The Dumb Waiter* or *The Birthday Party* and *Old Times, Betrayal, A Kind of Alaska,* or *Mountain Language.* But--and this seems to me to single him out among many of his contemporaries who have deteriorated under the impact of their success--Pinter has remained singularly faithful to the integrity of his inspiration. The very fact that he does not write any plays when no overwhelmingly powerful image obsesses him, and thus avoids repeating himself or falling into self-parody of his own style, testifies to that. It is surely highly significant that when he uses his outstanding skill as a technician of dramatic writing in his work as a screen-writer he always exercises it on basic material provided by the imagination, and perhaps "inspiration," of other writer-novelists.

Thus he can retain his reliance on the deepest wellsprings of his art for the work that is his most personal field of expression--the live theatre.

THE ECONOMY OF *BETRAYAL*

Ruby Cohn

Before the arrival of Goldberg and McCann in Act I of *The Birthday Party*, Stanley reminisces (or fictionalizes?) to Meg:

I once gave a concert....[1] It was a good one, too. They were all there that night. Every single one of them. It was a great success. Yes. A concert. At Lower Edmonton....I had a unique touch. Absolutely unique. They came up to me. They came up to me and said they were grateful. Champagne we had that night, the lot. (*Pause.*) My father nearly came down to hear me. Well, I dropped him a card anyway. But I don't think he could make it. No, I--I lost the address, that was it. (*Pause.*) Yes. Lower Edmonton. Then after that, you know what they did? They carved me up. Carved me up. It was all arranged. It was all worked out. My next concert. Somewhere else it was. In winter. I went down there to play. Then, when I got there, the hall was closed, the place was shuttered up, not even a caretaker. They'd locked it up. (*Takes off his glasses and wipes them on his pyjama jacket.*) A fast one. They pulled a fast one. I'd like to know who was responsible for that. (*Bitterly.*) All right, Jack, I can take a tip. They want me to crawl down on my bended knees. Well I can take a tip...any day of the week. (I,32-33)[2]

13

A few minutes later Meg satisfies Goldberg's curiosity about Stanley:

> He once gave a concert.... (*falteringly*). In...a big hall. His father gave him champagne. But then they locked the place up and he couldn't get out. The caretaker had gone home. So he had to wait until the morning before he could get out. (*With confidence.*) They were very grateful. (*Pause.*) And then they all wanted to give him a tip. And so he took the tip. And then he got a fast train and he came down here. (I, 42)

Meg's abridgement is a betrayal. She eclipses Stanley's two concerts--one in the unlikely London suburb of Lower Edmonton, and the other terrifyingly unplayed--into a single triumph in an unlocalized hall. She ignores the fine distinction between the unnamed "they" who came *up* to Stanley, and his father who came *down*. She couples Stanley's father with champagne, oblivious of the filial fears in the original. She reverses Stanley's position with respect to the locked door, for in his own account he is literally and metaphorically out in the cold. Stanley reports that an unnamed they "*said* they were grateful," but for Meg the gratitude shifts from report to fact. She omits Stanley's hesitation, interrogation, repetition, humiliation. Stanley's slang is utterly lost on Meg: She excises both his carving up and bended-knee crawl; she twists "fast" from deceit to speed, and "tip" from a revelation to remuneration. Above all, Meg imposes sequence, presence, and closure upon disjunction, absence, and unexplained terror.

Meg predicts Pinter criticism. For some three decades we critics have eased ourselves into his mysterious rooms, uncovered analogues of his mysterious intruders, assigned causes to the mysterious actions of his characters. Early warned away from the verifiable, we nevertheless frame Pinter in a plausible context--each of us in her or his own context. And that is as it should be, or what are critics for? Throughout Pinter's writing life critics have been struck--almost physically--by his hard-fisted language. Early reviewers, dumping him into the kitchen sink, praised his tape-recorder ear for the lower-class ideolect of East London. More recent reviewers clamor for his intellectuals to wrap their lexical sophistication around sturdier substance. Early and late, Pinter critics agree that, like Mallarmé, Proust, Eliot, and Beckett, he has purified the language of the tribe, by means of the techniques that blend into his signature--repetition, disjunction, jargon, cliché, hesitation, and sound play. Pinter's Spooner has often been quoted: "All we have left is the English language." English should be underlined, for Pinter savors that language, even while holding it at a critical distance: "I have mixed feelings about words myself" (I, 13). He caresses and teases the language; he rides roughshod over it or rolls single words on a sensuous tongue. From menace to mannerism, from brand name to braggart warrior, this pacifist writer commands a linguistic arsenal for his Lorenzian stage skirmishes.

Begin with his titles: "My plays are what the titles are about" (Packard, 82). Pinter's titles are direction-pointers into the heart of his polyvalence. *The Room*, a theme as well as a place, is a diminished version of Kafka's *Castle*. *The Dumb Waiter*, a character as well as a prop, is a curtailed version of Beckett's waiters for Godot. *The Birthday Party* climaxes in a festivity of sorts, which proves to be a wake of sorts. The wouldbe caretaker, doubly expelled from the room, has finally to take care of himself. *The Collection* is sexual rather than sartorial. With Ruth a home may be coming, in a double entendre that plays on the Janus-head of mother and whore. Rival claimants of *Old Times* are dirtily buried when a newly bathed Kate declares her independence. Expelled like the wouldbe caretaker, Spooner the wouldbe secretary finally delineates "a happy household" as an icy and silent no man's land. The lack of an article in the title *Betrayal* generalizes behavior, as each character betrays the other two. Although marital betrayal is not new in Pinter's drama, *Betrayal* pivots on that firm and slippery pole, and the set in the original London production turned literally from scene to scene. Moreover, as Elin Diamond has noticed, marital betrayal links three recurrent Pinter themes--the difficulty of verification, the invasion of private territory, and the masking of emotion. But *Betrayal* also betrays those themes: the past is verified for *us*, whereas the characters lack verification; the intruder does *not* upset an equilibrium; territory is not sought, but rather relinquished; the three main characters are at once monosyllabic and highly articulate. In John Arden's felicitous summary of Pinter: "The slantindicular observation of unconsidered speech and casual action ... illuminate[s] loneliness and lack of communication" (*Telling a True Tale*).

What is *not* betrayed in *Betrayal* is form in the part and the whole. Unlike Pinter's more recent interviews, his 1962 speech at the National Student Drama Festival bristles with quotable lines: "I think I can say I pay meticulous attention to the shape of things, from the shape of a sentence to the overall structure of the play. This shaping, to put it mildly, is of the first importance" (I, 14). Although a number of critics have enumerated the distinctive Pinter instruments of shaping--John Russell Brown, Peter Davison, Elin Diamond, Bernard Dukore, Martin Esslin, Arnold Hinchliffe, Andrew Kennedy, Austin Quigley--none of them has divided the devices quite as I propose to do, into the rhythmic and the lexical.[3]

Rhythmic shaping is evident even to those who do not understand the English language, for basic rhythms lie in sound. Anyone can hear the purr of Goldberg's: "She's not a leper, Webber," or Edward's "...you sit like a hump, a mouldering heap," or Spooner's "betwix twig peeper," or Foster's "a giggle and a cuddle." Rhyme, slant rhyme, alliteration--almost always the effect of sound play--is deflationary.

The phoneme is the smallest unit of Pinter's orchestrated repetition, but more telling is his repetition of word or phrase, whether exact, like Meg's: "This house is on the list," or variable, like Davies' "You see what I mean?... you know... you get my meaning?... you know?... what I'm getting at is... I mean... You know what I'm talking about then?... you see what I'm getting at?... Won't you listen to what I'm saying?... what do you think of this I'm saying?... Do you see what I'm saying?" Pinter's dramatic repetitions are sometimes immediate, sometimes separated by stretches of stage time. Occasionally, a single character will indulge in repetitions; more usually, a phrase is bounced between two characters. Probably the most striking example of verbal repetition in Pinter's oeuvre occurs in *No Man's Land*, where the titular phrase is first uttered as a generalization by a hesitant Hirst. A similar passage virtually concludes the play when Spooner assigns his host Hirst to its bleak territory, replacing the three-dot series by commas, and intensifying the negatives to "never"s. As Bernard Dukore notes: " . . . changes . . . emphasise finality" (104).

More repetitive than any verbal technique in Pinter's plays are his units of silence--indicated in print by comma, period, three dots, pause, and silence, which can function like musical notation for the actor. The only wholly silent character in Pinter is the Matchseller of *A Slight Ache*, a play conceived for radio, but his quieter characters tend to dominate the prattlers--Bert in *The Room*, Ben in *The Dumb Waiter*, Ruth in *The Homecoming*, Kate in *Old Times*. In dramatizing a silence that confers strength, Pinter differs from Beckett, for whom silence is the voice of the void, so that his characters continually try to tell "another of those tales to keep the void out" (*That Time*).

Where Pinter's shaping most resembles that of Beckett is in the rhythm of verbal duels (Cf. Kennedy, *Dramatic Dialogue*). Of Beckett's stage plays only *Waiting for Godot* and *Endgame* resort to stichomythic duets, in shorter lines than the Greek dramatists anticipated.

Beckett's duologues are valiant strategies against the void. For Pinter, in contrast, the short-lined exchanges usually constitute an attack and defense--Mr. Kidd against Rose, Riley against Rose, Ben against Gus, Flora against Edward, and, most sharply in *The Collection*, James against Bill, Harry against Bill, and James against Harry. In these combats sheer speed endows a character with power, but the celebrated three dots predict defeat. Already by the time of *The Caretaker* (1959), Pinter counterpointed these rapid duologues against long monologues, of which Aston's recollection of shock therapy remains the most electrifying example. Pinter himself has cast doubt on Aston's veracity (Bensky, 362), but in the theater the monologue *sounds true*--if one understands English. In the main, Pinter's monologues break the rhythm of volleys, but not the mood of challenge. Mick's fantasy of interior decoration, Edward's tales of country squiredom, Lenny's rodomontade of cruelties to women, Deeley's version of *Odd Man Out*, Briggs' verbal labyrinth on Bolsover Street--are all calculated to turn the protagonist's ground to quicksand (cf. Pinter in "Writing for the Theatre" I, 12). *Old Times* opens on the duologue of Kate and her uneasy husband Deeley, but Anna breaks that rhythm with her entering monologue. In Act I of *No Man's Land* Spooner's garland of Victorian phrases is punctured by Hirst's monosyllables. In Act II, however, Spooner rises to an imitation of Hirst's Oxbridge Colonel Blimperie, before he is rhythmically deflated by the verbal thrusts of Briggs and Foster.

Monologue, duologue, stichomythic volley, varieties of repetition, all punctuated by measured pauses, compose the "Music in that Room" (Irving Wardle's phrase). Distinctively as Pinter shapes these several rhythms, his presence is even more apparent in the lexical skill of his dialogue. The pun by definition uses sound to multiply sense, depending as it does "on similarity of form and disparity of meaning" (Culler, 5). I have suggested the punning strength of Pinter's main titles, but puns are relatively rare in his dialogue. Still, Meg shifts the meaning of Stanley's colloquial signifiers. Bill taunts James: "I'm going to be Minister for Home Affairs" (II, 131). Although Pinter, unlike Beckett, stages few writers, other characters call attention to language. Not only do Gus and Ben argue about "light the gas, light the kettle," but Gus enthuses about a football match: "Talk about drama." Stanley teases Meg with the word "succulent." The faintly archaic monosyllables "gaze" and "lest" attract the attention of Deeley in *Old Times*, who pedantically explains his use of the word "globe," rather than "world." *No Man's Land* is exceptional in that three of the four characters are said to be writers, but it is Spooner alone who foregrounds language. Not only does he wax lyrical about the English language, but he is cheered by a metaphor, he boasts about his terza rima, and his locutions carry traces of Yeats and Eliot, e.g. "Experience is a paltry thing" and three repetitions of "I have known this before."[4]

From *The Room* to *No Man's Land* Pinter fondles certain words to endow them with a sexual edge. It can be as simple as Bert's feminization of his van on an icy road:

> But I drove her. *Pause.* I sped her. *Pause.* I caned her along. She was good.... I kept on the straight. There was no mixing it. Not with her. She was good. She went with me. She don't mix it with me. I use my hand. Like that. I get hold of her. I go where I go. She took me there. She brought me back. (I, 126)

Were "it" to displace "she," the sexual resonance would diminish sharply. Bert's verbs seem tangential both to driving and to sex in this early play, but Pinter would soon acquire explicit jargons to intensify his drama.

As early as *The Birthday Party* Goldberg reassures McCann in the Latinate diction of the organization man:

> The main issue is a singular issue and quite distinct from your previous work.   Certain elements,

however, might well approximate in points of procedure to some of your other activities. All is dependent on the attitude of our subject. At all events, McCann, I can assure you that the assignment will be carried out and the mission accomplished with no excessive aggravation to you or myself. (I, 40)

Flora of *A Slight Ache* has a polysyllabic garden: "You must see my japonica, my convulvulus...my honeysuckle, my clematis" (I, 199). Mick attacks Davies in *The Caretaker* as much with the lexicon of interior decoration as with the electrolux. And Teddy's family in *The Homecoming* offers Ruth emoluments of another class of interior decoration for her flat in or near Greek Street. Spooner applies the technical terms of cricket to Hirst's putative wife:

> How beautiful she was, how tender and how true. Tell me with what speed she swung in the air, with what velocity she came off the wicket, whether she was responsive to finger spin, whether you could bowl a shooter with her, or an offbreak with a legbreak action. In other words, did she google? (IV, 92)

The effect of such jargon is comically deflationary.

Families figure so often in the dialogue of Pinter's plays, that relationships take on the quality of technical jargon, from Mr. Kidd's Jewess mum to Spooner's malevolent mother, via Goldberg's expanded family and the all-male household of *The Homecoming*. Of the last of these plays Ronald Knowles has observed: "We find primarily family, dad, father, mother, mum, son, brother, wife, uncle, and secondarily sister-in-law, brother-in-law, daughter-in-law, nephews, grandchildren, grandfather. These words occur approximately 130 times in the play" (Bold, 118).[5] Almost always, the jargon of family relationships--at least until Pinter's political plays of the

1980s--subverts that residual nuclear unit of modern society.

More obstreperously than these nouns of kinship, the jargon of geography runs through most of Pinter's drama. His first two plays are unlocalized--"A room in a large house," "A basement room," and even *The Birthday Party* is set in an unnamed seaside town--but Goldberg has London in his veins, referring to the Ethical Hall of Bayswater and Lyons Corner House at Marble Arch. Fittingly, *The Homecoming* is set in "An old house in North London," but the references carry us around the city: Max and Mac once frequented the West End, Sam drives his clients to London Airport, the Savoy, the Caprice, the Dorchester, the Ritz Bar, and even Hampton Court. Lenny's haunts belong to another class--North Paddington, Greek Street, the Scrubs.

Place names can be weapons of attack. In *Old Times* Anna and Deeley duel with them; the former recalls bastions of culture--Albert Hall, Covent Garden, Kensington High Street, the Tate, Greenwich, Green Park. In contrast, Deeley goes to a pub off Brompton Road, notices the Edgeware Road gang and the Paddington Library. Asserting her independence, Kate consigns Deeley: "To China. Or Sicily." In *No Man's Land* Hirst having met Spooner at the (rather elegant) pub Jack Straw's Castle (named for the leader of the 14th century peasants' uprising), invites him home to a mansion in Hampstead, but Briggs relegates Spooner to a pub in Chalk Farm, called, like pubs all over England, the Bull's Head. It is against that background that Spooner boasts of his travels abroad to Lyon and Amsterdam, before admitting: "I wrote my Homage to Wessex in the summerhouse at West Upfield," where the pastoral atmosphere is undermined by the sexual suggestion of WesSEX and UPfield (IV, 135).

Jargon, in the fifth definition of the OED, is "applied contemptuously to the language of scholars, the terminology of science or art, or the cant of a class, sect, trade or profession." Essentially recondite, then, jargon is opposed by the cliché, or wellworn phrase. What Pinter does is combine the cliché with the strikingly original phrase, as in Goldberg's lucubrations on his family, or Hirst's on his upper-class past: "Constantine bowling, war looming" (IV, 127).

For all Pinter's artful manipulation of cliché from Meg's "Is it nice?" to Hirst's "As it is," his lexical brilliance gleams most brightly in inventive insults. In Pinter's first play Bert's insult is monosyllabic: "Lice" but two years later Mick attacks Davies vitriolically: "...You're violent, you're erratic, you're just completely unpredictable. You're nothing else but a wild animal, when you come down to it. You're a barbarian. And to put the old tin lid on it, you stink from the arse-hole to breakfast time" (II, 82-3).

Four years after that, in *The Homecoming*, insults proliferate, beginning with a father-son exchange:

> Lenny: Plug it, will you, you stupid sod, I'm trying to read the paper.
>
> Max: Listen! I'll chop your spine off, you talk to me like that ! (III, 25)
>
> Sam [about Mac]:   He was a lousy stinking rotten loudmouth. A bastard uncouth sodding runt. Mind you, he was a good friend of yours. (III, 34)
>
> Max [about Ruth]:   We've had a smelly scrubber in my house all night. We've had a stinking pox-ridden slut in my house all night.... They come back from America, they bring the slopbucket with them. They bring the bedpan with them. (III, 57, 58)

In *No Man's Land* insults carry class resonance. Hirst's are upper class Victorian: "I'm beginning to believe you're a scoundrel.... I'll have you blackballed from the club!" (IV, 134). But Briggs is vulgarly contemporary about Spooner: "To him? To a pisshole collector? To a shithouse operator? To a jamrag vendor? What the fuck are you talking bout? Look at him. He's a mingejuice bottler, a fucking shitcake baker" (IV, 146). Although my quotations are rife with obscenities, Pinter calculates their shaping power, as he does all the instruments of his varied lexicon.

Between *The Room* and *No Man's Land* (both metaphor and setting), separated by seventeen years, Pinter came to tower over the British theater landscape, and his very name was adjectivized to Pinteresque.[6] Although the several theater glossaries do not define that adjective, its main features are the unverifiable and the disjunctive, which are only glancingly attained by the devices I have enumerated. As every Pinter critic has remarked, however, *Betrayal* (1978) represents a new departure for Pinter. First and foremost, the past is not only verified, it is staged. And instead of disjunction, each line of *Betrayal* feeds the next sequentially, although pauses still abound. No other play in the Pinter canon offers a better illustration of his "meticulous attention to the shape of things, from the shape of a sentence to the overall structure of the play."

In *Betrayal* Pinter's sentences are briefer than ever before, and the overall structure of the drama is strikingly symmetrical, as Austin Quigley first observed (*The Modern Stage and Other Worlds*, 230). The play begins with the end of an adulterous affair, and it ends with the beginning of that affair. Although the nine scenes of *Betrayal* move roughly backward through nine years, they are arranged symmetrically about the single scene set outside of London, where Robert the husband confronts his wife Emma with his discovery of her affair with his best friend Jerry.

1. 1977--Emma and Jerry in a pub.

2. 1977, later--Jerry and Robert at Jerry's house.

3. 1975--Emma and Jerry in a flat.

4. 1974--Emma, Jerry, and Robert in Robert's house.

5. 1973--Emma and Robert in Venice.

6. 1973--Emma and Jerry in a flat.

7. 1973, later--Jerry and Robert in a restaurant.

8. 1971--Emma and Jerry in a flat.

9. 1968--Emma, Jerry, and Robert in Robert's house.

It is in scene 5, just before Robert's revelation of his discovery of his wife's adultery, that he voices the play's theme and title in a one-word sentence: "Betrayal."

To dramatize betrayal--of love, trust, and friendship--Pinter economizes on his usual instruments. Dialogue is still counterpointed against silence, but Pinter is less prodigal of the former. Duologues are still counterpointed against monologues, but the former run to monosyllables and brief phrases; the latter to subdued images and clipped length. As implied by the scenic breakdown above, the duologue remains Pinter's building-block, but although these exchanges are conducted in sentences so brief that they stop short of the margin, they are rarely stichomythic.

Monologues do not exceed the half-page, so that they contrast subtly with the duets. Moreover, the monologues are inequitably distributed among the three characters: Emma speaks none, and Jerry speaks inconsequentially until his final drunken declaration of love.   Robert's three monologues all bear obliquely on Emma's adultery, but their surface subjects are the game of squash, Italian carelessness about correspondence, and a confession of hatred of books.   The famous Pinter pause is ubiquitous in *Betrayal*, and silences punctuate tense moments, cementing the rhythm.   The distinctive three dots are reserved for the most disturbed moments of each of the three characters:

> Emma: You see, in the past...we were inventive, we were determined, it was...it seemed impossible to meet...impossible...and yet we did. (IV, 194)
>
> Robert: A flat. It's quite well established then, your...uh... affair? (IV, 223)
>
> Jerry: It is quite right, to...to face up to the facts...and to offer a token, without blush, a token of one's unalloyed appreciation, no holds barred. (IV, 267)

Concommitant with these economies of emotional expression is that of sound play, which is reserved for the men.   Jerry's first monologue about men drinking together burbles in p's and b's: "For example, when you're with a fellow in a pub... from time to time he pops out for a piss... if he's making a crafty telephone call... you can sense the pip pip pips" (IV, 172).   Robert, braving Jerry about betrayal, jabs with short i sounds: "You don't seem to understand that I don't give a shit about any of this. It's true I've hit Emma once or twice... The old itch...you understand" (IV, 185).   Perhaps the most lethal example of sound play occurs in the Jerry-Robert confrontation of Scene 2, with its volleying of "know" and "No."
    If Pinter is abstemious of such sound play as rhyme and alliteration in *Betrayal*, he is prodigal of repetition, which erupts in such banalities as questions, exclamations, and routine courtesies.   Occasionally, however, a sonic repetition brings us up short, when it underlines or

undermines lexical repetition. Emma in Scene 4 criticizes Casey's novel as "dishonest," and this is questioned by Jerry and repeated by Robert, who within a few moments labels Casey as a "brutally honest squash player." Within another few moments Robert opens his monologue that bars Emma from a game of squash: "Well, to be brutally honest...." (IV, 209). The subtext is honesty in marriage. After the interval, in the central discovery scene, Robert begins his second monologue: "To be honest..." but he still avoids direct reference to honesty in marriage (cf. Ben-Zvi, 231).

Instead of accusing Emma of adultery, Robert inquires about the contents of Jerry's letter: "Has he discovered any new and original talent? He's quite talented at uncovering talent, old Jerry."

> Emma: No message.
> Robert: No message? Not even his love?
> *Silence*
> Emma: We're lovers. (IV, 222)

The repetition of the slender phrases subvert the favorable resonances of both "talent" and "love." On the frontier of the sonic and the lexical, Pinter compensates for a paucity of sound play by a sharp increase of repetition.

Otherwise, however, *Betrayal* is linguistically spare. No words are savored for their own sake, and the clichés are those of polite society: How are you? What do you mean? That's funny. Obscenities are rare: Once Jerry calls Robert a bastard and is warned not to do so. Once Robert inveighs against Venice: "They really don't give a fuck there." When Emma utters the word "fucking," she means it literally, but Jerry amends it to "loving."

Although Robert is a publisher and Jerry a literary agent, Pinter deprives us of the jargons of publishing and publicity, as well as that of the game of squash, but a residue remains of the jargons of family and geography. In the very first scene Jerry reminds Emma: "You remember the form. I ask about your husband, you ask about my wife" (IV, 161). And both lovers link their affair with Jerry's throwing Emma's daughter in the air and catching her: "Yes, everyone was there that day, standing around, your husband, my wife, all the kids, I remember" (IV, 166). Pinter has been called the poet of London transport, and yet he provides no location for Jerry's house or Robert's; or for Emma's gallery, Robert's publishing firm, or Jerry's literary agency. We know the location only of the flat for adultery--31 Wessex Grove, off Kinsdale Drive in Kilburn--"Who ever went to Kilburn in those days? Just you and me" (IV, 169). It may be pressing the lower middle-class area to read the ironies of Kill and Burn into a love affair so domesticated that the Sex of Wessex Grove soon peters out. Exceptionally in Pinter's jargon of geography, London actually sports neither a Wessex Grove nor a Kinsdale Drive, although Kilburn is alive and well.

In the lexical economy of *Betrayal* the few images are all the more telling. Jerry and Robert in Scene 4, while waiting for Emma, prattle comically about the reluctance of boy babies to leave the womb, and this primes us to witness the reluctance of each of them to leave the womb of habit. A more insistent image is that of Jerry in Robert's kitchen (confused by Emma with Jerry's kitchen) throwing her daughter Charlotte up and catching her. Three times this image is linked with the love affair between Emma and Jerry. By the end of the play Jerry has thrown over Emma (whom Charlotte resembles), and he has not caught her. Not has her husband Robert. Perhaps she will be caught by Casey, the dishonest honest writer who brings profit to both men. Perhaps not.

Betrayal has been read as a comedy of modern manners (Diamond). It is that, but it also indicts such manners as a betrayal of a richer, more instinctual life. Although Jerry and Robert are to some extent mirror images of one another, Robert Downs is more of a rake, who has betrayed Emma for years, while adhering to the convention of marriage. Urbane and witty, he reads Yeats, vacations abroad, and keeps fit--the modern man about town who doesn't even have a nickname. Jerry, in contrast, is a nickname, and we never learn his surname. To rent the flat of his trysts he chooses the pastoral pseudonym of Green. Although Jerry went to Cambridge and Robert to Oxford, and both made conventional marriages within their class, Jerry seems to betray literary talent less often than Robert, who accuses Jerry: "You know what you and Emma have in common? You love literature" (IV, 250). In short, the lovers are romantic.

The play's final scene confirms Robert's judgment. When a drunken Jerry woos Emma, his lexicon is the richest in the spare play--"All these words I'm using, don't you see, they've never been said before" (IV, 265). Paradoxically, Jerry woos with verbal rape: "I should have blackened you, in your white wedding dress," although Emma insists that she did not wear white at her wedding. Jerry then gains verbal momentum in a rich rush, enhanced by slippage of the word "state." He climaxes a series of miseries he will suffer if rejected by Emma, with banishment to "a state of catatonia." Surging on, Jerry shifts "state" from a condition to a country ruled by a prince--"the prince of emptiness, the prince of absence, the prince of desolation. I love you." With Robert's implicit acquiescence, Emma rescues her prince from his lonely domain, but the previous scenes have dramatized Jerry's betrayal of that rescue. Romance fades, and the prince malingers.

In *Betrayal* Pinter is so abstemious of the language techniques he has burnished over two decades that it would be only a slight exaggeration to state that he betrays them, but he is all the truer--all the more brutally honest--to "the shape of things," from treacherous one-word sentences-- Really?... Darling.... Cheers.... Dreamland.... Good.... Beautiful.... Absolutely--to the symmetry of the nine scenes. *Betrayal* is Pinter's wholly creative betrayal of his earlier themes and devices, in contrast to his three most recent brief plays, which illustrate his December 1988 statement to Mel Gussow: "I understand your interest in me as a playwright. But I'm more interested in myself as a citizen." However we admire the citizen, we may regret

Pinter's (necessary?) betrayal of our most finely tuned playwright.

NOTES

1.   In quotations from Pinter, my ellipses are spaced, but Pinter's dots are unspaced.

2.   All quotations from Pinter's work are taken from the 4-volume Methuen edition. Volume and page number are indicated in parentheses in my text.

3.   See Bibliography.

4.   "An aged man is but a paltry thing,
     . . . unless
     Soul clap its hands and sing . . ."
          ("Sailing to Byzantium")

     "I have known them all already"
          ("The Love Song of J. Alfred Prufrock")

5.   Also suggestive in Bold is Steven H. Gale, "Harold Pinter's *Family Voices* and the Concept of Family."

6.   Cf. ". . . Pinter's Plays are indeed Pinteresque; the causes, motives and implications of his characters' most clear-cut gestures, though undulating with significance on stage, remain hidden in a London fog" (Bold, 96).

BIBLIOGRAPHY

Arden, John, "Telling a True Tale," *Encore* (May, 1960); reprinted in *The Encore Reader*, eds. Charles Marowitz, Tom Milne, and Own Hale (London: Methuen, 1965).

Bensky, Lawrence, "Harold Pinter: An Interview," *Paris Review* (Fall, 1960); reprinted in Ganz.

Ben-Zvi, Linda, "Harold Pinter's *Betrayal*: The Patterns of Banality," *Modern Drama* (September 1980).

Bold, Alan, ed., *Harold Pinter: You Never Heard Such Silence* (London: Vision Press, 1984).

Brown, John Russell, *Theatre Language: A Study of Arden, Osborne, Pinter, and Wesker* (London: Allen Lane, 1972).

Culler, Jonathan, *On Puns* (Oxford: Blackwell, 1988).

Davison, Peter, *Aspects of Drama and Theatre* (Sydney: Sydney University Press, 1965).

Diamond, Elin, *Pinter's Comic Play* (Lewisburg: Bucknell University Press, 1985).

Dukore, Bernard, *Harold Pinter* (London: Macmillan, 1988, second edition).

Esslin, Martin, *Pinter: A Study of His Plays* (London: Eyre Methuen, 1977, third edition).

Gale, Steven H., *Butter's Going Up: A Critical Analysis of Harold Pinter's Work* (Durham, N. C.: Duke University Press, 1977).

Ganz, Arthur, ed., *Pinter: A Collection of Critical Essays* (Englewood Cliffs: Prentice-Hall, 1972).

Hornby, Richard, *Drama, Metadrama and Perception* (Lewisburg: Bucknell University Press, 1986).

Kennedy, Andrew, *Six Dramatists in Search of a Language* (Cambridge: Cambridge University Press, 1975).

_____, *Dramatic Dialogue* (Cambridge: Cambridge University Press, 1983).

Packard, William, "An Interview with Harold Pinter," *First Stage* (Summer, 1967).

Quigley, Austin, *The Pinter Problem* (Princeton: Princeton University Press, 1975).

_____, *The Modern Stage and Other Worlds* (Methuen: New York, 1985).

Wardle, Irving, "There's Music in That Room," *Encore* (July, 1960), reprinted in *The Encore Reader*.

TIME FOR CHANGE IN *NO MAN'S LAND*

Austin E. Quigley

No Man's Land has received more than its fair share of the adverse criticism directed at Pinter's plays. Like many of the others this one, too, has been attacked for being puzzling and obscure, but *No Man's Land* has proved to be a play more difficult than most to defend against the usual criticisms. Indeed, a series of comments from otherwise sympathetic critics suggests that the play lacks a coherent structure, that the characters are out of harmony with the plot, that the ending is puzzlingly inconclusive, that the treatment of time oscillates oddly between a concern for fixity and a concern for flux, and that character interaction gives the impression of dramatic abstraction rather than emotional engagement. Various attempts to accommodate the play's structural peculiarities have led to conclusions that it is about old age, death, stasis, a waste land, modern alienation, unconstrained fantasy, time, memory, nihilism, absence, and a variety of other things whose relevance seems indisputable but whose centrality is less so. Their local importance is easier to establish than either their various relationships or their collective significance. Indeed, there is a serious question to be asked about the possibility of establishing a coherent theme for the play until a better understanding of its structure is achieved.

    Three specific comments by Wardle, Nightingale, and Collins suggest something of the problem that needs to be addressed. Irving Wardle has noted the play's tendency toward abstraction and suggests that Pinter is lapsing into stylization by making his own techniques more than

usually explicit. He cites as an example Briggs announcing
that Foster will contradict his version of events rather than
Foster, in more characteristic Pinter fashion, simply
providing the contradictory account that Briggs alludes to.[1]
This tendency toward abstraction and contradiction rather
than exemplification and integration also generates
Nightingale's concern about an apparent structural
disharmony in the play, one that leaves the audience feeling
that in the character of Spooner Pinter has "written a part
rather more memorable than the play that contains it."[2]
Somehow there seems to be more to Spooner than is ever
exemplified in his engagement with the episodic events of
the action. This second comment is given more general
application in the third comment by R. G. Collins who
argues that the point is true not just of Spooner but of all
the characters in the play. (Indeed, he suggests, it is to
some extent true of characters in other Pinter plays.)
Spooner, Hirst, Briggs, and Foster seem to Collins to be
"excessive to the plot's need of them" for "they create
expectations that they never really fulfill," and in some
sense "they stick out beyond the edges of the play."[3]

Collins's readiness to generalize these issues
suggests that the structural disharmony in *No Man's Land*
differs in degree rather than kind from that encountered in
other Pinter plays. It has often been pointed out that one of
the characteristic features of Pinter's plays is a disharmony
exemplified in the unbridgeable distance between
characters who have difficulty understanding each other.
Their mutual opacity tends to affect the scope and
consistency of character development and often produces a
radical disparity between earlier aspects of a character and
those exhibited later when circumstances change.
Consequently, Pinter's plays lack the kind of unbroken
continuity we are always inclined to anticipate in the
development of social relationships and individual
personalities, and where such continuity begins to emerge,
it is sooner or later disrupted. Rose's life in *The Room* is
disturbed by an intruder who calls her by another name and
invites her to some other home. Stanley in *The Birthday*

Party is transformed from a slovenly, talkative, aggressive individual into a smartly dressed, silent, and passive one. Disson, initially a confident leader in *Tea Party*, degenerates into a helpless victim. Ruth in *The Homecoming* switches from being an apparently loyal wife and mother to being a self-concerned, power-hungry matriarch. The personalities, clothing, and behavior of Richard and Sarah in *The Lover* change quite markedly from one time of day to another. Beth and Duff in *Landscape* talk obliquely to each other as if they existed in separate time zones. The commitment of Jerry and Emma to each other in *Betrayal* is one that seems able to flourish only if they can isolate it from the rest of their lives. Characters in one play after another find themselves having to adjust, in fairly radical ways, to circumstances that require them or force them to change what they are and who they have been. Their ability to effect or resist such change varies from case to case, as do the benefits and liabilities involved in their attempts to adapt to changing circumstances. It is in this context that communication problems regularly occur, but these are usually manifestations of equally important issues to do with commitment, continuity, and control.

The issue of continuity is the one that tends to provide most problems for audiences, and in this respect the sense of disharmony in *No Man's Land* is like that in every other Pinter play. But the recurring disruption of the temporal evolution of both character and plot, which is the cause of so much of our difficulty with Pinter's work, is one that occurs so frequently in *No Man's Land* that it attracts special attention. Hirst invites Spooner home and then can't remember who he is; Foster appears without introduction and produces a dizzying variety of unconnected information; Briggs supplies an elaborate version of his first encounter with Foster prefaced by the acknowledgment that Foster will deny it; Hirst recalls different pasts at different times and addresses the other characters by different names. So fragmented is the nature of their interaction that none of the characters seems the least surprised when required to switch rapidly from one embryonic form of relationship to another. Spooner responds without a flicker of resistance to being addressed as Wetherby and Briggs does likewise when addressed as Denson. This pervasive discontinuity in the action is the major source of the atmosphere of abstraction that surrounds character interaction. Anticipating the possibility of further radical change, the characters seem reluctant to become deeply involved in the present action or with each other. And this has consequences for character interaction that are both puzzling and potentially misleading. For much of the play the characters adopt a strategic stance of disengagement that registers their evident uncertainty about the nature and implications of the reported past and about the consequences of the present for the emerging future. They thus give the appearance of going through the motions of interaction rather than committing themselves to it. Even as Hirst and Spooner discover a common interest in interweaving aesthetic and pragmatic concerns, they display little interest in the kind of long-term relationship that might follow from it. In spite of the intricate and extensive nature of their discussions, Spooner and Hirst register pragmatic concerns that seem primarily to be those of the moment and of the self, and community exists, where it exists at all, to be exploited locally for personal ends. Their varied interaction displays little that hints at mutual goals, long-term hopes, emerging sympathies, or shared aspirations. Indeed, when such possibilities do arise, they are immediately rejected. Spooner, encountering so many rapid and recurring changes, registers disdain for any larger hopes and takes his own posture of disengagement to what appears to be the logical extreme.

Rejecting experience in general as a paltry thing and an inadequate means of prophesying the future, Spooner congratulates himself on his ability to live comfortably without enduring relationships and without "any kind of expectation" (p. 80).[4] He describes himself as a wise observer of life rather than a struggling participant, as a free man who is liberated from the claims of the past and from desires for the future, and as an independent person who admires the "serenity" of those who have made themselves similarly immune to the contingencies of life. In the face of so much contingency, Spooner has, he claims, abandoned the pursuit of lasting relationships and thus made the best kind of adjustment to life as he has known it. This adjustment, he argues, is based not upon weakness but upon the strength of achieved independence. Spooner seems, in fact, quite determined to avoid what we are inclined to seek in the play, the kinds of steadily growing relationships that will reduce its atmosphere of abstraction and resolve its problems of structural discontinuity. And Spooner has past as well as present reasons for preferring a stance of independence, reasons graphically rendered in his recollection of his relationship with his mother: "I looked up once into my mother's face," he recalls, and "what I saw there was nothing less than pure malevolence. I was fortunate to escape with my life" (p. 88). The enduring impact of this rejection on Spooner's subsequent life derives less from its involving his mother than from its having become characteristic of so many of his other relationships. As he makes clear to Hirst from the outset:

> Spooner: I shan't stay long. I never stay long, with others. They do not wish it. And that, for me, is a happy state of affairs. My only security, you see, my true comfort and solace, rests in the confirmation that I elicit from people of all kinds a common and constant level of indifference. . . . To show interest in me or, good gracious, anything tending towards a positive liking of me, would cause in me a condition of the acutest alarm. Fortunately, the danger is remote. (p. 79)

As the action of the play goes on to make clear, the danger is, indeed, remote, and Spooner's retreat towards independence seems more than justified. His recollections of earlier disruption and discontinuity are soon replicated in the rapid and recurring changes that characterize his interaction with Hirst, Foster, and Briggs.5   What is puzzling, however, about a play so characteristically constituted by diversity and discontinuity is that it has attracted so much critical discussion in quite different terms, terms that its title seems, indeed, to invite: those involving fixity, finality, and immobility. In spite of the rich variety of incident, such discussion seeks to interpret the play's structural multiplicity as an exemplification of variation on a single theme, one of unchanging limitation.

The title of *No Man's Land* suggests what two brief comments on it appear to imply: that it is a kind of waste land into which individuals may venture but in which no one can establish a sense of belonging and within which no communities can establish themselves or flourish. Here, indeed, appears to be a world of unchangingly prosaic limitations: "No man's land . . . does not move . . . or change . . . or grow old . . . remains . . . forever . . . icy . . . silent" (p. 96). At the close of the play Spooner repeats with small variations Hirst's words about no man's land, and the title, the repetition, and the emphasis provided by Spooner's final words all serve to give the image special prominence in the play. The question is whether it is then right to regard this image as the governing motif that characterizes the whole action of the play and which in some sense summarizes the implications of the play's diversity of incident and discontinuity of action. It is this procedure that leads Jones to conclude that the play is primarily about stasis in the sense of "total, final immobility." He argues that Spooner effects no change in the play, that there is no development or alteration of character or situation, that all the play's images convey a single impression, and that the chief linguistic device of the play is one of repetition.6 Though such an argument seems quite compatible with the larger stances of disengagement that the characters adopt, it seems less compatible with the rapid changes that characterize their interaction from moment to moment. If we are inclined to base our conclusions on the title image of the play, we cannot avoid first looking closely at the other images the play has to offer. When we do so, we encounter not widespread confirmation but widespread challenge to any conviction that fixity and repetition govern either the action of the play or the character of its images. What is immediately evident is the remarkable diversity of the images invoked in the dialogue and also the tendency of several of them to depict not fixity but motion. Briggs, in famous words, presents an elaborate image of the intricate perils awaiting anyone foolish enough to drive into the one-way system surrounding Bolsover Street. Foster, not to be outdone, describes at one point a man walking with two umbrellas in the Australian outback and, at another, a naked beggar somewhere out East making a coin vanish as it flies through the air. Spooner's anecdotes likewise invoke in pictorial terms events that have lodged in his mind. These include his encounter with the Hungarian emigré who purportedly changed Spooner's life, the episode in which his mother responded so malevolently to her son, the summer evening gatherings at a country cottage where Spooner and his wife entertained young poets, and a moment in Amsterdam when a canal, a waiter, a child, a fisherman, two lovers, and a whistling observer came briefly into evocative juxtaposition. Hirst makes his own contribution to the proliferation of images with recollections of a ceremony involving garlands in a village church, of a dream in which someone may be drowning in a waterfall or a lake, of cricketers in action at Lord's just before the war, of Spooner's golden athletic moment breasting the tape at Oxford, of an affair with Spooner's wife Emily, and of a photograph album consisting of further evocative images of lives and times gone by. These are but a few of the images so graphically described in the play, and it is difficult indeed to try to convert their diversity into repetition or to regard them all as variants upon a single theme suggested by the play's title. If anything, their impact is not to reinforce our initial understanding of the nature of no man's land, but to complicate it and force us to consider it further.

Just as important as the diversity of the images is their remarkable number. The play is riddled with images and we find ourselves forced to consider both what the characters are doing with them and why Pinter, in this play, makes such extensive use of them. Obviously enough, they are often deployed to strategic effect by all the characters who, in characteristic Pinter fashion, seek to keep each other off balance. When Foster, for example, tries to make it clear to Spooner that he does not belong in Hirst's home and has no claims on his friendship, he resorts to a string of local images to make his point:

> Foster: Listen.   Keep it tidy.   You follow?
> You've just laid your hands on a rich and powerful man. It's not what you're used to, scout. How can I make it clear? This is another class. It's another realm of operation. It's a world of silk. It's a world of organdie. It's a world of flower arrangements. It's a world of eighteenth century cookery books. It's nothing to do with toffeeapples and a packet of crisps. It's milk in the bath. It's the cloth bellpull. It's organisation. (p. 111)

In similar fashion Hirst's images of the seduction of Spooner's wife and Spooner's images of his own remarkable capacities and experiences are often moves in the characteristic Pinter activity of social manipulation. But some of the images, as we will see later, have a poignancy that exceeds, without excluding, the strategic activity of combat and conquest. These various uses of a remarkable variety of images serve not only to challenge the primacy of the play's title image but also the most obvious implications of the posture of disengagement all of the characters adopt. This appearance of disengagement that gives the play its atmosphere of abstraction can easily reinforce convictions that no significant changes occur in the play in spite of its variety of incident. But the image of disengagement is an image as strategically employed as all the others, one designed to disguise visually not only what the characters are attempting to achieve verbally but the fact they are actually trying to achieve anything at all.

If we are inclined to doubt the latter point, we should note that Spooner's first extensive remarks in the play explicitly warn us to be suspicious of the authenticity of strategic posturing.

> Spooner: I was about to say, you see, that there are some people who appear to be strong, whose idea of what strength consists of is persuasive, but who inhabit the idea and not the fact. What they possess is not strength but expertise. They have nurtured and maintain what is in fact a calculated posture. Half the time it works. It takes a man of intelligence and perception to stick a needle through that posture and discern the essential flabbiness of the stance. I am such a man. (p. 78)

Hirst, of course, is rightly puzzled by the ambiguity of the final sentence, which leaves Spooner situated uncertainly between the roles of adopting a pose and exposing a pose. Or, to put it another way, between adopting the pose of a posturer or adopting the pose of an exposer of posturers. But however we resolve the matter in Spooner's case, his remarks on posturing explicitly alert us to the nature of such posturing, inadvertently warn us to be wary of his own, and indirectly alert us to the visual complexity that is to characterize the narrative action. What is manifest in his own subsequent behavior is not only a pose of disengagement but also a readiness to deploy this and other images to serve local strategies of self-advancement and social control. To conclude that the play is primarily about a no man's land of fixity and repetition within which no significant changes are sought or achieved is thus to take at face value the pervasive posture of disengagement. But it is also to fail to reconcile what appears to be happening globally in the play with what appears to be happening locally. In an action riddled with local discontinuities there exists a larger and persisting discontinuity between the postures of disengagement the characters regularly adopt and the manifestations of engagement that characterize their interaction from moment to moment. Indeed, the question of whether the play is primarily about fixity or about flux is really a question of why Pinter has structured the play in such a way as to make what appears to be happening globally in the play the opposite of what appears to be happening locally.

A little further thought suffices, however, to revise this version of the play's structure and to clarify the reasons for Pinter's extensive use of images in the play. Things are not quite as fixed globally as the characters' postures of disengagement and the play's title image might at first suggest. Spooner's own words on the ambivalent nature of posturing help us recognize that postures are images deployed for action and that the posture of disengagement is itself inherently unstable. It not only limits loss when changes occur but also limits the gains that local maneuvering makes possible. There is thus a constant tension between local change and larger fixity that has the double effect of slowing ongoing change at the local level while also introducing it at the larger. And change at the larger level, though comparatively slow, does indeed take place. The characters may be going through the motions of interaction but the motions occur, they may announce the rejection of expectation but expectations arise, they may be opposed to the passing of time but time continues to pass, they may be resisting change but change irresistibly occurs. The play, indeed, displays a slowly unfolding action whose development it is not difficult to trace. Throughout a variety of episodes Spooner persists in exploring different ways of establishing himself in Hirst's home, Hirst endeavors to clarify the consequences and value of his presence, and Foster and Briggs invest in various defenses of their own interests and positions. By the end of the play it is clear that Spooner is failing and that the other three are closing ranks against him. But this is a different situation than the one with which the play began. Hirst may finally seek refuge in a no man's land that excludes Spooner but it was Hirst who initially invited Spooner home. Hirst may remark with distaste that he finds himself "in the last lap of a race . . . I had long forgotten to run" (p. 94), but this is an acknowledgement that Spooner has, in fact, managed to draw him out into the battlefield of contested and conceded terrain.

Cohn is thus quite right to point out that "though stasis has been named as the theme of *No Man's Land*, the play moves forward from its [opening] event."[7] The pose of independence, disinterestedness, and disengagement defended in such heroic terms by Spooner and exhibited less grandly in both his behavior and that of the other characters turns out to register not a global commitment to fixity that contrasts with a local interest in change but a general uncertainty about the appropriate speed and probable value of potential change. The apparent conflict between the global posture of disengagement and the local actuality of intricate engagement is, in fact, a contrast between two different attitudes towards change exhibited in two different speeds of change.

This reformulation of a key contrast in the play is essential if we are to find a way of reconciling not only the global and the local in the action but also the repeated conflicts between one local detail and the next. And this reformulation will also help us understand the nature of the conflict between the two major characters. Their richly various strategies of interaction register not only an initial uncertainty but also a growing disagreement about the value of the various changes the quixotic Spooner seeks to introduce. Hirst, who invited Spooner in, speaks of the fear of being alone but also of the fear of being controlled by someone else. His initial response to Spooner is to incline more toward the former than the latter, but Spooner's erratic behavior eventually serves to reverse the balance between his competing inclinations. Spooner, while more than ready to pose as someone without goals or expectations, is always much more deeply entangled in the local possibilities whose long-term consequences he is at pains publicly to dismiss. In spite of his defensive protestations he reveals a readiness to play out the possibilities that this or any other situation provides, and in this respect he seems very different from Hirst who appears to be more ready to contemplate than to initiate change. Although Spooner recognizes that the potential value of particular changes in a constantly changing world is likely to be rather limited, he pursues possibilities with a tenacity that registers the persistence of hope in the face of contradictory experience. His is not, indeed, a cynical game-playing. If life consists of playing out the hand that has been dealt, Spooner takes pride in playing it with imagination, elegance, and flair. "Temperamentally," claims Spooner, while announcing his readiness to serve as Hirst's friend, literary agent, secretary, companion, servant, or cook, "I can be what you wish" (p. 147). He consistently displays a readiness to change along with change that throws into relief Hirst's unwillingness to do likewise.

These persisting contrasts between the two main characters replicate the contrast between competing speeds of change that permeates the play. The difference between their attitudes toward and capacities to adapt to change is not one that proceeds from different preferences for fixity or for flux, but one that reveals contrasting evaluations of the probability that impending change will involve gain rather than loss. It would be easy but erroneous to conclude that Hirst's greater resistance to change is merely a consequence of his superior social position giving him more to lose. Hirst, we must remember, invited Spooner home and pays him considerable attention. There is something that he sees in Spooner or through Spooner that makes him more interested initially than he is finally in what Spooner has to offer. What Hirst initially sees in Spooner has, of course, much to do with the images Spooner so imaginatively invokes and portrays, images designed to enhance the one exhibited by his own rather seedy and shabby appearance. In the midst of an action riddled by discontinuity and characterized by contrasting attitudes toward change, the deployment of images becomes the key to the promotion and control of change, the successful acquisition of desired self images, and the conquest of all contested terrain. To recognize the characters' strategic use of images is not, however, to exhaust the variety of their application. The image of no man's land is only one such image and many of the others, as we noted earlier, are images not of immobility but of action. If we are to make sense of the structure of *No Man's Land*, we must explore further the ways in which these images function and the reasons why Pinter relies so extensively on them.

The relationship between the visual and the verbal in Pinter's plays is a matter of some controversy. He himself tends to take little credit for his use of the visual resources of the stage: "I'm not a very inventive writer in the sense of using the technical devices other playwrights do--look at Brecht! I can't use the stage the way he does, I just haven't got that kind of imagination."[8]   He may, indeed, lack the kind of theatrical imagination that would allow him to employ the visual resources of the theater in the ways that Brecht does, but Pinter is constantly experimenting with the visual in his plays. The action in a particular scene or a whole play is often concluded by a stare, a smile, or a tableau, and the stage sets for plays like *The Dumb Waiter*, *The Caretaker*, *The Homecoming*, or *Landscape* confirm what Pinter's film scripts also confirm: that he has a rich visual imagination. In *Landscape* Beth explicitly remarks on an intriguing aspect of images, the relationship between their origin and their impact, and her comments have wider implications:

> I remembered always, in drawing, the basic principles of shadow and light. Objects intercepting the light cast shadows. Shadow is deprivation of light. The shape of the shadow is determined by that of the object. But not always. Not always directly. Sometimes it is only indirectly affected by it. Sometimes the cause of the shadow cannot be found. *Pause.* But I always bore in mind the basic principles of drawing. *Pause.* So that I never lost track. Or heart.[9]

The notion that the causes and consequences of a picture are not always rendered explicitly within the picture's frame is directly linked to the evocative nature of many of Pinter's images and to the particular use he makes of them in *No Man's Land.*

The images in *No Man's Land*, we should note, are more often invoked rather than displayed; they are repeatedly drawn from the past as a means of influencing the present, and they often depict a particular kind of action. Indeed, what gives them their enigmatic power is the characteristic form of action they display. Instead of being completed, the actions are regularly arrested at some key point in their evolution. What these images often suggest is interrupted rather than completed processes whose origins and consequences remain elusive. Furthermore, in the context of their recollection they appear to function again in ways they functioned previously, by promising more than they are finally able to deliver. The present action repeatedly displays characters initiating actions that they are unable or unwilling to complete, and many of the images they invoke display similarly interrupted action in the past. In particular, the images described in Hirst's much-described, but never produced, photograph album tend to depict instances of

actions which have a narrative potential that is prematurely
terminated. What the album so described displays and
exemplifies is the irreducible variety of an aggregation of
images that never fulfill their promise to achieve what Hirst
at times seems to want them to achieve, something larger
than a mere local significance.

Hirst: In the past I knew remarkable people.
            I've a photograph album somewhere. I'll
            find it. You'll be impressed by the faces.
            Very handsome. Sitting on grass with
            hampers. I had a moustache. Quite a
            few of my friends had moustaches.
            Remarkable   faces.   Remarkable
            moustaches. What was it informed the
            scene?   A   tenderness   towards   our
            fellows, perhaps. The sun shone. The
            girls had lovely hair, dark, sometimes
            red. Under their dresses their bodies
            were white. It's all in my album. I'll
            find it. You'll be struck by the charm of
            the girls, their grace, the ease with which
            they sit, pour tea, loll. It's all in my
            album. . . . My true friends look out at me
            from my album. I had my world. I have
            it. Don't think now that it's gone I'll
            choose to sneer at it, to cast doubt on it,
            to wonder if it properly existed. No.
            We're talking of my youth, which can
            never leave me. No. It existed. It was
            solid, the people in it were solid,
            while . . . transformed by light, while
            being sensitive . . . to all the changing
            light. When I stood my shadow fell upon
            her. She looked up. . . . It's gone. Did it
            exist? It's gone. It never existed. It
            remains. . . . What was it? Shadows.
            Brightness, through leaves. Gambolling.
            In the bushes. Young lovers. A fall of

water. It was my dream. The lake. Who
was drowning in my dream? It was
blinding. I remember it. I've
forgotten. . . . She looked up. I was
staggered. I had never seen anything so
beautiful. That's all poison. We can't be
expected to live like that. (pp. 106-8)

Hirst's sudden denial of the possibility of living a life in
terms suggested by one or all of the images in the album
registers the persistence of the very expectation he rejects.
But his intermittent efforts to attribute a larger significance
to the local images are unsuccessful. His attempt to locate
a benevolent something that would link all the images
together founders on their manifest variety; his attempt to
make of their aggregation something not only unified but
also permanent founders on his acknowledgment that they
represent the experience of his youth and not of his old age;
his attempt to make of life exemplified in the album
something not only unified and permanent but potentially
all-encompassing founders as the voice of experience
challenges the voice of youth: "She looked up. I was
staggered. I had never seen anything so beautiful. That's
all poison. We can't be expected to live like that" (p. 108).

Hirst's uncertainty about the status of the images is
registered in the inconsistent stance he takes toward them.
Indeed, his description of the images in the album is as
discontinuous as the images the album is said to contain.
The album so described remains a record of local events
that fail to cohere into something larger, an aggregate of
promising local images that fail to provide individually or
collectively a global model. But what the album fails to
supply to Hirst's changing needs it nevertheless supplies to
the play--an analogous text whose structure guides us
toward an understanding of the structure of Pinter's text
and the function of images within it.

As we have noted, the play, riddled by
discontinuity, lacks a temporal flow sustained enough and
wide enough to encompass the diversity of the episodes it

contains. The strategic disengagement of the characters from the actions they initiate allows the narrative to swerve from one line of development to another. Instead of seeking to establish an all-encompassing narrative that unifies the flow of events, Pinter provides us with an image of an analogous text that displays forms of coherence without explicitly or uniformly linking all of the elements it contains. There is an insistence upon emerging but suspended narrative lines, upon fragmentary episodes that suggest more than they can ever confirm, upon moments of shared significance whose potential value remains potential but nevertheless remains.

These aspects of the play's images are also displayed in several outside the album. Spooner's projected but never completed painting of an episode in Amsterdam exemplifies the disrupted potential that characterizes many of the other narrative images that appear in the play, and his anecdotes along with those provided by Hirst, Foster, and Briggs include images as evocative and enigmatic as those Hirst describes in his album. The Hungarian emigré, the eastern beggar, the Australian in the outback, the cricketers at Lord's just before the war, the young poets on the lawn, and the athlete breasting the tape are images that repeatedly suggest what the remarkable faces in Hirst's album and the beautiful young woman who looked up at him also suggest-- interrupted narratives and arrested actions. It is neither necessary nor possible to believe that each such episode had more to offer than circumstances allowed. It is only necessary to recognize what Hirst's description of his album and Spooner's investment in imaginative anecdotes suggest they both share--an embattled belief that one such episode might perhaps be life fulfilling and life encompassing. Hirst's "we can't be expected to live like that" acknowledges in its denial the persistence of an expectation that he can never quite extinguish, a persistence whose strength is also exhibited in his readiness to explore the past and present once more with a character like Spooner. Shabbily dressed, advanced in years,

acknowledging a checkered career, and confessing to a life
of insult and deprivation, Spooner soon confirms Hirst's
skepticism, but the latter's readiness to try, however
tentatively, to construct something new with someone like
Spooner confirms also the continuing strength of his
intermittent expectations.

We thus see in the posture of apparent
disengagement adopted by Hirst and Spooner a larger
skepticism that is at odds with local expectation, and this
serves to exhibit in the current action a discontinuity
analogous to that displayed in the narrative images. Such
discontinuity is the recurring experience of characters
whose present lives and previous experience are made up
of local episodes that fail to fulfil their initial promise. It is
precisely this aspect of experience that the play seeks to
capture and explore. The repeatedly arrested motion of the
action and the characteristically arrested motion of the
images exemplify Pinter's interest in portraying the
discontinuous aspects of lived experience.

When Jones began his article on stasis in *No Man's
Land*, he began by alluding to the term's implications of
stagnation, of forces held in check, of suspended animation.
Stasis as a balance between conflicting forces soon gives
way, however, in his argument to stasis as something static,
as something implying "final immobility."[10]   This is
unfortunate because the term stasis invites extension in the
other direction of increased rather than decreased
instability. In the stasis of balanced and competing forces
small changes can produce large consequences, and in such
a context it is as necessary to exert force to maintain
stability as it is to disrupt stability. Fixity and change in
such a context are thus reciprocally related rather than
radically opposed, as the recurring images of arrested
motion in *No Man's Land* suggest. A no man's land of
fixity and immobility is not there to be had for the asking.
Control of fixity in the play is as challenging as control of
change, and where there is putative stasis in the action it is
the enforced stasis of arrested motion not the tensionless
stasis of absent motion. The interruption of movement

before it can fulfill its potential is thus characteristic of the images and the action of a play in which two old men review and renew a life of recurring discontinuity. The interaction between Spooner and Hirst exhibits what Hirst's description of his album exhibits--life seen from the perspective of old age as an aggregate of intriguing but discontinuous moments rather than as a unified pattern of continuous flow. And it is the importance of perspective that makes it essential for the images deployed strategically or otherwise to be presented indirectly as narrative images rather than directly as pictorial images.

The depiction of lived experience as an aggregate of discontinuous moments is by no means unknown to modern and postmodern literature, but Pinter is not content to recapitulate what others have suggested before him. The key feature of the discontinuous moments in *No Man's Land* is that they exemplify not just fragmentation but thwarted potential, and the key feature of the perspective offered on old age is that its implications spread well beyond their immediate context of origin.[11] But it is the relationship Pinter establishes between these two issues that gives the play its coherence and its power. As we encounter the album's images of Hirst's youth through his descriptions of moments of unfulfilled promise, it is important to recognize that these images of arrested motion revive both the initial promise and its subsequent failure. The imagined camera freezes action, and in so doing, it records the trace of motion in the image of its cessation. Hirst's revival of the images renews both stages of the process. His "we can't be expected to live like that" is both a repetition and a renewal of a denial for which the necessity has again arisen. And his initial invitation to and subsequent rejection of Spooner reenacts in the present his own decisions of the past. In one local episode after another the various actions of the present characters replicate those of characters in the past by repeatedly being interrupted without being completed. But what repeatedly renews the repeatedly interrupted action is the readiness of Hirst and Spooner to contemplate locally what they are so skeptical about globally: the possibility that the flux of events may yet generate possibilities large enough to restore continuity to discontinuous experience. The recurring tension in the discontinuous action derives from the capacity of the two old men to include in the predominantly skeptical perspective of age the optimistic perspective of youth.

Throughout the play we witness the painful interaction of two men of advanced years whose experience of life is that what is gained locally is what is lost locally, whether it be friendship, love, or youthful achievement. But in those earlier episodes that provide the focus of discussion we encounter images that exemplify the capacity of youth to believe in what the older characters can be only intermittently believe in--the possibility that current achievements might have lasting consequences. The optimistic young faces, the moments of athletic success, the achievement of serenity, and the display of beautiful proportion all provide the context for a current interaction constantly revived by the potential of local moments to have lasting effects. The interaction between Hirst and Spooner is renewed by the reminders the images provide of local and potentially lasting belief, but the interaction is, in turn, disrupted by the other reminder the same images provide of episodes that foundered in the context in which they first flourished. That disruption is, in turn, made more powerful by the defensive postures of disengagement that the characters adopt and by their mutual readiness to convert the images of potential intimacy into weapons of conquest and destruction. Spooner is quick to invent anecdotes about Hirst's impotence and Hirst responds with anecdotes about Spooner's cuckoldry. Even as they reach out to each other, they prepare to withdraw the proffered hand before the opportunity for rejection is exploited. Foster and Briggs, parasites on the action and dependent on its outcome, feed the negative side of the interaction with every form of disruption they can think of. At the end of the First Act, Foster walks about the room, stops at the door, turns to

Spooner, and says: "Listen. You know what it's like when you're in a room with the light on and then suddenly the light goes out? I'll show you. It's like this" (p. 115). And he turns the light out. The Act ends on a moment of renewed interruption, but the interaction between Hirst and Spooner begins again on the basis of a renewed pursuit of continuity.

In old age Hirst and Spooner behave inconsistently because they continue to be intrigued by episodes about whose larger consequences they are deeply skeptical. But more than mere inconsistency is at issue in Pinter's depiction of past and present discontinuity. The potential superiority of the perspective of old age is registered in Hirst and Spooner's capacity to observe from outside as well as inside the significance of moments within which youthful characters appear to be trapped. They can see what youth is unable to see, that the discontinuity of life is as large a factor as any continuity that is ever likely to emerge. But it is their capacity in such a context to renew their interest in moments of unfulfilled promise that exemplifies the stasis of conflicting and arrested motion in the play. The conflict between their larger disengagement from and their local fascination with promising moments displays both the power of skepticism in the perspective of experience and the power of local moments to challenge and disrupt it. The action of the play depicts neither the static immobility of absent motion nor the static fragmentation of unrelated episodes. Rather it displays the repeated renewal of an interaction about which both characters are deeply ambivalent.

Torn between a larger skepticism based on long experience and a local optimism that once was overwhelming, the characters constantly renew an uncertainty they are unable to resolve. It is a nostalgia for their earlier belief that continuity might eventually conquer discontinuity that promotes their re-entry into a race they had long forgotten to run, and it is that same nostalgia that makes each see intermittently in the other more promise than either seems able to fulfill. To see what they see we must share not only the images they repeatedly invoke but also the perspective that gives those images their poignancy and their power.[12] It is the capacity of each character not so much to restore that earlier promise but to remind the other of its earlier existence that reactivates their nostalgia for and their renewed interest in moments of vague but unspecified promise. Too old to regard such moments as fully credible, they adopt postures of disengagement to disguise their fascination with past and present moments that promise more than they ever manage to deliver. In their erratic behavior we see memories of the past and hopes for the future alternately flourish and fail. And as we do so, we come to understand the ambivalent status of the no man's land that provides the title of the play.

The dominant perspective of the old age depicted in the play is one in which disengagement and doubt contaminate social participation, limit it, and threaten to eliminate it. This is the process that leads Hirst towards a no man's land "which never moves, which never changes, which never grows older, but which remains forever, icy and silent" (p. 153). But this is not the sole perspective of old age exhibited in the play. The very images that display collectively the discontinuity of life continue to display individually a potential for life to be otherwise. Hirst and Spooner repeatedly recall earlier moments which once promised and in some residual way continue to promise another kind of world and another kind of life. Their recollections play their part in a discontinuous action that depicts a persisting tension between local engagement and general disengagement, between the competing demands of youthful hope and later doubt, between social intimacy and social distance, between revived hope and recurring fear, between renewed movement and repeated arrest. The no man's land of the title is the destination toward which the action moves but it is not the culmination of the action nor is it the image that governs either the world of the play or the world of the play's conclusion. A world of fixity is no more free from the possibility of flux than a world of flux is from the possibility of fixity. In the final moments of the action as in the initial moments, the claims of continuity and the claims of discontinuity are in persisting conflict. Hirst's determination never to change again the subject of the conversation is set in contrast to his renewed recognition of the insistent promise of change.

The sound of birds that disturbs and disrupts the diminishing discourse restores life's challenge to the skepticism of old age, insisting that eternal change might not be just another symptom of discontinuity but, even now, a sign of Hirst's capacity to learn, grow, and change.

> Hirst: It's night.
> Foster: And will always be night.
> Briggs: Because the subject--
> Foster: Can never be changed.
> *Silence*
> Hirst: But I hear sounds of birds. Don't you
>   hear them? Sounds I never heard before.
>   I hear them as they must have sounded
>   then, when I was young, although I never
>   heard them then, although they sounded
>   about us then.
> *Pause*   (pp. 152-53)

At the end of the play, as throughout the action, Hirst's desire for final disengagement conflicts with his desire to reexamine a past in which engagement promised something ill-defined but indispensable: "Did it exist? It's gone. It never existed. It remains" (p. 108). These affirmations of conflicting possibilities, these manifestations of opposing and arrested movements, leave us with the sense of a past that in some sense both persists and disappears. The moments of arrested motion in the anecdotes, the album, and the action of the play depict a mode of existence in which the potential of change and the purposelessness of change are locked in persisting conflict. The discontinuity of social experience is exemplified in the play as in the album by lives impinging without combining, incidents achieving local value without establishing larger scope, and relationships registering local contact without promoting long-term convergence. The continuity of individual experience is registered in the characters' repeated reexamination of moments they can neither make do with nor do without. It is in this sense that the characters, in Collins's phrase, stick out beyond the edges of the play, for they register, in spite of their denials, expectations that exceed the boundaries of every episode in the action. It is the characters' capacity to envisage what the episodic images suggest but are unable to supply that makes them seem more memorable than any of the local episodes in which they participate. And it is their intermittently renewed desire to exploit the possibilities that the narrative images locally affirm and globally deny that gives the play its unexpected form of coherence, a coherence that finds room for continuous and discontinuous action and for contrasting speeds of change.

NOTES

1. Irving Wardle, "In a Land of Dreams and Actuality," *The Times* (London), 24 April 1975, p. 10.

2. Benedict Nightingale, "Inaction Replay," *New Statesman*, 2 May 1975, p. 601.

3. R. G. Collins, "Pinter and the End of Endings," *Queens Quarterly*, 85, Spring 1978, p. 116.

4. Harold Pinter, *No Man's Land, Complete Works: Four*, New York, 1981. All page references are to this edition.

5. Steven H. Gale traces the variety of literary allusions that contribute to the diversity of character interaction. *Butter's Going Up: A Critical Analysis*

of Harold Pinter's Work, Durham, N. C., 1977, pp. 199-221.

6. John Bush Jones, "Stasis as Structure in Pinter's *No Man's Land,*" *Modern Drama,* 19, September 1976, pp. 291-304.

7. Ruby Cohn, "Words Working Overtime: *Endgame* and *No Man's Land,*" *The Yearbook of English Studies,* 9, 1979, p. 193.

8. Harold Pinter, "Harold Pinter: An Interview" (with L. M. Bensky, 1967), in *Pinter: A Collection of Critical Essays,* ed. Arthur Ganz, Englewood Cliffs, N. J., 1972, p. 22.

9. Harold Pinter, *Landscape, Complete Works: Three,* New York, 1978, pp. 195-96.

10. John Bush Jones, "Stasis as Structure in Pinter's *No Man's Land,*" p. 294. Though I disagree with his conclusions, Jones provides a precise and detailed argument. He perceptively juxtaposes but unfortunately seeks to equate arrested motion and immobility. He argues that photography and painting "render the active static," that "suspended animation" is simply a more precise description of "inaction," and that a "fixed" moment of activity is not readily distinguished from one that is "continuously replayed." As a consequence Jones can make little of Spooner's interest in being "eternally present and active." For Jones "there is little evidence . . . for the verity of the final word" (p. 300). Spooner's verbal activity, of course, provides ample evidence of complex social action, as does that of the other characters seeking to relate in various ways the past to the present and to the future.

11. The play's lack of clear lines of temporal continuity
     and consistent narrative connection is directly
     related to Pinter's efforts to dramatize the
     discontinuous aspects of lived experience. But this
     does not mean that the play lacks coherence
     because life lacks coherence. Rather it implies that
     the play's coherence is located elsewhere. For
     further discussion of Pinter's use of discontinuous
     structures, see my article on "The Temporality of
     Structure in Pinter's Plays," *The Pinter Review*, 1,
     1987, pp. 7-21.

12. This is a matter that has generated some theoretical
     as well as interpretive debate. Whitaker, apparently
     misunderstanding what is at issue in Wittgenstein's
     discussion of the reference theory of meaning,
     concludes that there is a necessary inconsistency
     between the positing of a problematic and
     negotiated reality and the assignment to characters
     of motives, goals, and strategies. Describing the
     latter as a manifestation of "naive realism" he offers
     as an alternative an anti-realism which seems a
     rather more suitable candidate for the term "naive."
     No Man's Land presents in this view "a world
     where the past is unknowable, the future
     unpredictable, the present a room of loveless wills
     constructing themselves out of fictions, and each
     fiction a mocking symbol of that world." In a play
     in which "existence has become words, words,
     words," characters are reduced to voices, or more
     accurately to a single voice, for there is only one
     thing to be said in this "hell of echoing absence"
     and each character keeps saying it, and every scene
     repeats it (Thomas R. Whitaker, "Playing Hell," *The
     Yearbook of English Studies*, 9, 1979, pp. 184-86).

          In spite of its theoretical sophistication, this
     argument offers a variant on the theme of
     unchanging fixity in *No Man's Land*, but it exhibits

a form of linguistic skepticism that has more in common with Derrida's philosophy than Wittgenstein's. As I have argued elsewhere ("Wittgenstein's Philosophizing and Literary Theorizing," *New Literary History*, XIX, Winter 1988, pp. 209-37), Wittgenstein is as much opposed to such skepticism as he is to referential foundationalism. Like Saussure, Wittgenstein recognizes that the characteristic of non-referential arbitrariness, which multiplies the complexity of the sign, reinforces rather than relaxes the constraints of convention upon it. There is nothing in Wittgenstein's philosophy or Pinter's dramatic practice that precludes the assigning of motives, the determining of preferences, or the attribution of goals, needs, and desires. Wittgenstein's philosophy does not present us with an unattractive choice between a naive realism and a naive anti-realism. Rather it points the way to a non-naive realism, one that enables us to recognize that discontinuity in the drama can be of many kinds and for many purposes. An alternative movement in literary theory that seeks to illuminate texts by converting different kinds of discontinuity into the same kind of discontinuity, different characters into clones of the same character, and different plays into variants of the same play seems, like many of the episodes in *No Man's Land*, to be promising more than it will ever manage to deliver.

LAST TO GO:
A STRUCTURALIST READING

David Lodge

"Last to Go," a revue sketch first performed in 1958, is a microcosm of Harold Pinter's dramatic universe. It presents in a condensed form the central paradox of his work. How is it that dialogue superficially so banal, repetitive and full of silences, and a narrative so ambiguous and exiguous can interest and entertain an audience or reader? (That Pinter's work succeeds in doing so, I take for granted.)

The fact that this text (reprinted at the end of this essay) is so short allows us to ponder the question with the whole "play," as it were, present to our consciousness, and this is the reason I choose it for analysis. It has already been the object of an acute commentary by Deirdre Burton in her book *Dialogue and Discourse: a Sociolinguistic Approach to Modern Drama Dialogue and Naturally Occurring Conversation* (1980). What I have to say here is indebted to her work and also, I hope, complementary to it. As her subtitle implies, her approach derives primarily from applied linguistics; mine from structuralist poetics. Behind the question, what makes "Last to Go" a work of dramatic art, there is for me a larger question: what makes *any* text a work of art?

For Deirdre Burton, the value of "Last to Go" inheres in the way it identifies and dramatically exploits certain features of "real" conversation, notably what the anthropologist Malinowski called "phatic communion," that is, speech whose primary function is to maintain contact between the interlocutors rather than to convey information.   Usually this is a one-sided operation, as when a psychiatrist murmurs "Mmm, mmm," to indicate to the patient that he is listening to the latter's outpourings.   But "Last to Go" presents a conversation that is mutually and simultaneously phatic for both interlocutors, maintaining contact but not conveying much information between them. This accounts for the extraordinary amount of repetition in the dialogue.   As Deirdre Burton observes, "the characters are continually questioning and confirming matters that they both already know, that they must surely know they both know, and that the audience certainly knows that they know."[1]

The presence of the audience is, of course, crucial, making the dialogue an object of aesthetic rather than sociolinguistic interest; or, to put it less solemnly, funny and moving for us, but not for the speakers.   We can formalise this point by putting the category of "phatic" in the perspective of Roman Jakobson's structuralist model of the speech act:[2]

CONTEXT

ADDRESSER   MESSAGE   ADDRESSEE

CONTACT

CODE

The ADDRESSER (speaker, writer) sends a MESSAGE (utterance, text) to the ADDRESSEE (interlocutor, reader) referring to a CONTEXT (the world, physical and mental, they both inhabit) using a CODE (*e.g.*, the English language) and a means of CONTACT (which Jakobson defines generally as "a physical channel and psychological connection" (it might be a book or a telephone line or, as in conversation, the mutual presence-to-each-other of the interlocutors).   The function of a given speech act, or of an entire discourse, can be classified according to which of the component elements is emphasised, thus:

CONTEXT
(referential)

ADDRESSER   MESSAGE   ADDRESSEE
(emotive)   (poetic)   (conative)

CONTACT
(phatic)

CODE
(metalingual)

A "message" focussed primarily on Context (like this essay) is Referential; a message focussed on the Addresser, such as an expletive, is Emotive; a message focussed on the Addressee (an order or instruction, for instance) is Conative; a message focussed on its own code (such as a dictionary definition) is Metalingual; and a message that is focussed on Contact (of which examples have already been given) is Phatic. But there is a final category, the Poetic, when the Message is focussed on itself. "The set (*Einstellung*) toward the message as such, focus on the message for its own sake, is the POETIC function of language." Under "poetic," Jakobson includes all discourse considered as verbal art. Utterances that in a non-aesthetic context might be classified as dominantly referential, emotive, conative, etc. acquire a different status when they occur in an aesthetic context. Language that is phatic for the Barman and the Newspaper-seller is poetic for us. How does this happen? It is another version of the question with which we started.

Before we pursue it, let us look more closely at what Jakobson says about the category of the phatic:

There are messages primarily serving to establish, to prolong, or to discontinue communication, to check whether the channel works ("Hello, do you hear me?"), to attract the attention of the interlocutor or to confirm his continued attention ("Are you listening?" or in Shakespearean diction, "Lend me your ears!"--and on the other end of the wire, "Um-hum!"). This set for contact, or in Malinowski's terms PHATIC function, may be displayed by a profuse exchange of ritualised formulas, by entire dialogues with the mere purport of prolonging communication.[3]

This last observation seems very applicable to "Last to Go." The sketch, we might venture to say, is on one level about two lonely people who rather than face their own solitariness, late at night, desperately keep a conversation going although they have nothing substantial to communicate. Neither of them wants to be the last to go (home).

It is important to recognize that Jakobson's typology of speech acts is based on *dominance*. That is to say, speech acts are rarely focussed exclusively on one function; it is a question of which function is dominant. The opening line of Pinter's sketch for instance,

> MAN: You was a bit busier earlier

is ostensibly referential, though we infer from the triviality of its content and the silence (indicated in the stage direction) preceding it, that its real function is phatic. The Barman's reply, "Ah," (line 2) is, however, manifestly phatic, since it neither confirms nor disconfirms what the Man has said, but merely establishes that the former has heard the latter. The dialogue proceeds in this way for some lines--a pseudo-referential message from the Man being phatically acknowledged by the Barman, until the Barman ventures a referential confirmation, and the Man (redundantly) confirms it yet again:

BARMAN: Yes, trade was very brisk here about
            ten.
MAN: Yes, I noticed. (8-9)

This slight reversal of roles in the conversation brings the
first phase of movement of the piece to an end. The Man
now begins a new but parallel topic, concerning the time
and nature of his last sale of the evening. This is a
sublimely vacuous topic, spun out by the Man's repetition
of the same information and the Barman's redundant
checking:

MAN: I sold my last one about then. Yes.
            About nine forty-five.
BARMAN: Sold your last then, did you?
MAN: Yes, my last "Evening News" it was.
            Went about twenty to ten.
            (*Pause*)
BARMAN: "Evening News," was it?
MAN: Yes.
            (*Pause*)
            Sometimes it's the "Star" is the last
            to go. (9a-13a)

In performance, the pauses add greatly to the comic effect
of the two men's effort to keep this contentless
conversational ball rolling. Having covered all the possible
variations of which newspaper is the last to go, the topic
seems to be exhausted, but after a silence the Man
doggedly revives it by repeating what he has already said,
and confirmed, earlier (11, 13):

            (*Pause*)
MAN: All I had left tonight was the
            "Evening News". (17a)

Then, after *another* pause, the Barman *again* checks this
useless piece of information:

                        (*Pause*)
        BARMAN: Then that went, did it?
        MAN: Yes.
                        (*Pause*)
        MAN: Like a shot. (18-19a)

This phrase is so incongruous, both in application to the
sale of the last newspaper at such a late hour, and in the
context of the leaden-paced conversation, that it is sure to
raise a gust of laughter from an audience in performance.
Another reason for such an effect is that the opportunity to
laugh provides relief from the tension of wondering
whether the speakers will succeed in keeping the
conversation going--a suspense heightened by the
concentration of pauses at this part of the text. Silence, a
characteristic feature of Pinter's drama, is extraordinarily
potent on the stage, because of the audience's assumption
that drama consists of speech or significant action.

An additional reason why "Like a shot" has a
powerful effect is that, although a cliché, it is a figure of
speech, a simile to be precise, and the first to be used by
either speaker. One way of putting this is to say that the
phrase "Like a shot" is *foregrounded* against a background
of more literal, denotative language used by the speakers
up to that point. For the Man, it constitutes a heroic effort
(comically, pathetically heroic in the audience's
perception) to dignify the banality of the last sale by a
rhetorical flourish. In a livelier linguistic context it would
hardly register as such. But that background of dull,
repetitive, denotative language is itself foregrounded
against the kind of language traditionally expected from
drama--pointed, well-formed, eloquent, profound, witty,
etc.--and thus makes "Last to Go" a modern or
experimental piece of drama.

The poetic function of language is partly a matter of
the way a given discourse is framed and perceived. A
declaration of love in verse, for instance, might be
primarily emotive for the addresser (a relief for his
feelings) or primarily conative if sent to the addressee

(persuading her to reciprocate) but if it is published in a literary magazine it is poetic, read "for its own sake." But you cannot turn *any* discourse into a work of verbal art simply by reading the message for its own sake. A railway timetable stubbornly remains a referential message, a dictionary remains a metalingual message, unless you select from and manipulate their component parts--in which case they would no longer perform their original functions.

What kind of selection and manipulation would be entailed? What is it that poetic messages, or messages capable of being received as such, have, that other messages do not have? Jakobson had a highly technical answer to this question: "The poetic function projects the principle of equivalence from the axis of selection to the axis of combination."[4] To expound this fully would take too long here,[5] but in effect it means that discourses which are either designed as works of verbal art, or capable of being read as such, are characterised by parallelism, symmetry, repetition, contrast, and other kinds of binary patterning. The most obvious example is the metrical and phonological patterning of regular verse, which is not required for the referential, emotive, and conative functions of the message. In prose fiction and "prose drama," the system of equivalences is more difficult to spot, because prose and realistically rendered speech do not exhibit the formal patterning of verse, and because the variety of discourses and voices in these forms obscure what patterning there is. Nevertheless it can usually be discovered.

We receive "Last to Go" as a "poetic message," as a work of verbal art, on both the grounds referred to above: first because we encounter it in an aesthetic frame--as performed in a theatre or as read in a book of plays and sketches; and secondly because it stands up to being read as a message for its own sake, a quality which turns out on examination to have something to do with patterns of equivalence that can be perceived in it. Like all drama, this sketch is an imitation of various speech acts that can be classified according to the functions they would have in reality (referential, phatic, etc.), but that considered together, as a whole, constitute a poetic message, which we attend to "for its own sake"--that is, for the meanings it generates independently of any "real" context. And both the plethora of meanings and the unification of them into a "whole" are related to the pattern of equivalences discoverable in the text. Like much modern realistic or naturalistic writing, "Last to Go" disguises its aesthetically necessary patterns of equivalence as contingency, as mere representation of typical behaviour. The surface justification for the amount of repetition in the dialogue is that people do actually repeat a good deal in dominantly phatic conversations. But the diagram that Deirdre Burton draws to show how repetition of information is used by the Man and the Barman "to ensure that . . . the conversation will keep going,"[6] can also be used to point to an effect in the dialogue something like echo and refrain in poetry:

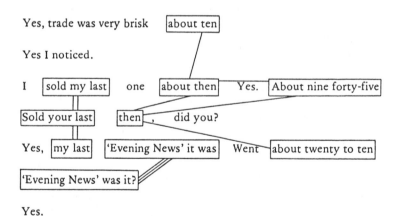

Yes, trade was very brisk | about ten

Yes I noticed.

I | sold my last | one | about then | Yes. | About nine forty-five

Sold your last | then , | did you?

Yes, | my last | 'Evening News' it was | Went | about twenty to ten

'Evening News' was it?

Yes.

There is a high degree of artifice here as well as an acute ear for the character of colloquial, uneducated speech. It would probably be possible to deceive someone into thinking that this dialogue was recorded from life, if one got two actors to tape-record it in a certain way--with much humming and hahing, coughs, grunts, overlapping of lines, elisions of words, nongrammatical pauses, background noise and suchlike features of "naturally occurring conversation." But, as written, the dialogue invites a much more stylised performance, bringing out its symmetries and echoes: *about ten/about then*; *sold my last/sold your last*; *"Evening News" it was/"Evening News" was it?*

I have not yet mentioned the most obvious equivalence in the sketch--that between its beginning and ending, marked by the difference of its middle. Drama is a form of narrative, and narrative entails process. Whereas a lyric poem can simply express a steady state in a pleasing arrangement of lexical and phonic equivalences ("Hey nonny nonny, this life is so jolly" etc.), there must be some change, however minimal, in a story whether written, recited, or performed. At first "Last to Go" presents a purely static situation. Two men are talking for the mere sake of talking. They endlessly recycle the same trivial information. Statements and questions that seem superficially to be referential in function are in fact purely phatic. But this stasis, and the pattern of verbal equivalences that underpin it, are disturbed in line 25:

BARMAN: You didn't stop here, though, did you?
MAN: When? (24-5)

This is a deviation from the previous pattern of the text, whereby only the Barman asks the questions, and they are pseudo-questions, checking formulae which contain their own answers (though they are answered anyway): "Ten, was it?" (4); "Sold your last then, did you?" (10); "Evening News" was it? (12). The Man's "When?" in line 25 is a breach in the tacit rules of the game the pair are playing. It also implies that the Man is either extraordinarily stupid (since there is no doubt about what time is being referred to) or that his attention is wandering. The latter seems the likelier explanation. The Barman tries to pull the

conversation back on to its safe course ("I mean, you didn't
stop here and have a cup of tea then, did you?" 26) but the
Man moves on to another topic:

> MAN: No, I went up to Victoria.
> BARMAN: No, I thought I didn't see you.
> MAN: I had to go to Victoria. (29-31)

The "No" in line 29 is foregrounded against all the "yeses"
scattered earlier through the dialogue, and the Barman is
compelled to repeat this negative word in expressing
agreement. He tries desperately to keep the conversation
anchored to the previous topics ("Yes, trade was very brisk
about then," 32) but the Man is mentally retracing his
journey to Victoria, and the Barman has reluctantly to
follow him.

> MAN: I went to see if I could get hold of
>   George. (33)

This dialogue now begins to take on a different character
from the pattern previously established. With the
introduction of the topic of George, statements and
questions become genuinely referential. But the possibility
of disagreement also raises its head, and with it, the
possibility of confrontation, challenge and termination of
the conversation. Either one of the men is wrong about
George, or they are each thinking of a different George. In
either case, the continuity of the conversation is
jeopardised. In the event the desire to maintain phatic
communion triumphs over the desire to establish the truth,
but there is dramatic suspense about this outcome for some
lines.

> BARMAN: George who?
> MAN: George . . . whatsisname.
> BARMAN: Oh.
>   (*Pause*) (37-8)

When the Man uses the expression "whatsisname" previously, the Barman was able to supply the missing name (15-16). Clearly unable to supply it in this case, he chooses to pretend that he knows who the Man is referring to.

BARMAN: Did you get hold of him?
MAN: No. No, I couldn't get hold of him. I couldn't locate him.
BARMAN: He's not much about now, is he? (38a-40)

This last line has the grammatical form of those earlier questions from the Barman that are ostensibly referential, but in fact phatic, merely recycling interrogatively the information that has just been stated declaratively, like "Sold your last, then did you?" (10) and "'Evening News,' was it?" (12). But this time the Barman has hazarded additional information on his own account, and thus laid himself open to referential challenge.

MAN: When did you last see him, then? (41)

The Barman equivocates and the Man, instead of pressing him, identifies himself with the answer.

BARMAN: Oh, I haven't seen him for years.
MAN: No, nor me. (42-3)

Emboldened by this admission, the Barman makes a very specific referential assertion:

BARMAN: Used to suffer very bad from arthritis. (44)

Why does he say this? Assuming that he doesn't really know whom the Man is referring to, it could be because he actually knew a George who suffered from arthritis, and is convinced that the Man knows so little about *his* George that the two can be happily fused into one for the phatic purpose of the conversation; or it could be that he is reinforcing his claim to know George by inventing this detail, as a writer will give a fictitious character an air of reality by what Henry James called "solidity of specification." At any rate, it proves a rash move in terms of the conversational game they are playing, because it leads to a direct challenge:

MAN:	Arthritis?
BARMAN:	Yes.
MAN:	He never suffered from arthritis.
BARMAN:	Suffered very bad.
	(*Pause*) (45-48)

This is obviously the dramatic climax of the sketch, the only moment of conflict between the two *dramatis personae*. There is a danger that if the topic is pursued much further it will be revealed that one or both of the interlocutors is misinformed or misunderstanding or lying, and the conversation will end acrimoniously.

MAN:	Not when I knew him. (49)
	(*Pause*)

This seems to continue the challenge, though it also offers a face-saving solution of their disagreement, *viz*, that they must have known George at different times. If the Barman had replied aggressively, "Well, he did when *I* knew him," it would be necessary to establish when that was and to settle other factual matters to do with the identity of George, probably revealing the incompatibility of their respective accounts of him, and thus jeopardising the continuance of the conversation. But in fact the Barman backs down:

BARMAN:	I think he must have left the area. (50)

This refers back to an earlier topic, namely, the Man's failure to "locate" George. It is by way of being a confirmation of information already received, and thus brings the potentially divisive topic of George to an amicably indeterminate conclusion. The Man collaborates by reverting to the safe, manageable topic of the last newspaper to go:

> MAN: Yes, it was the "Evening News" was the last to go tonight. (51)

To which the Barman eagerly responds with one of his typically redundant questions, reformulating information already received:

> BARMAN: Not always the last though, is it, though? (52)

To which the Man replies:

> MAN: No. Oh no. I mean sometimes it's the "News." Other times it's one of the others. No way of telling beforehand. Until you've got your last one left, of course. Then you can tell which one it's going to be. (53)

Superficially, the Man's reply seems another recycling of information already communicated in lines 11-16. But in fact there is a significant difference. Whereas in the earlier lines the Man had merely commented on which paper was the last to go, here he is talking about *predicting* which will be the last paper to go. This point is given emphasis by the fact that it is made in the longest single speech of the entire play. The phrase "last to go," which is the title of the whole piece thus begins to acquire additional resonances, or equivalences.

The phrase, "Last to Go," I suggested earlier, applies to the two men--neither wanting to be the last to go home, the last to be alone. But there seems to be another possible metaphorical meaning: death, and the fear of death. Out of a given set of people, you never know who is going to be the next to die, until there is only one left: "then you can tell which one it's going to be." This might explain why the Man reverts, somewhat unexpectedly, in the very last line of the play, to the topic of George, adopting a line of the Barman's as if it is his own:

MAN: I think he must have left the area. (55a)

George's departure may have been from this life, not just from Victoria.

According to A. J. Greimas[7] all concepts are semantically defined by a binary relationship with their opposites, (*e.g.*, life versus death) or their negatives (*e.g.*, life versus non-life), yielding the basic semiotic model, A:B::-A:-B (*e.g.*, Life is to Death as Non-life is to Non-death), and all narrative can be seen as the transformation of such four-term homologies into characters and actions. In "Last to Go" the life/death theme is represented as presence/absence. Life is presence, death is absence. Speech requires presence, and in phatic communion is used chiefly to maintain presence. The opposite of speech is silence, absence of speech, the "pause" that is such a characteristic feature of Pinter's drama. The negative of presence is represented by George, who is named in the dialogue but not physically present, thought to be in Victoria, but not "located" there; and the negative of absence is presence-about-to-be-terminated, such as the last newspaper to go, just before it goes. The semiotic structure of the sketch might therefore be summarised as: Speech is to Silence as George is to the last newspaper to go.

NOTES

1. Deirdre Burton, *A Sociolinguistic Approach to Modern Drama Dialogue and Naturally Occurring Conversation* (1980), p. 13.

2. Roman Jakobson, "Linguistics and Poetics," in *Language in Literature*, edited by Krystyna Pomorska and Stephen Rudy (1987), p. 66 ff.

3. Jakobson, p. 68.

4. Jakobson, p. 71.

5. For further discussion, see my *The Modes of Modern Writing* (1977), *passim*.

6. Burton, p. 17.

7. A. J. Greimas, *Semantique Structurale* (Paris 1966), *Du Sens* (Paris, 1970) and Maupassant, *La semiologie du texte: exercices pratique* (Paris, 1976). I am indebted to Ann Jefferson's explication of Greimas' method in her review of the last-named book in *Poetics and Theory of Literature* II (1977), pp. 579-88.

LAST TO GO

A coffee stall. A BARMAN and an old NEWSPAPER SELLER. The BARMAN leans on his counter, the OLD MAN stands with tea. Silence.

MAN	You was a bit busier earlier.	1
BARMAN	Ah.	2
MAN	Round about ten.	3
BARMAN	Ten, was it?	4
MAN	About then.	5
	(Pause)	
	I passed by here about then.	5a
BARMAN	Oh yes?	6
MAN	I noticed you were doing a bit of trade.	7
	(Pause)	
BARMAN	Yes, trade was very brisk here about ten.	8
MAN	Yes, I noticed.	9
	(Pause)	
	I sold my last one about then. Yes. About nine forty-five.	9a
BARMAN	Sold your last then, did you?	10
MAN	Yes, my last 'Evening News' it was. Went about twenty to ten.	11
	(Pause)	
BARMAN	'Evening News', was it?	12
MAN	Yes.	13
	(Pause)	

	Sometimes it's the 'Star' is the last to go.	13a
BARMAN	Ah.	14
MAN	Or the . . . whatsisname.	15
BARMAN	'Standard'.	16
MAN	Yes.	17

(*Pause*)

| | All I had left tonight was the 'Evening News'. | 17a |

(*Pause*)

| BARMAN | Then that went, did it? | 18 |
| MAN | Yes. | 19 |

(*Pause*)

| | Like a shot. | 19a |

(*Pause*)

| BARMAN | You didn't have any left, eh? | 20 |
| MAN | No, Not after I sold that one. | 21 |

(*Pause*)

BARMAN	It was after that you must have come by here then, was it?	22
MAN	Yes, I come by here after that, see, after I packed up.	23
BARMAN	You didn't stop here though, did you?	24
MAN	When?	25
BARMAN	I mean, you didn't stop here and have a cup of tea then, did you?	26
MAN	What, about ten?	27
BARMAN	Yes.	28

MAN	No, I went up to Victoria.	29
BARMAN	No, I thought I didn't see you.	30
MAN	I had to go to Victoria.	31
	(*Pause*)	
BARMAN	Yes, trade was very brisk here about then.	32
	(*Pause*)	
MAN	I went to see if I could get hold of George.	33
BARMAN	Who?	34
MAN	George.	35
	(*Pause*)	
BARMAN	George who?	36
MAN	George . . . whatsisname.	37
BARMAN	Oh.	38
	(*Pause*)	
	Did you get hold of him?	38a
MAN	No. No, I couldn't get hold of him. I couldn't locate him.	39
BARMAN	He's not much about now, is he?	40
	(*Pause*)	
MAN	When did you last see him then?	41
BARMAN	Oh, I haven't seen him for years.	42
MAN	No, nor me.	43
	(*Pause*)	
BARMAN	Used to suffer very bad from arthritis.	44
MAN	Arthritis?	45

BARMAN	Yes.	46
MAN	He never suffered from arthritis.	47
BARMAN	Suffered very bad.	48
	(*Pause*)	
MAN	Not when I knew him.	49
	(*Pause*)	
BARMAN	I think he must have left the area.	50
	(*Pause*)	
MAN	Yes, it was the 'Evening News' was the last to go tonight.	51
BARMAN	Not always the last though, is it, though?	52
MAN	No. Oh no. I mean sometimes it's the 'News'. Other times it's one of the others. No way of telling beforehand. Until you've got your last one left, of course. Then you can tell which one it's going to be.	53
BARMAN	Yes.	54
	(*Pause*)	
MAN	Oh yes.	55
	(*Pause*)	
	I think he must have left the area.	55a

MONOLOGUE: THE PLAY OF WORDS

Linda Ben-Zvi

> Do you remember--of course she does!--the conversation--or rather, perhaps I should say, monologue?
> "Monologue?" She was hostile all of a sudden. "What's that? Something to eat?"
> "Oh" he said, "words that don't do any work and don't much want to. A salivation of words after the banquet."
> > Samuel Beckett, *Dream of Fair to Middling Women*

    Like a minimalist sculpture or painter, Harold Pinter has always taken great pleasure in making much of little. A woman making breakfast, a man reading the daily newspaper, a couple killing an annoying wasp have carried the burden for his unfolding investigation of contemporary life. Pinter has also displayed a parallel spareness in his language. Only Samuel Beckett among contemporary dramatists has set more stringent restrictions on the variables in his works and his words. Yet even for Pinter, *Monologue*, his television play written in 1972 and presented on the BBC on April 13, 1973 (coincidently, Beckett's 67th birthday), is restrictive. It is a work of only 1,253 words, a monologic outpouring delivered by a man who sits alone on a stage, addressing his words to an empty chair, affixed to which he imagines a male friend. In 29 short fragments, some only a line long, punctuated by pauses and one full silence, he tells the story of their friendship and of the woman whom they both desired. Hardly the residue of banquets past, the monologue reflects the paltry life of the speaker, the equally reclusive life of the friend, and the fleeting moments of love. Perhaps because of its brevity or its single video presentation to date, the play has received almost no critical attention.[1] It is, however, an important work in the Pinter canon. A sustained dramatic piece in its own right, it is also a catalogue, pared to its essentials, of the major preoccupations in all Pinter plays: the loss of love, the isolation experienced in maturity, the desire for male bonding, and the slippages caused by the vagaries of memory and the imprecision of language. Written ten years after *The Collection*, *Monologue* illustrates that the central connections in the Pinter world are still between men and that women provide an intrusive force that threatens to destroy any male camaraderie. Coming six years before *Betrayal*, it acts almost as an outline for the more detailed depiction of the same themes in that work.

"The thing I like, I mean quite immeasurably, is this kind of conversation, this kind of exchange, this class of mutual reminiscence," the speaker says to his imagined friend in the empty chair, midway through the play. Self-address disguised as conversation is nothing new in Pinter; it is found in *A Slight Ache*, *The Examination*, *Landscape*, and *The Homecoming*. In *Monologue*, however, the technique is unadulterated, with no ostensible receiver present; and the sign of absence--the chair--is placed on the stage, providing a visual metaphor of the self-reflexive nature of the character's speech.

While *Monologue* is standard Pinter writ small, it is also--precisely because of its length--an excellent vehicle to use when analyzing Pinter's consummate attention to language and the ways in which lexical, syntactical, and grammatical elements support his themes. Since there is no physical movement in the play, the speaker never leaving his chair, the only marks of time's passage are linguistic, and the familiar Pinteresque tensions between past and present are played out exclusively through language, a situation implied in other Pinter plays but often masked by accompanying stage business. The patterns of past and present marked by word choice are established in the initial speech of the play when the unnamed speaker, played in the BBC production by Henry Woolf--the man for whom *The Room* was written--talks to his unseen friend:

> I think I'll nip down to the games room. Stretch my my legs. Have a game of ping pong. What about you? Fancy a game? How would you like a categorical thrashing? I'm willing to accept any challenge, any stakes, any gauntlet you'd care to fling down. What have you done with your gauntlets, by the way? In fact, *while we're at it,* what happened to your motorbike?

The words refer to a challenge, one man taking on another in some game. Typical of the world that Pinter usually draws, it is not a physically demanding engagement that is being suggested, but rather a game of ping-pong, described in an offhanded way as an extension of the need for physical activity. Reminiscent of the same game between Disson and Willy in *Tea Party* and the marble bowling in *The Basement*, the encounter seems to be threatening only insofar as it provides an opportunity for some sort of confrontation between men who are friends. However, unlike the earlier examples, but similar to the form of male confrontation described in the later play *Betrayal*, the game only exists in discussion; it is never depicted. The very hesitancy of the words framing the challenge undermines the seriousness implied in these earlier confrontations. "I think I'll nip down" is more tentative than the mock duel in *The Collection*, where the weapons may be relatively harmless but the malignity with which they are wielded is not.

A world where men test their prowess through ping-pong, marbles, or fruit knives, however, is a far cry from some earlier period when physical mastery was made manifest on larger fields of action, with more deadly instruments. What Pinter does in *Monologue* is to sketch linguistically both the modern, enervated world of the speaker and some previous age to which it is implicitly being compared.

"Nip down" and "Fancy a game" is the vernacular of today: colloquial, slang. The abbreviated sentences-- "Stretch my legs," "Have a game"--are imperatives but self-addressed, a prod to action, to get going, in this case to "the games room," the assigned place of combat in the modern society Pinter depicts. In juxtaposition to the present situation evoked in these few verbal, clichéd brushstrokes, Pinter calls up another time through his vocabulary and grammatical choices. "I'm willing to accept any challenge, any stakes, any gauntlet," the speaker proclaims, underlining his desire by using three seemingly synonymous words. However, they are not interchangeable; they create very different images. The synecdoche of throwing down the gauntlet offers just enough of a past time--medieval knights, jousting, heroism--to illuminate the absurdity of its present use when attached to ping-pong. Where are the gauntlets of yesteryear, Pinter seems to ask; and where is the surety of a past when combat determined--in lore if not in fact--"the better man," who, by receiving a "categorical thrashing," could be finally and absolutely defeated. Such vanquishing is impossible in the world of the play where a challenge, even the tentative suggestion of a ping-pong match, is rendered impossible, since the speaker directs his words to an empty chair. The only combat possible is that undertaken inside the skull.

Pinter continues to build on the juxtaposition of present and past and the decline of the former, by introducing the word "stakes," positioned as if it too were a synonym for challenge and for gauntlet. This word also carries resonances of earlier specificity connected with objects used in situations of action: execution, torture, and boundary marking. Its present usage bears the mark of the modern world: unspecified items waged in commercial combat, challenge equated with financial rather than physical activity and conquest. With consummate skill, Pinter goes ever further in this brief opening fragment. Grammar as well as vocabulary indicates the enervated world he describes. The first action--the only action--in the play is thinking. Pinter chooses to show this condition by employing in the first sentence a stative verb, "think" which disallows the progressive. He then couples it with a modal, setting up the important dichotomy between inaction and the attempt to "will" activity into some vague future tense. The very construction encapsulates the dilemma of the speaker: his volition thwarted by the frozen form of his thoughts, the future nullified by the static state of the present which refuses the dynamic alteration of the modal construction. The speaker is thus caught in an unchanging and unchangeable present, the stative verb providing a grammatical foreshadowing of his inability to alter his situation. With economy Pinter describes a world with no future, only the past linguistically replayed over and over in the present. Even a count of the verb tenses in *Monologue* illustrates the situation: 48 are past tense, 18 present, and only 6 future.

The one possibility of melioration in the play is provided by the modal form: conditional words which attempt to change the situation in the present by altering its truth in some way. In the speech above there are two: "would" and "will." Their use becomes pervasive as the play continues, stop-gap grammatical measures to alter the construction of the memory being replayed. The use of conditionals also indicates the irony of the situation of the speaker. He may be willing, or think that he is willing, to take on his friend in combat, but his "will" is contingent on the modal "would," controlled finally by the will of the absent antagonist. Two of the three questions that the speaker asks above illustrate that he is able to carry out the action that he first indicates--playing ping-pong--only if the absent friend assents. Even stretching his legs seems somehow connected to the acquiescence of his friend.

Since the man's stated desire can be met only by the compliance of a listener who is not there, defeat becomes linguistically as well as visually determined from the outset of the play. This opening speech sets up the condition of the modern world--paralysis, alienation, and decline--and contrasts it to a vague, romantic vision of an earlier world of combat, action, and surety. Pinter continues to build upon this dichotomy in the next speech, where the modern avatar of knight-on-steed is described. He is the motorbikist in black:

> You looked bold in black. The only thing I didn't like was your face, too white, the face, stuck between your black helmet and your black hair and your black motoring jacket, kind of aghast, blatantly vulnerable, veering towards pitiful.

Pinter has used this image of romanticized hero/friend before. He is Hawkins in *The Collection*, Cavendish in *A Slight Ache*, MacGregor in *The Homecoming*, and Whipper Wallace, who went "rolling down by the banks of the Euphrates" in the short 1959 review sketch "Dialogue for Three."2 All these friends seem to have certain elements in common: they are physically stronger than the speaker; they are either more successful, more cultured, or more brutal; and they are always absent.

In *Monologue*, Pinter does more than merely evoke an absent male, however; he also wields his double-edged pen, pointing to both the world of the present, where motorbikists play knights, and the chivalric past where knights played gods. The starkness of the phrase "bold in black" with its strong assonance seems to activate the image of the powerful, physical friend; but the picture is quickly blurred by five repetitions of the pronoun "it," which becomes progressively less connected to a clearly delineated antecedent. Once more the manipulation of grammar allows Pinter to say something about society and language, both of which alter and shift in time, the former worn down by collapsing values, the latter by imprecise constructions.   Societal decline mirrored by lexical shifts is illustrated in even more dramatic fashion in Pinter's choice of vocabulary in the passage above.   "Kind of aghast," "blatantly vulnerable," and "veering towards pitiful" are adverbs strangely coupled with adjectives.   Yet, Pinter seems to have carefully chosen these words to underline the themes of displacement, decline, and loss of surety that he established in the grammatical structures of the first speech.

The *Oxford English Dictionary* indicates that the three words "aghast," "vulnerable," and "pitiful" have something in common: they all meant the opposite of what they have come to mean in modern vernacular.   "Aghast" originally indicated "frightening"; "vulnerable," "having the power to wound"; and "pitiful," "full of or characterized by pity."   In the present the words mean the opposite, no longer denoting action but rather the state of being acted upon.   To illustrate how such reversals may occur, Pinter places the words in phrases where the modifying words are imprecise or where they point to the nature of the problem of societal or grammatical dislocation.   For instance, "kind of," a modern slang, distorts through its ambiguity any word with which it comes into contact.   "Blatantly"-- "unpleasantly loud, offensively conspicuous, obtrusive"-- has resonances introduced in the first fragment, where combat is waged for "stakes."   The final modifying words, "veering towards," meaning "capricious changing," become a coda for both verbal and societal slippage: knights into motorbikists, active words into passive, slang into accepted lexicon; categories blurred and confused.

It is possible to go through the play and indicate the repeated use of vocabulary, cliché, and grammatical forms which point to the disparities between present and past usage--the linguistic ping-pong game of the monologue. What Pinter seems to be showing is the difficulty, if not impossibility, of the monologist's attempt to call up memories of the past, since that past has changed in its form and values, and the meanings of the words which might retrieve and revivify it are likewise continually shifting and altering in time.

When, for example, the speaker moves from the man in black to the black woman whom they both desire, he describes her and his friend as forming "some kind of link-up, some kind of identical shimmer, deep down in your characters, an inkling, no more, that at one time you had shared the same pot." Again the word choice conveys more than is immediately apparent. "Link-up" is appropriated from space-age jargon; "shimmer" is one more example of a word altering in time, once denoting "gleaming brightly," now the opposite, "waning light." Pinter may be suggesting that "link-up," describing connections with space travel, will be clear only as long as its origins are understood, that is, only for a given period of time. Then it too will become unfixed and may eventually carry the obverse of its present meaning.

Slippage occurs in language; it is also built into the sequence of fragments in the play. When the speaker once more attempts to engage his friend in a game, the language shows a marked deterioration in specificity from the first attempt, a skillful touch on Pinter's part that allows the audience to experience the very process of the mind's slow alterations forced on it by language's inevitable obfuscation:

> All the same, you and I, even then, never mind the weather, weren't we? we were always available for net practice, at the drop of a hat, or a game of fives, or a walk and talk through the park, or a couple of rounds of putting before lunch, given fair to moderate conditions, and no burdensome commitments.

In this section, the speaker no longer describes the possibility of a game, even of ping-pong, but simply practice for a game, and then only if the weather is fair and the time right. There is a commensurate tentativeness created by the syntactic displacement, ellipsis, and hyperbation of the initial phrase. The "weren't we/we were" inversion leaves unanswered the central question: "What were we?" It is the question that lies at the heart of the monologue. Later in the play, the speaker attempts to answer the question, again using grammatical inversion: "Sometimes I think you've forgotten me. You haven't forgotten me who was your best mate, who was your truest friend." Here, through a conflation of interrogative and declarative, the speaker seems to be willing the friendship to life by the tensions generated by grammatical manipulations.

When he turns to the two scenes in which he describes the woman, the language changes once more. The first scene seems almost squeezed out of memory in the past tense, with few words, and those delivered as if by rote with the speaker creating the picture as he goes along: "She was tired. She sat down. She was tired. The journey. The rush hour. The weather, so unpredictable."

The second evocation of the woman is more glib because more removed; she is the subject for disquisition or composition: "As for me, I've always liked simple love scenes, the classic set-ups, the sweet . . . the sweet . . . the sweet farewell at Paddington Station." The "simple" love scene takes shape as he continues: "My collar turned up. Her soft cheeks," are details sufficient to temporarily thrust the woman into the present, where she becomes "my ebony love, she smiles at me." However, the image does not last, and the speaker concludes the sequence once more reverting to the past tense, "I touched her."

For the two men, speaker and friend, the woman seems--as all Pinter's women seem--little more than an object to be won or the ball in some sexual ping-pong game. The speaker makes just this point: "I loved her body. Not that, between ourselves, it's one way or another a thing of any importance. My spasms could be your spasms. Who's to tell or care?" One might imagine Jerry in *Betrayal* saying the same thing to Robert. In *Monologue*, however, Pinter's use of language reveals that the speaker doubts this masculine interchangeability. After the requisite pause, he continues, "Well . . . she did . . . can . . . could. . . ." Again the play of modals chips away at the previous statement, one the speaker is unwilling or unable to fix in a final form.

It is clear in this brief exchange--and throughout the play--that the desired connection in the play is between men with the speaker attempting to find words which would allow such a condition to exist, if only in his mind. Near the end of the play, in the longest sustained speech, he pours forth a torrent of words, larded with the jargon and hyperbole that Pinter often reserves for those moments of greatest revelation: "I keep busy in the *mind*, and that's why I'm still sparking, get it? I've got a hundred per cent more energy in me now than when I was twenty two." Cliché follows cliché: "But now I'm sparking, at my peak. . . . I'm a front runner. My watchword is vigilance." The speech, a last ditch effort to get the images and the words right, ends with the speaker finally revealing the impossibility of his entire monologue:

> Even if you're too dim to catch the irony in the words themselves, the words I have chosen myself, quite scrupulously, and with intent, you can't miss the irony in the tone of *voice*!

Here is Pinter at his most playful--and most bleak: having his monologist talk about the irony of voice while talking only to himself! At the same time, Pinter has him assert the scrupulous choice of words, which the playwright has in fact "scrupulously" chosen in the play to indicate the impossibility of verbally fixing the past in place.

The outpouring leads to what is presumably the climax of the work, marked in the text by the only silence that follows a section and by additional spaces setting it off: "What you are in fact witnessing is freedom. I no longer participate in holy ceremony. The crap is cut." What better way to indicate the impotence underlying the modern cry for freedom than with the modern, debased language illustrated in "the crap is cut."

The play, however, does not end with this cry; it concludes with a denouement that gives pathos to the entire work and saves it from being another parody of the limits of language in the modern world. The speaker turns yet again to his true subject: his connection with his friend. He employs a relationship that Pinter will develop more fully in *Betrayal*, when Jerry repeatedly recalls that moment in the kitchen when he threw Robert's child up in the air. In *Monologue* the image of children is more fragmentary but equally indicative of the unity the speaker desires:

> I'd have died for them.
> *pause.*
> I'd have been their uncle.
> *pause.*
> I am their uncle.
> *pause.*
> I'm your children's uncle.
> *pause.*
> I'll take them out, tell them jokes.
> *pause.*
> I love your children.

This section begins with the speaker still in the thrall of the clichés that colored the preceding speech. However, he soon turns one last time to his ritual of calling up modals to alter the past. The "could have" addressed to the absent friend becomes the "would have" addressed finally to himself. Once having made this linguistic transference of person, he is able to move into the present tense, turning conjecture into fact. He gains through his words a veracity from which to launch one final time into a hoped-for future before coming to rest finally in the reconstituted present without conditions or conditionals, where the only possible connections between two men is that provided through the agency of procreation--

heterosexual coupling--with the speaker becoming an imagined child's uncle, that is the friend's brother.

This desire for intimacy and love between men that shapes so many of Pinter's plays is nowhere more succinctly delineated than in *Monologue*. In the work Pinter articulates not just a wish for love but for the return to some edenic state, before maturity and sexuality reared their fractious, male heads. And nowhere in the Pinter canon does he make as clear the problems that thwart such return. The world of the past, finally, resides only in memories, framed in the monologues one speaks to oneself, framed in language. These word pictures alter and smudge through handling, just as language alters and smudges through general usage and time. The "churn of stale words in the heart again," Beckett called such attempts to talk the past into being. And like Beckett's tireless monologists, Pinter's speaker keeps reworking the past in order to find a way of living in the present. The effort--a salivation at best--never abates the hunger.

NOTES

1. Martin Esslin makes only passing reference to the play, providing little more than plot summary in his *Pinter: A Study of his Plays* (189-191). Bernard F. Dukore goes into more detail in *Harold Pinter* (99-102), and his subsequent article,"Pinter's Staged Monologue," focuses directly on the work (499-504). The only other article I have found on *Monologue* is Paul Goetsch, "Pinter's *Monologue* und Shakespeare's Sonette" (349-355).

2. There are many similarities between "Dialogue for Three" and *Monologue*, besides the fact that both works indicate in their titles a form of discourse. In the 1959 sketch, the main speaker, a man labeled only 1st Man, seems intent on monologue, despite

the presence of the other two who say little. The other man utters only one line, and this completely removed from the subject of the 1st Man's speech; the woman's few words seem to arouse only the most cursory of answers. Both plays also use the same image: the woman as "a spider caught in a web."

WORKS CITED

Beckett, Samuel. "Cascando." *Collected Poems in English and French.* New York: Grove P, 1977.

_____. *Dream of Fair to Middling Women.* Beckett Archives, University of Reading, England.

Dukore, Bernard F. *Harold Pinter.* New York: Grove P, 1982.

_____. "Pinter's Staged Monologue." *Theatre Journal* 32 (1980): 499-504.

Esslin, Martin. *Pinter: A Study of his Plays.* London: Methuen, 1976.

Goetsch, Paul. "Pinter's *Monologue* und Shakespeare's Sonette." *Archiv für das Studium der neueren Sprachen und Literaturen* 218 (1981): 349-355.

Pinter, Harold. *Monologue.* London: Covent Garden Press Ltd., 1973. N. pag.

_____. "Dialogue for Three." *Complete Works: Volume 3.* New York: Grove P, 1977-78.

THE DUMB WAITER, THE COLLECTION, THE LOVER, AND THE HOMECOMING: A REVISIONIST APPROACH

George E. Wellwarth

One of the few advantages of growing older is that one becomes wiser; and one of the few disadvantages of becoming wiser is that one is forced to look back in embarrassment and regret on the intellectual indiscretions of one's past. Especially if one has published them. The worst aspect of this mess, of course, is that one no more knows that one is right now than one did then. It is simply statistically more probable that the revision is more sensible than the original. It is in this spirit that I offer revised views of aspects of Pinter's *The Dumb Waiter, The Collection, The Lover,* and *The Homecoming* twenty-five years later.[1]

Among the most puzzling aspects of Pinter criticism is its extraordinary variety, ranging from disapproval through bafflement to a conviction that Pinter is one of the great modern playwrights. The last-mentioned is the most common view, leading scholars to see in Pinter's plays universal avatars of the human condition. Finding universal avatars in new writers is a little like panning for gold: all too often it turns out to be fool's gold. Unfortunately, scholars tend to be dazzled and blinded by the appearance, whereas prospectors soon have to face reality. Hence some of the extraordinary interpretations of Pinter's plays that have been foisted on us by scholars drunk on appearance instead of sobered by reality. To a

certain extent this is understandable. Pinter has clearly
been influenced by authors of intellectual stature, notably
Beckett. It is no wonder, therefore, that he has been
regarded as a playwright whose works seem to be more
than meets the eye instead of the opposite and that he has
become the victim of romanticizing critics who insist on
seeing apocalyptic visions in his plays in much the same
way that Beckett has been ludicrously misinterpreted by
critics who see him as a Christian author.

I suggest that the time has come to recognize the
fact that Pinter is the only critic who has made any sense of
Pinter. In one of the interviews that he has given over the
years Pinter, on having read to him a particularly
convoluted example of *academese* and being asked to
comment, replied, "I don't know what the hell he's talking
about." In its way this is just as severe and just as deserved
as Nigel Dennis's remarks in a review article on Martin
Esslin's *The Peopled Wound* and James Hollis's *The
Poetics of Silence*: ". . . writers like Mr. Esslin and Mr.
Hollis . . . give no particular value to any word: when they
talk of 'deep and organic connections between the multiple
planes' [Esslin] or 'the world navel and vortex of all
beginnings' [Hollis] they are using language with the same
contempt and ignorance as the illiterate soldier who
depends completely on four-letter obscenities."2   One
wonders what Pinter's comment on these two quotations
would be.

However, none of this gets us any nearer to an
understanding of Pinter's own view of his plays. This has,
in fact, been clear from the very beginning of his career.
As early as 1961 Pinter explained that his central image is a
room which for him serves as a microcosm of the world. In
the room people feel safe. Outside are only alien forces;
inside there is warmth and light. The conflict in his plays
occurs when one of the outside forces penetrates into the
room and disrupts the security of its occupants. Pinter's
role is that of dispassionate observer, and much of the
apparent difficulty of his plays stems from the fact that he
writes them as if he were eavesdropping on his characters

and recording their often pointless stream of consciousness. At first glance this seems obscurantist, but, as Pinter put it elsewhere, "I only formulate conclusions after I've written the plays . . . "3 and "I don't know what kind of characters my plays will have until they . . . well, until they are. Until they indicate to me what they are. I don't conceptualize in any way . . . "4 This seems the exact opposite of the way a playwright of ideas works. The playwright of ideas supposedly begins with an idea or thesis and creates characters and situations to illustrate it. In other words, he works objectively. A perfect example of such a playwright would seem to have been George Bernard Shaw. Yet it was Shaw who said that it was his method to imagine characters together and then to take down their conversation. He saw himself as a stenographer recording the words of the characters he had imagined. In his mind they assumed an independent dimension and spoke of the ideas that were obsessing him at the time. Shaw even found himself under the necessity of explaining the meaning of what he had recorded his characters as saying in lengthy prefaces to his plays afterwards. The difference in Pinter's method is that he imagines characters in a room and then asks himself what they would do; Shaw asked himself what they would say. The many different interpretations of Pinter's plays, not all of them invalid, might indicate that there *is* no "correct" interpretation, no precise meaning to his plays--only a vague allusiveness stretching tentative tentacles in diverse directions. In a letter he wrote to Peter Wood, director of the disastrous first production of *The Birthday Party*, Pinter clearly enunciated his theory of the play as a separate entity concerned only with itself. There is no connected philosophy running through his plays: each play, like each life, is an entity with no meaning beyond itself--and each play has a different meaning, just as each life has a different and self-sustaining meaning: "The play is itself. It is no other. It has its own life. . . . I take it you would like me to insert a clarification or moral judgment or author's angle on it, straight from the horse's mouth. I

appreciate your desire for this but I can't do it. . . . I believe
that what happens on this stage will possess a potent
dramatic image and a great deal of this will be visual. . . .
The curtain goes up and down. Something has happened.
Right? . . . Where is the comment, the slant, the
explanatory note? In the play. Everything to do with the
play is in the play."5

Pinter has often been praised for his realism,
particularly for the realism of his speech patterns, and
justly so. But realistic speech patterns are logically
inextricably bound to realistic action; and in the light of
Pinter's remarks to Wood it is worth considering what,
exactly, realism in the theater is. Realism is an unfortunate
term, implying, as it does, photographic reproduction,
which is impossible on the stage and would be undesirable
even if it were possible. Theatre is the selective
exaggeration of reality. It is not reality. Only reality is.
And perhaps a Warhol movie, which is consciously a
precise reproduction of reality and thus supererogatory.
Realism in art, as one writer has put it, "has, strictly
speaking, nothing to do with life 'as it is'; it is, like
expressionism or surrealism, a way of seeing things, a
convention."6 Its purpose, in other words, is to *explain*.
When it attempts to explain the inexplicable it fails, of
course. It cannot explain the surreal or irrational aspects of
life; it cannot, in short, explain chance, the moving
principle of all life. But by concentrating on the
interpersonal minutiae of life it can impose the illusion of
logic on it. Human beings are ultimately inscrutable in
depth, even to themselves (on the surface, of course, they
are perfectly clear: in life we deal in façades), but the
theatre of realism gives us the comforting, if illusory
assurance that human beings are explicable in depth. The
spectator at a realistic play can understand the characters,
what they do and what happens to them, because they are
planned, squared away, and boxed-in by the God of the
theatre, the playwright. Outside the theatre human beings
are incomplete, mysterious even to themselves, and

anything but logical. Most people feel they need relief from that--hence, theatre. Pinter gives his audiences neither the illusion of control over life nor relief from its inscrutability. Worse: he assures them that there is neither a hidden meaning nor any superior force that might be hiding a putative meaning. Philosophically, he is, of course, following Beckett here with the sole difference that the surface reality that Beckett eschews makes Pinter's plays more ambiguous and has resulted in the strange and largely lamentable outpouring of interpretation of his works on the part of academic critics.

What is long overdue in Pinter criticism is the elimination of the philosophical façade erected to obscure the simplicity of his writing, which is to a very great extent random as far as the action is concerned and null as far as the ideas are concerned. Pinter's plays are situation pieces that encapsulate an atmosphere or mood, often vague in its specifics but emotionally pervasive, thus leaving his audiences puzzled after having been totally caught up in the action and emotion during the performance.[7] This is due to the fact that Pinter's plays are set within the context of contemporary reality, upon which they depend for their form and content and to which they refer; but they exist *in vacuo* as exemplary slices of reality but without the stresses and far-reaching interconnected motives of everyday reality as we know it. Nigel Dennis in his review essay[8] rather harshly describes Pinter's plays as acting exercises. They are much more than that, of course, but they are that too. Actors, Dennis points out, love Pinter's plays. Having played Gus in *The Dumb Waiter*, Harry in *The Collection*, and Richard in *The Lover*, I can attest to that. The reason actors like playing Pinter gives us another clue to his dramaturgy. The plays exist *by themselves*: they are entirely self-contained entities. The actors find their characterizations in the lines. Everything is laid out for them. They do not have to worry about motivations because their motivations are obvious within the closed world of the play. To seek motivations through memory recall or through attempted connections with the external world would be ruinous to the production. There is no place in a Pinter play for the Method actor, in other words. And that is significant for an understanding of the plays since the Method actor is constantly trying to wrench the life of the play away from the author's imagination and sprinkle it with the dust of the streets, drape it with his own personal problems, and generally lower its meaning from the general to the specific.

In the light of the foregoing we can ask what, for example, *The Dumb Waiter* is about. Does the floating, motiveless situation of Ben and Gus have a meaning outside itself or is the play a mood piece contrasting deadly menace with quotidian ordinariness: a tacit commentary on "motiveless malignity" and "the banality of evil"? It is all too easy and tempting for critics seeking "profundity" and a spurious originality to interpret *The Dumb Waiter* as a variation on the theme of Godot, who, when he finally comes, turns out to be a sardonic joker sending whimsical and purposeless orders down on the dumb waiter and destroying--instead of saving--those who are bewildered by his demands for food-offerings. Or perhaps we might see the dumb waiter as being a parody of the Biblical altar from which burnt offerings are fragrantly floated up to placate an uncaring deity. Such interpretations are amusing but pointless. There is no justification in the text for this desperate lusting after symbols on the nonsensical premise that if it's good literature it *must* have symbols. The dumb waiter isn't God, and Ben and Gus are not mankind.[9] A more sensible view is that the play is about hierarchical domination, a universal aspect of the human condition as shown by the menacers menaced, the butcher butchered, and the potential rebel cut down. Gus becomes conscious of himself, he begins to wake up from the primal torpor in which he has passed his life so far, he wants to find out *what it all means*; and the search for meaning destroys him for it leaves him no belief to rely on, no explanation for anything. This has to be shown *dramatically*--hence the play. Gus is a modern Woyzeck, and the play in which he appears is a definition of life as a temporary state where domination--the exercise of power--is the supreme human motive. In a slightly higher stratum of the eternal domination hierarchy are the two mysterious intruders in *The Birthday Party* who might as well have been called Ben Goldberg and Gus McCann.[10] Like them, Ben and Gus are basically ordinary and rather amusing fellows, but, then, as we know from the newspapers, mass murderers are *always* people who were not only liked but well-liked by all who knew them.

The Collection is about the attempt to verify the story of one of the four characters to the effect that she had a one-night affair with one of the others while they were showing their collections at a dress designers' convention in the north of England. Nobody ever finds out, nobody here being the remaining two characters and the audience. *The Collection* has often been compared to Pirandello's *Così è se vi pare,* but the comparison is not entirely valid. Pirandello brings audience participation into the theatre by implying that the truth of the plot is no more the audience's business than it is the prying townspeople's, thus neatly eliminating dramatic irony. But Pirandello's point is privacy, not the verifiability of truth. It is obvious that in the situation that Pirandello has set up either Ponza's wife is his first or his second (or she is someone else altogether) and either she is or she is not Sra. Frola's daughter.

Pirandello's other belief was that truth is subjective and that therefore there is no truth, only a myriad of truths. This is nonsense (if it isn't, everything else is). Pinter makes neither the point about privacy, nor does he believe that truth is subjective. He believes that truth is unverifiable: "The desire for verification is understandable but cannot always be satisfied. There are no hard distinctions between what is true and what is false. The thing is not necessarily either true or false; it can be both true and false. The assumption that to verify what has happened and what is happening presents few problems I take to be inaccurate."[11] This seems to me to make no sense whatsoever, either in general or in the context of the play. Stella and Bill in the play amuse themselves by making up constantly changing versions of what happened between them in Leeds but *they* know. One can forget details of what happened this morning, but if one has been unfaithful to one's lover less than a week ago--the case with both Bill and Stella--one does not forget. In his attempt to establish the general unverifiability of truth Pinter has taken absent-mindedness to ludicrous lengths. That at least is less despairing than Pirandello's taking subjectivism to virtually infinite lengths.

Twenty-five years ago I wrote that *The Lover* shows a typical modern couple illustrating the malaise of the age by being able to achieve physical communication only through an elaborate by-passing of emotional communication: "The sterility, both physical and emotional, of this typical modern couple is so great that they can come close to each other only in a fantasy world."[12] This seems to me now not only immature drivel but a complete misinterpretation of the play. Far from being either misanthropic or critical of the values attributed to Richard and Sarah, *The Lover* seems to me now to be Pinter's masterpiece. Unlike all of his other plays, *The Lover* is not a play of amorphous meanings and atmosphere, but rather a play of straightforward psychological observation and a celebration of life. Richard and Sarah are a prosperous upper-middle class suburban couple who, two or three times a week, play a fantasy game in the afternoons in which Richard, transformed from the staid and stuffy husband in whom decorum and deportment reach their full flowering into the sporty and devil-may-care Max, returns home and plays a series of interlocking and presumably ever-varying sexual games with Sarah, also transformed, in her case from the mousey, dutiful housewife into a glamorous and desirable seductress. The games are mainly based on domination, which flows effortlessly from one to the other as seductress becomes timid victim and solicitous protector becomes seducer. The fantasy climaxes with sex under the tea table, a nicely ironic juxtaposition of that symbol of staid and stodgy English middle-class life with the freedom of asocial sex: the tea table sheltering with tablecloth as curtain the riotously free animalism underneath it. In the course of the play Richard, the less adventurous partner, makes a concerted effort to stop the fantasies and the parallel life he leads as Max. The games have been going on almost since they were married some ten years ago, and although he is good at them and clearly enjoys them, Richard is a little too much the English public school boy, a little too much the well-to-do upper middle class equivalent of whatever the English call Yuppies to feel entirely at ease with having a secret life. The scenes in which he tells his wife, as Richard, that he has no mistress, only a whore and in which, as Max, he invents a private life for that character involving a wife and children and says he can no longer bear to betray them are devastating in their duplicity and cruelty. The play is about the psychological conflict in Richard, who is torn between his quite genuine love for and infatuation with Sarah, who, for her part, returns both feelings completely sincerely. The fantasy life these two have constructed for themselves does not regulate and encompass their whole lives: there is no reason to assume that their fantasy sex life necessarily excludes any other form of sex life. Fantasy is the variation on the basic theme of sexual love. Nor need we assume that Pinter sees lust as being incompatible with love. Richard and Sarah, as she perceives and he does not, live richer and fuller lives than other people. They are *more* alive than their compatriots in precisely the way the Actor as Absurd Man in Albert Camus' *The Myth of Sisyphus* is more alive than others because he lives parallel lives along with his own. The Absurdist measures life quantitatively as well as qualitatively *because life is all that there is.* To live as many lives as possible, no matter how temporarily, how spuriously, how self-deludingly, is to enrich the basic life we live. Richard and Sarah live their real life, but they play variations on it and give these variations equal stature with their real, outward life while they are living them; furthermore, these variations are their own creations so that in their fantasies they are--

momentarily--the gods of their own destiny. To fantasize in mutual confidence and abandonment is already to be liberated, for it creates an alternative world inhabited only by the fantasizers. Richard succumbs helplessly to his wife's spell in the last scene (a fiendishly difficult one for the actor):

SARAH:	. . . Take off your jacket. Mmmnn? Would you like to change? Would you like me to change my clothes? I'll change for you, darling. Shall I? Would you like that? *Silence. She is very close to him.*
RICHARD:	Yes. *Pause.* Change. *Pause.* Change. *Pause.* Change your clothes. *Pause.* You lovely whore. *They are still kneeling, she leaning over him.*

CURTAIN

When Richard is vanquished here at the very end of the play, helplessly engulfed in the overwhelming sexual allure of his wife, he is saved because he remains far more fully alive than the respectable husband for whose state he had yearned.

The Homecoming has stimulated more speculation and criticism than any other Pinter play so far. Eighteen years ago, in writing about the play, I quoted Richard Schechner as saying that it was "a probe of the dark male attitudes toward the 'mother-whore' and the equally compelling female desire to play this double role."[13] I described this as "a provocative suggestion that is definitely on the right track."[14] I began this essay by remarking that one of the few advantages of growing older is that one becomes wiser, as an illustration of which I offer the information that if asked now what I think of this I would emulate Pinter himself by replying, "I don't know what the hell he's talking about."

The problem with most criticism of *The Homecoming*, once again, is the urge to seek a specific meaning. *The Homecoming* is not a semantically cohesive play. It does not have a "point," nor was it written in order to expound a particular idea or point of view. If considered as a play with a linear plot line--a plot impelled by logical cause-and-effect progression--it is seen to be riddled with inconsistencies. *The Homecoming* does not have a linear structure; it has a nuclear structure. In other words, it starts from a central node--or theme or atmosphere--and effloresces randomly from there. It is best described as a play of familial atmosphere, though this should not be taken to mean that it is a statement about the nature of the family as such. *The Homecoming* is a play about certain aspects of family life and relationships that are common to all families in greater or lesser degree--in some cases to a degree that makes the family relationship virtually unbearable to some of its members (to Teddy in *The Homecoming*) and in others to such a minimal degree that it makes that relationship a preponderantly happy one. *The Homecoming* is a play about the centripetal tentacular grasp of family relationships: the suffocating pressure of unwanted emotion and social expectation from the family and the conflict between the infantile and the independent as the adult seeks his own identity. As Pinter himself has noted, ". . . if ever there was a villain in the play, Teddy was it."[15] And it is indeed quite obviously Teddy who is the central character despite the fact that he plays a comparatively minor part: one could almost say that Teddy is the stage manager rather than the protagonist. Teddy approaches the meeting with his family with trepidation, half hoping for the friendly reception that he envisages in the words he speaks to Ruth with nervous reassurance as they enter the house like thieves in the night. When he sees that this was a delusive hope, he immediately erects impenetrable psychological palisades around himself and lets events take their course. Ruth's decision at the end of the play to remain with the family, implausible in realistic terms though it is, is a reversion to her original way of life-- a resumption of the profession it is broadly hinted that she practiced before marriage. It is also her revenge on Teddy by treating him as he has treated her, with stony, unemotional indifference. Teddy returns to the comfortless yet comforting (because he is in control) sterility of academia in the American desert, cut off forever from his family and free to brood on whatever branch of philosophy *is* his province.

The problem, it has always seemed to me, with *The Homecoming* is not with what happens in it but with Pinter's description of Teddy. Teddy, we are told, is the oldest son of this family of brutish grotesques who straddle the working class and the underworld. Six years earlier, having picked up a local "nude model" and married her without informing any member of his family, Teddy disappeared and has been almost incommunicado ever since (he seems to have written from America that he has received a Ph.D., but has not mentioned either his marriage or his fatherhood). Pinter seems to know nothing of American academia or of philosophy, but he does seem to have a corrosive contempt for both--by no means an untenable or reprehensible point of view. Still, the idea of a scion of this family as the possessor of a Ph.D. in philosophy and as the occupant of a professorial post at an American university and as the author of "critical works" on philosophy is risible at best and totally incredible at worst. Were it not for the fact that when Teddy and Ruth are alone it is evident from their remarks that Pinter does indeed intend them to be married and parents living in America, where Teddy really is a professor, a Ph.D., and a published scholar, one would be tempted to suggest an alternative and more credible background for the pair. In this scenario the marriage, the children, the Ph.D., the professorship, and the publications would all be part of a cover story intended to aid Teddy's carefully planned revenge on his family. Six years earlier Teddy met Ruth and took her to a city in the industrial North. Brainier than his father or Lenny, he has become head of the underworld or chief pimp in, say, Blackpool or Scunthorpe with Ruth as his chief helper. The "homecoming" is a plot between him and Ruth, whom he has paid bounteously for her acquiescence, to destroy his family, all of them already impotent, as Teddy is also. When Ruth will have done her work, the octopus of the family will finally be torn apart, and Teddy, as he thinks, will be vindicated, revenged, and liberated.

Whatever interpretation one can give it and however one might think that Pinter was mistaken in his portrayal of the leading character, *The Homecoming* represents the quintessence of Pinter's dramaturgy. It is a play that does not *mean* anything: it simply *is*. And what it is is a baffling, unresolved and unresolvable human situation. Reality, not an escape from it.

NOTES

1. Cf. my *The Theatre of Protest and Paradox* (New York: New York University Press, 1964), pp. 197-211, and (New York: New York University Press, 1971), pp. 224-242.

2. *New York Review of Books*, XV, xi (1970), p. 22.

3. *Ibid.*, p. 21.

4. *Paris Review*, XXXIX (1966), p. 24.

5. Harold Pinter, "A Letter to Peter Wood," in Michael Scott, ed., *Harold Pinter: The Birthday Party, The*

Caretaker, The Homecoming. A Casebook (London: Macmillan, 1986), p. 80.

6. L. A. C. Dobrez, *The Existential and its Exits* (London: The Athlone Press, 1986), p. 336.

7. Leonard Powlick describes this situation very well in his essay "What the Hell is That All About?" in Steven H. Gale, ed., *Harold Pinter: Critical Approaches* (London and Toronto: Associated University Presses, 1986), pp. 30-37.

8. Cf. *supra*, p. 2.

9. The only thing in the play that borders on the supernatural, although I have been unable to find any commentary on it and must confess it drove me round the bend when I played the part, is Gus's entrance at the end through the door from the corridor, beaten up and stripped of his gun (not an easy thing to do soundlessly to a professional killer), although he left the room by the door that leads to the kitchen and toilet.

10. "Goldberg and McCann? Dying, rotten, scabrous, the decayed spiders, the flower of our society." See Scott, p. 81.

11. *The Theatre of Protest and Paradox*, 1st ed., p. 209.

12. *Ibid.*, p. 211.

13. Richard Schechner, "Puzzling Pinter," *Tulane Drama Review*, XI, ii (1966), p. 183, quoted in *The Theater of Protest and Paradox*, 2nd ed., p. 239.

14. *Ibid.*

15. Peter Hall, "A Director's Approach" in John Lahr, ed., *A Casebook on Harold Pinter's "The Homecoming"* (New York: Grove Press, 1971), p. 20.

DISPLACEMENT IN TIME AND SPACE: HAROLD PINTER'S *OTHER PLACES*

Katherine H. Burkman

At the heart of Harold Pinter's plays, *Family Voices* (1981), *A Kind of Alaska* (1982), and *Victoria Station* (1982), collected in a volume he calls *Other Places*, are displacements in what one might call realistic time and space. In *Family Voices* the protagonist, a young man who on a realistic level has ostensibly left home and is writing to his mother, is actually suspended in space. Initially a radio play, *Family Voices*, as the title suggests, involves us in the interplay of three voices, that of a son and his mother and father. Subsequent staging of the play tends to emphasize that interplay as if we are dealing not with characters in a specific time or place but with disembodied voices who define where they are in psychological rather than physical terms.

The setting of *A Kind of Alaska* is initially more realistic. Here, a victim of a sleeping sickness, encephalitis lethargica, has been treated with a drug that brings her out of a 29-year state of sleep. While the protagonist does not know where she is or what time she inhabits, the doctor who has awakened her purports to know; with him we watch another who is disoriented about time and space. The effect of the play, however, is to draw us into Deborah's experience of disorientation, so that by the end as she becomes more sure of where and when, we somehow become less sure.

The final play of this arresting trio, *Victoria Station*, is something of a cross between the other two. Although

109

on a realistic level we are introduced to the two characters as taxi driver and taxi dispatcher or Driver and Controller, their immobilization, one in his cab, the other in his "office" and the nature of the exchanges between them again suggest a suspension of ordinary time and space. The Driver has never heard of Victoria Station where the Controller informs him his next fare awaits him "under the clock." At first the Driver doesn't know where he is, but he eventually locates himself by "a little dark park underneath Crystal Palace" (55); the Controller, however, informs him that Crystal Palace "burnt down years ago old son" (57). By the end of the play the Controller has given up Victoria Station with its specificity of time and place in favor of a possibly endless search for the Driver in some far more mythical location.

In Pinter's earlier works there is often an invasion of realistic space and time by some outside, disruptive force, *A Slight Ache*'s Matchseller, *The Homecoming*'s Ruth, *Old Times'* Anna, *No Man's Land*'s Spooner. *Other Places* differs from such plays by only glancing at realistic time and setting rather than firmly establishing and then disrupting them. The invasion of space that Pinter began to dramatize in his first play, *The Room*, has been so complete that we now begin outside the room in other places, other more frankly interior spaces. Here, the efforts of the characters to orient themselves, to re-locate themselves in time and space, are not entirely different from such efforts in earlier Pinter dramas, but their struggles do provide a fascinating progress, a kind of three act exploration of the quest for self in the modern world. In each case, the ironies have to do with the falseness of attempts at realist orientation.

The son in *Family Voices*, Voice 1, valiantly tries to negotiate the journey from childhood to adulthood, to leave home and become independent. His unsent missives to his mother about his new home are, however, like interior monologues that reverberate in the void that isolates him. As Elin Diamond notes, the new family sounds so much like the old that "through internal echo and parody, Pinter suggests that the Witherses are the demonic double of the son's family, his projection of his own familial dreams and fears" (215). At one moment Voice 1 claims a happiness that condenses past, present, and future; surrounded by the three Withers women, he asserts that he has taken an endless seat in their midst. "I took a seat. I took it and sat in it. I am in it. I will never leave it" (76). Such bliss almost immediately gives way, however, to Mr. Withers' perception of Voice 1's location "in a diseaseridden land" (77).

The kind of incestuous possessiveness of both mother and father that the son recalls in his past are what he reports in his missives home to be happening again, so that time and place are conflated into a single, inescapable trap. At the same time that Mr. Riley reports to Voice 1 that he has sent his visiting mother and sister packing as intruders, he is himself intruding on the young man in the bathroom, the door of which Voice 1 is sure he locked. The bathroom, which Voice 1 had earlier praised as a place in which the entire family bathe--"They all lie quite naked in the bath and have very pleasant baths indeed" (67)--is now revealed as a place of nakedness and exposure that leaves Voice 1 vulnerable to menace. Delivered from his former family, he is now menaced by the new one.

Absence, however, as well as possessiveness characterize Voice 1's family relationships in new and old home alike, the son wondering why his father has not accompanied his mother and sister on their visit reported by Riley. Speaking from the grave, the Father, Voice 3, gives the impression that he has always been absent or dead from his son. "I have so much to say to you. But I am quite dead," the father announces; "What I have to say to you will never be said" (83). The mother feels equally isolated and articulates the combined possessiveness and absence that are at the core of the displacement of the family's experience when she speaks about her dead husband and absent son. She recalls that even in a happier past when she washed her son's hair and saw in his eyes that he "wanted no-one else, no-one at all" (76), she was still alone: "I sometimes think I have always been sitting like this, alone by an indifferent fire, curtains closed, night, winter" (76).

As unable as his dead father or grieving mother to connect, the son remains arrested in a dependent state, the sense of absence from home he experiences reflecting his sense of absence from self. Because he has somehow always been displaced, suspended and isolated outside of time or space, this condition undermines his "realistic" descriptions of his stay with his new family and his projected journey home. In the final interplay of speeches at the play's conclusion, the son says in one breath that he is coming home to his mother, in the next that he is there, looking for his father: "I've looked in all the usual places, including the old summerhouse, but I can't find him. Don't tell me he's left home at his age? That would be inexpressibly skittish a gesture, on his part. What have you done with him, mother?" (82). Perhaps the son is wistful as he wonders if even at his father's age one can attempt to leave home, although the accusation that his mother may have done away with his father suggests the danger the son feels to himself. After describing this search for father and questioning of mother, the son again says he is "about" to take the journey home, but the play concludes with his total rejection by both parents; the mother says she has given him up "as a very bad job" (83) while the father laments his inability to communicate with him from the grave. Apparently the son can neither leave home nor return to it, suffering a permanent displacement.

Pinter's "place imagery," according to Leo Schneiderman, whose comments on other Pinter dramas offer important clues to Pinter's use of time and space in this play, "throws the theater audience back upon itself, forcing it to confront its own suppressed desires, including its nostalgia for the lost stasis of the past and the seeming security of childhood" (187). The home in Pinter's plays, accordingly, is not really a symbol of security but of the "failed or absent mother" (202) for whose possession the preoedipal characters are generally too weak to fight their fathers (192). Certainly the son in *Family Voices* would seem to evolve from earlier Pinter characters, such as Teddy in *The Homecoming*, who are equally unable to make the return trip because they have never developed a strong enough sense of self to leave in the first place. Pinter's dramaturgy in this play suggests that movement in time and space is false; as the family voices speak past each other, the lack of connection becomes a trap that leaves each one suspended in a void.

Schneiderman, however, tends to reduce Pinter's characters to case histories, neglecting to place them in terms of the kind of existential anguish that they endure or to consider the political overtones that we have become more aware of since the more overtly political *One For the Road* (1984) and *Mountain Language* (1988). In *A Kind of Alaska*, Deborah refuses such reduction, questioning and mocking the doctor who would treat her as a case.

Making a more valiant effort to negotiate a journey of growth than the son in *Family Voices*, Deborah, who has fallen into a trance-like sleep at age sixteen and is presently emerging at age forty-five, has more success in her return to "reality" than Rose R. had, the patient whose case history, related by Dr. Oliver Sacks in his book *Awakenings*, inspired Pinter to write the play. Rose R. was one of many patients who suffered from a sleeping sickness that had its onset in the 1920s but became treatable through the drug L-DOPA in 1969. When first roused from her very withdrawn condition, the patient became much excited, but she was, Dr. Sacks suggests, "a sleeping beauty whose 'awakening' was unbearable to her, and will never be awoken again" (79). Unable to imagine what it was like to be older than twenty-one, Rose R. proceeded to block out what Sacks calls "an intolerable and insoluble anachronism--the almost half-century gap between her age as felt and experienced (her *ontological* age) and her actual or *official* age" (79).

Dr. Hornby's fascination with Deborah's interior journey to what he calls a kind of Alaska and Deborah's resistance upon her return to the world presented to her as "real" by him serve, in the play, as a critique of the society that would help her. While Dr. Sacks speaks confidently about the intolerable anachronism faced by Rose R., for Pinter's Deborah the nature of what are considered the norms of reality is what may be truly intolerable. When Deborah complains that the dog who has awakened her with his "turning about" is dreaming and "not himself up" (7), the suggestion is that the doctor who has awakened her is himself dreaming and not himself awake. Dr. Hornby has apparently left his wife, Deborah's sister, to watch over Deborah, proclaiming his wife a widow. The implication here is not only that Hornby is in one sense dead, but that his fascination with the sleeping woman must have to do with his own desired awakening from the male kind of Alaska in which he dwells.

Indeed, Ann Hall suggests that the play offers a critique of a patriarchal society in which Deborah does not have the happy ending of the Sleeping Beauty fairy tale because she speaks out. "To some extent," Hall writes, "Deborah describes the place of the feminine in the patriarchy or phallocentric thought--confined, other, silent, and even a bit tortured" (11). But if Hall is correct in suggesting that Hornby has cast Deborah in the role of the mirror, thus turning her into an object (15), Deborah refuses to be so cast. As her sense of time fluctuates, she moves from reliving her confinement--"Oh my goodness, oh dear, oh my goodness, oh dear, I'm so young. It's a vice. I'm in a vice. It's at the back of my neck. Ah. Eyes stuck. Only see the shadow of the tip of my nose. Shadow of the tip of my nose. Eyes stuck" (38)--to planning her rebirth--"I'm going to run into the sea and fall into the waves. I'm going to rummage about in all the water" (33), though she questions whether she will have one; "Is it my birthday soon?" (35). Suspended between her past captivity and the moving in of realistic walls that may promise another kind of captivity, another kind of Alaska, Deborah complains of being cold and suggests that she wants "to go home" (35).

Certainly Deborah's desire to "go home" when she is supposedly there is related to the son's sense of displacement in *Family Voices*, but Deborah's travels seem to be more authentic. Her disorientation indicates a condition of lostness and fragmentation (the fragmentation of the modern predicament?) but also a possible progress toward a fundamental reorientation or rebirth, a true awakening. Pinter focuses this idea in terms of Deborah's upcoming birthday and her description of a womb-like condition in her "sleep" state, where all is silent except for the dripping of a tap. Her desire to run into the sea, "to rummage about in all the water" (33), also contributes to the sense of the play's action as a struggle with rebirth. By his obsessive dedication to charting Deborah's "itinerary" into "quite remote . . . utterly foreign . . . territories" (35), Hornby would seem to be involved in the struggle for a new awakening for himself as well as for Deborah.

Then, too, unlike the son in *Family Voices*, Deborah seems to assess her predicament very clearly and to accept it. When she puts together some of the lies and truths that the doctor and her sister have told her, she speaks in such a way as to question what she says she accepts--"You say I was not dreaming then and am not dreaming now. You say I have always been alive and am alive now. You say I am a woman" (40). Deborah's strength may be in her continuing to question even as she seems to accept answers, her legacy to the audience who are made to question the nature of "home" and the degree to which we are "women," human beings, or awake. For those of us who believe that Shakespeare's shrewish Kate is never truly tamed, Deborah becomes a descendant.

The Driver in Pinter's brief play, *Victoria Station*, is not instructing his sleeping beauty as Dr. Hornby does in *A Kind of Alaska* but is enthralled by this POB or passenger on board, who sleeps on the back seat of his cab. He plans, he says, to marry her and live the rest of his life in the cab with her. Never having heard of Victoria Station with its clock and schedules, to which his Controller would send him, the Driver is rooted in a fantasy-reality that turns out to be exactly what the Controller, isolated and lost in his booth and his "function," craves. The Driver, stationary in his car but imaginatively wedded to a slumbering princess, remains one of Beckett's *Godot* tramps, whose disorientation in time and space leaves them paralyzed but rooted by a moving faith in the possibility of transformation.

As in *Family Voices* and *A Kind of Alaska*, displacement in time and space leads to the central problem of identity. As the Controller, identifying the Driver as a number, tries to locate him ("Where are You?") and receives little information ("What?" is the Driver's response), the questions behind such attempts at location in space are clearly both "Who are you?" and "Who am I?" (45-46). Again, too, efforts at location of self in time and space are hampered by questions of domination; the Controller begins by thinking of himself as the Driver's controller in every sense, his "local monk" (50), who would rule, aid, and save him, but ends up on a quest for the Driver that would seem to have become his own quest for salvation.

While the inhabitants of the son's initial home are doubled in his adopted home in *Family Voices*, the protagonist is doubled in *Victoria Station*, in which the intrapsychic nature of the conflict adds dimension to the interpersonal level of the action. Controller can obviously not operate without a driver and so questions him about the nature of his vehicle, making every effort as his "local monk" (50) to control him. When he has trouble with 274 and is ready to turn to 135, the Driver refuses to be left, slowly wooing his other self away from all such numbering, with its impersonal relationship to clock time and Victorian space and into his own fantasy realm with its lure of possible integration of the self.

Pinter's characters in these dramas are, then, displaced, suspended outside of the norms of realistic time and space. If this stance proves fatal to the son in *Family Voices*, who by hanging on to realistic markers remains unaware of his lost condition, it is not so for Deborah in *A*

Kind of Alaska, who makes a superb effort to re-locate herself in realistic time and space without losing the self she has nurtured in her retreat to a kind of Alaska. The Controller in *Victoria Station*, on the other hand, begins to learn to let go of those realistic markers of time and space that have isolated him in his office. He loses interest in "this man coming off the train at Victoria Station--the 10:22," whom, he suggests, "can go fuck himself" (61). Although his forthcoming journey to other places, the unspecified dark park by which the Driver is parked, is undertaken with an ambivalent rage ("Don't move. Stay exactly where you are. I'll be right with you," 62), the Driver's new-won Beckettian disorientation about realistic time and space offers the possibility of re-orientation to the Controller. *Victoria Station* becomes, then, a kind of third act in *Other Places* that leads the audience to this more hopeful stance. Pinter's dramaturgy in all three plays draws us into the characters' disorientation about realistic time and space, from which stance we, too, may feel terribly lost, but at the same time more able to seek a new way.

WORKS CITED

Diamond, Elin. *Pinter's Comic Play*. London and Toronto. Associated University Presses. Bucknell UP, 1985.

Hall, Ann. *A Kind of Alaska: The Representation of Women in the Plays of Eugene O'Neill, Harold Pinter, and Sam Shepard*. Ph.D. dissertation, Ohio State University, 1988.

Pinter, Harold. *Other Places: Three Plays by Harold Pinter*. New York: Grove Press, 1987.

Sacks, Oliver. *Awakenings*. New York: E. P. Dutton, 1983.

Schneiderman, Leo, Ph.D. *The Literary Mind: Portraits in Pain and Creativity*. New York: Insight Books, Human Sciences Press, 1988.

FILM AND DRAMA:
THE OPENING SEQUENCE OF THE
FILMED VERSION OF HAROLD PINTER'S
THE CARETAKER (THE GUEST)

Steven H. Gale

Since very early in cinematic history, stage plays have served as sources for motion pictures. One of the first instances of this practice occurred in 1908 when the French movie company Film d'Art produced its inaugural offering, *The Assassination of the Duke of Guise.* The most famous of these early films, and the first from Film d'Art to be screened in the United States, was the Sarah Bernhardt vehicle, *Queen Elizabeth.* Featuring members of the Comedie Française and directed by Louis Mercanton, *Queen Elizabeth* was released in 1912.

From early on, too, there has been a critical discussion about the relationship between film and drama as well as the characteristics and nature of filmed plays. The initial attempts to translate serious drama to a cinematic medium were unimaginative, noncinematic, wooden exhibitions. While the declamatory nature of stage acting was clearly not suited to the exaggerating intimacy of the camera lens, even more disappointing is the fact that directors ignored the potentialities of their new medium to interpret material in innovative ways that would be effective because of the very nature of the medium in which they were working. They seldom employed any of the characteristics of the film art other than the simple utilization of a camera. Takes were long and static. Little movement of the camera occurred, and very few shots were included that underscore or amplify the dialogue of the original play text. In many scenes the stationary camera merely turned on to record what was taking place on an essentially theatrical stage, and the cuts seemingly came only at the end of the scene. Even today there are disheartening examples of this approach to filmed drama.

In Pinter's screenplay for the movie version of *The Caretaker*, however, it is clear that the screenwriter exults in the possibilities that the film medium provides him to go beyond his own original text. For example, as Arnold P. Hinchliffe implies, the significance of the glance between the two brothers, Aston and Mick, at the end of the drama when the intruding tramp, Davies, is rejected is more emphatic (especially the hint of triumph on Mick's part) than it is on stage because of the camera's focusing ability--in the play there is only a slight indication of Mick's underlying emotional reaction.[1] In the play, the stage directions read: "*Aston comes in. He closes the door, moves into the room and faces Mick. They look at each other. Both are smiling faintly.*" Discussing the film in an article that he co-wrote with Clive Donner, the movie's director, Pinter acknowledges the superiority of the film in conveying the bond between Aston and Mick when he writes, "I think in the film one has been able to hit the relationship of the brothers more clearly than in the play."[2] First screened at the Berlin Film Festival on June 27, 1963, Harold Pinter's *The Caretaker* was released publicly in February 1964. In the United States the film appeared under the title *The Guest* (perhaps to avoid being confused with Hal Bartlett's *The Caretakers*, which had been released in 1963). His second film, and the first from a screenplay based on the adaptation of one of his own stage plays, *The Caretaker* won critical acclaim, being awarded the Berlin Film Festival Silver Bear (in 1963) and the Edinburgh Festival Certificate of Merit (1963).

This black and white film, with a running time of 105 minutes, is notable for its distinguished crew and cast. Directed by Clive Donner, edited by Fergus McDonnell, and photographed by Nicholas Roeg, it features a cast of

Alan Bates in the role of Mick, the younger brother; Robert Shaw as Aston, the older brother; and Donald Pleasence in the part of Davies, the tramp (Bates and Pleasence were reprising their roles in the original stage version). In choosing a play to transform onto film for his second attempt at screen writing, Pinter faced a different set of problems than he had in adapting Robin Maugham's novel, *The Servant*, to the screen. Many of the visual images were already incorporated in the stage play script, and the drama was the right length for a feature film. Stage drama, however, depends much more heavily on dialogue than does film, and, indeed, as implied above, stage plays tend to become wooden when presented on film exactly because of the importance and preponderance of words. Either the film is relatively static, with long takes of characters delivering dialogue, or the dialogue is delivered in a series of short takes that is unsatisfactory because this chops up the dialogue and the camera seems to jump around. Added to this is the fact that drama takes place in a confined space, both literally and figuratively. Sets tend to be indoors, and there are often not many scene changes. In Pinter's stage version of *The Caretaker*, for instance, everything takes place in a single room. A stage play is also an excellent vehicle for presenting intellectual and psychological themes due to the preponderance of and dependence on words and the confined nature of the set. In contrast, film can more easily produce emotional reactions in the audience due to the immediate impact of the visual images that do not, cannot, first be filtered through the observer's mind.

Theoretically, the initial sequence of a movie (some critics even say the opening shot) should contain the essence of the film visually symbolized. The first scene in *The Caretaker* is both a departure from the original stage script and an opening out of that script. It also serves the purpose of conveying the movie's thematic substance. The titles are run over a shot of Mick's car parked at night, outside the building in which Aston lives. The sound of a train is heard over. Since Mick is his brother's keeper, all of the action takes place in or about his house, and the intruder/guest, Davies, is a tramp--and tramps are associated with trains and, in contrast to Mick, they have no fixed abode and are constantly on the move. This all sets the stage for what is to follow.

As the scene develops, Mick emerges from the car, the interior of which is so dark that he has not been seen previously. Not only is he watching the house, then, but he also appears somewhat menacing. His leather jacket as well as the cascading, atonal music that accompanies him as he crosses the street support this impression.

On-screen movement is one of a filmmaker's primary tools. Albeit a subtle element, it can be an important component in the comprehensive development of a montage, with a potentially profound and powerful effect on an audience's subconscious. It is revealing to see how movement is utilized in this sequence which was not included in the stage version. The first indication that the audience has that the car is occupied is when there is a flicker of Mick's hand, lifting a cigarette to his unseen mouth, observed through the driver's-side window. A beat later this is followed by the casual tossing of the cigarette out the window. The audience is now aware that someone is present, but tension is created because neither the identity nor the intent of the person can be discerned. While the disposal of the cigarette may be merely a continuation of the process of drawing attention to the automobile (although the car is in the foreground, the house across the street in the backyard is lighted so that it is the dominant feature in the frame), littering is a thoughtless, antisocial act, so it increases the audience's concern about who is in the car and what is being done in there. Perhaps there is also a nod to the gangster or cowboy film convention of a character discarding a cigarette just before initiating a violent action, often involving gunplay.

When Mick gets out of the car, he momentarily moves off screen, then walks quickly left to right across the frame and again off screen for an instant before reappearing and walking across the street, his back to the camera.

Mick's face is seen so briefly, and in profile, that it is difficult to determine what he looks like. His disappearance from the screen increases the mystery, and his movement away from the camera further distances him from the audience both physically and psychologically. At the same time, it appears that the threat is withdrawing. Collectively, Mick's movements are sending mixed signals, thereby intensifying the audience's subconscious discomfort. A left to right movement across the screen is considered natural and, therefore, comforting; movement off of the screen is disturbing and suggests that the character does not abide by socially imposed restrictions-- he determines his own course and limitations. The movement away from the camera is also confusing because the threatening figure is retreating, but at the same time this movement reduces the audience's ability to verify the nature of the character. The ambiguity is compounded when Mick mounts the steps, for an upward movement in film signifies positive attributes, such as freedom, strength, control, and hope, but there has been a cut and the camera has been placed to the left of the stairs (i.e. a directorial choice has been made) so that this movement is simultaneously from right to left. Lateral movements are diminished by vertical movements, yet the right to left progression conveys the unnatural, stimulating a sense of uneasiness. The right-left movement can also imply that Mick is a man of action and represents the character's determination, so there is an internal tension between these contradictory impulses.[3]

When Mick arrives at the top of the stairs there is another cut and Mick is shown in a medium close up--but the closed form and the tight framing, together with Mick's three-quarter-turn positioning, is confining and retains an atmosphere of mystery because he is still partially concealed. The audience may even feel that the character is antisocial, consciously avoiding them or hiding something. Mick's threatening anonymity is undercut, however, when he produces a set of keys and unlocks the door. The discordant musical tones that accompany him on his walk across the street indicate that he is up to no good, yet it is suddenly apparent that he belongs here. As will be revealed during the course of the movie, Mick is a complex character, and all of the contradictory and unsettling features in the opening segment demonstrate this while concurrently containing thematic kernels. The entire sequence, from the first movement observed through the car window to Mick's entrance into the house, takes approximately thirty-four seconds.

In Pinter's early plays there was a thematic cluster that parallels the effects created through the movie's opening and to which the meaning of *The Caretaker*, which premiered on the stage on April 27, 1960, is clearly related. Typically, someone is in a room when an intruder arrives. Since the intruder figure implicitly contains an element of menace, the room's inhabitant must verify whether the intruder is a friend or a foe. To do this, communication must be established but the room's inhabitant is fearful of revealing a point of personal vulnerability through the communication. As a consequence, communication is inhibited, increasing the need for verification, the lack of which magnifies the existence of the menace and requires further communication for verification purposes. This circularity feeds on itself and creates an impossible situation for the inhabitant.

One of the interesting phenomena of Pinter scholarship is the lack of consideration given to how the dramatist's stage plays differ from his film versions of the same works.[4] A major difference between how Pinter approaches adapting someone else's work to the screen and how he approaches his own stage plays is that when he uses another author's writing as the basis for his screenplay he picks out the thematic elements that most appeal to him and emphasizes them. Thus, while he may well be being true to his source, that truth may be established in much the same way that he creates realistic dialogue. From the beginning of his career, critics have commented that he has a tape-recorder ear and that he accurately reproduces realistic sounding dialogue on stage. The key, though, is that he picks out certain quintessential elements and emphasizes them.[5] Real language literally reproduced on stage does not sound as real as Pinter's artificial dialogue; in a sense he has created a supra-realistic dialogue that captures and expresses the essence of normal speech. In his cinematic adaptations of novels his intent is likewise to focus on those components that comprise the essence of the work as opposed to faithfully reproducing the novel on film detail by detail. In treating his own works, while he may exercise the opportunity afforded by the medium of film to open them out, to reinforce with cinematic techniques and devices what was already there, basically he relies on what is there and does not try to focus on certain elements in order to express the essence of the drama. Therefore, the meaning of the film version of *The Caretaker* is the same as the meaning of the stage version of the play. As a matter of fact, the film, then, confirms, emphasizes, and further elucidates the meaning gleaned from the drama. This raises an interesting critical question, to wit, is the information gathered from this extraneous source (the film) valid in interpreting the play? Or, are the film and the play separate, though related, entities that perforce must stand on their own? In examining the play in retrospect, after having viewed the film, are elements introduced that are foreign to the original? And, if this is the case, how does a critic know this?[6]

Because I assume that the reader of this study will be somewhat familiar with *The Caretaker*, I am relegating little space to the discussion of the stage version. In addition, I have dealt with the meanings of and techniques in the play elsewhere so there is no need to go into an exhaustively detailed analysis of the play here.[7] As is typical with most of Pinter's scripts, the plot of *The Caretaker* is simple.[8] In fact, Donald Pleasence, who created the role of Davies in the original production and then gave up a part in George Stevens' *The Greatest Story Ever Told* in order to reprise the part in the film version, has comically reduced the plot to a six-word summary: "boy meets tramp, boy loses tramp."[9] As is also typically true with Pinter's dramas, a minimal plot provides few clues but this does not mean that it contains a simple meaning--instead, a number of possible alternatives come into play. In *The Caretaker* two brothers (one a former mental patient) and an old tramp become locked in a battle of wills when the recuperating brother rescues the tramp from an unpleasant situation and invites him into his room, which is in a house owned by the younger brother. The drama evolves in a series of confrontations between these three characters as they try to establish relationships between one another. The result of these confrontations is the expulsion of the old man.

In interpreting the play the items to be considered include the questions of identity and verification clustering around Davies; Aston's attempted reorientation, as well as his suggested Christ-figure qualities and his role in the society-versus-artist conflict; and the problem of communication and interaction between individuals. The last element is probably the most important in determining the ultimate meaning of the play, for the actions of the three characters make sense when one realizes that each is trying to establish an attachment with one of the others. Simultaneously, each is trying to protect that relationship from an outside interference, the third member, which threatens to destroy it by forming a new pairing.

The initial shots in *The Caretaker/The Guest* are significant in establishing the meaning that the author will develop during the course of the film. The importance of the house, Mick's potential strength, watchfulness, and patience, and his ability to force Davies to force himself out of his refuge, the relationship between the brothers, the underlying tensions, the ambiguity of the situation, the gritty reality of a theatrical world opened out--all of this has been suggested or prepared for through the use of cinematic devices in the opening sequence of the film. When, for example, we see Mick cross a street, we are outside the house and the room which is the only locale in which the stage play takes place. When Mick enters the building, climbs the stairs, and goes into the room tracked by the camera, besides the sense of menace described above, a sense of the size of the house and the existence of other rooms is imparted to the audience so that Aston's shutting himself off is more starkly recognized. The details and refinements of the plot and themes that constitute the movie proper will be dealt with in much the same way. For instance, the stage directions for the play suggest that Davies is following his host like a lost dog when they first enter the room at the beginning of the play. This comparison is obviously indicated in the first appearance of Aston in the movie, walking down the street with Davies shuffling back and forth after him. The most interesting thing about the opening sequence of the film version of *The Caretaker*, then, is that in adding it Pinter not only symbolically captures and conveys the essence of his stage play, but in doing so he demonstrates that he understands how film functions and that he can control this medium as surely as he controls the dramatic medium.

NOTES

1. Arnold P. Hinchliffe, *Harold Pinter* (New York: Twayne, 1967), n. 16, p. 175.

2. Harold Pinter and Clive Donner, "Filming 'The Caretaker,'" *Transatlantic Review*, no. 13 (Summer 1963), p. 20.

3. A valuable introduction to the mechanics of cinematic kinesthesia can be found in Chapter Three of Louis D. Giannetti's *Understanding Movies* (Englewood Cliffs, N. J.: Prentice-Hall, 1987, fourth ed.).

4. See *Butter's Going Up*, pp. 81-95.

5. See discussions of this technique in *Butter's Going Up*, pp. 256-75, and in Martin Esslin's *Pinter: A Study of His Plays* (New York: Norton, 1976), Expanded Edition, pp. 242-45.

6. Space does not allow for the consideration of such an extensive subject in this article, but these are some of the questions that are discussed in my forthcoming book-length examination of Pinter's films to be published by Greenwood Press.

7. See *Butter's Going Up*, pp. 81-95.

8. *Ibid.*

9. Quoted in Henry Popkin, Introduction to *Modern British Drama* (New York: Grove, 1969), p. 24. There are also several interesting stories about how financing was obtained for the film, who was involved in that financing, where the movie was shot, and other incidents related to transferring the play to celluloid; some of these are recounted in *Butter's Going Up*.

PINTER AND POLITICS*

Susan Hollis Merritt

Though acknowledging a "shift" toward political drama in Pinter's recent dramatic works *One for the Road*, *Precisely*, and *Mountain Language*, some critics question whether it is genuine. Judging the authenticity of any such change of direction is more complex than giving an account of Pinter's views or of his dramatic plots. Such judgments are contingent on the perspectives of the critics, on their particular politics or ideologies. From different critical vantage points, Pinter's politics can seem to have undergone a radical shift on the one hand, while maintaining a somewhat conservative stance on the other. This double perspective on Pinter's shift to political drama reflects current conflicts in cultural studies between those writing from mainstream positions and those espousing Marxist, neo-Marxist, and post-Marxist views.

A feature of the academic study of drama and theater may have engendered the problem of assessing Pinter's position and classifying his plays. As Marvin Carlson documents, "a continuing point of debate in modern theatre theory has been over whether the theatre should be viewed primarily as an engaged social phenomenon or as a politically indifferent aesthetic artifact;

---

* This essay is from chapter 8 of *Pinter in Play: Critical Strategies and the Plays of Harold Pinter*, forthcoming from Duke University Press in 1990. It is being published with permission.

a significant amount of contemporary theoretical discourse can still be oriented in terms of this opposition" (454). Carlson's own historical account of twentieth-century theater details the opposition between theater based on Brechtian theory and practice ("political theatre") and theater based more on the theory and practice of Artaud ("absurd theatre," "theatre of cruelty").

Critics have difficulties "placing" Pinter and his drama because he crosses the "standard" boundaries delineated by such binary oppositions. At various stages throughout his career, Pinter himself has characterized his work in some of these terms, and Pinter's plays have been championed by one "camp" or another, leading to early critical claims that he is *either* a "social realist" *or* an "absurdist," *or* that his work is an oddly idiosyncratic mixture of *both* strains. It has been commonplace to quote Pinter's statement "what goes on in my plays is realistic, but what I'm doing is not realism" ("Writing for Myself," 174). Critics' different responses to this "paradox" inform controversies about how to assess any developments in his career.

The social realism perceived in his most recent work complicates the problem. Though Pinter dramatizes political concerns more overtly in *One for the Road*, *Precisely*, and *Mountain Language*, this "new interest" has strong roots in Pinter's early "comedies of menace" with their representations of individuals anxiously confronting the forces of social authority. What *political position* Pinter represents through his plays is difficult to situate on a conventional Left/Right spectrum. As we will see, Pinter gravitates less toward specific political ideological affiliations (rejecting even their terminology) than toward thinking matters out on his own, though he does ally himself with organizations that support his particular inclinations.[1] If a label is necessary for purposes of identification--and I am not so sure one is--I would call Pinter a social democrat and an advocate, even an activist, for peace, international human rights, and freedom of expression; his current political activities and his plays dramatize concerns with the protection of human rights and unilateral disarmament.   Perhaps the most conspicuous shift, however, involves his characterization of the source of these concerns as an unquestionable political "reality." Throughout most of his career it has been "against the grain" to discuss Pinter's drama as "political." For example, Henkle points to the relative isolation of Pinter's characters; "[t]he possible political dimensions of plays like *The Birthday Party* are remarkably abstract, and the sources of our response to them lie much more in our *personal* anxieties" (185).   But, in Germany, where *The Dumb Waiter* premiered in 1959 and *The Caretaker* was performed in 1960, the initial critical popularity of Pinter's plays was partly due to an appreciation of their social relevance.   Describing the first performance of Ionesco's *Rhinoceros* at the Düsseldorf Schauspielhaus, where *The Caretaker* also played, Esslin observes: "the German audience instantly recognized the arguments, used by the characters who feel they must follow the trend, as those they themselves had heard, or used, at a time when people in Germany could not resist the lure of Hitler. . . . Rhinoceritis is not only the disease of the totalitarians of the Right as well as of the Left, it is also the pull of conformism" (*Theatre of the Absurd*, 150-51).   Though Pinter has recalled spectacular choruses of "boos" accompanying his opening night curtain calls in Düsseldorf ("Between the Lines"), some Germans, focusing on the lower-class status of Davies, regarded *The Caretaker* as relevant socioeconomically.   In England, following *The Caretaker*, Taylor grouped Pinter with the "Kitchen Sink" playwrights--social realist and working-class drama of "the Angry Young Men" John Osborne and Arnold Wesker--in *Anger and After*, first published in May 1962 (cf. Anderson, "Harold Pinter").

Yet, in talking about the politics of such drama with Harry Thompson in 1961, Pinter rejected its dramatic viability (9).   When Bensky gave him another opportunity to discuss his political concerns in 1966, Pinter himself tended to deemphasize their importance to his early work.

Though qualifying the impression that he was "indifferent"
to politics and indicating that his political consciousness
was still developing, he nevertheless questioned the
relevance of politics to his social role as a playwright,
focusing on his violent dislike of politicians and political
ideologies and how such violence characterized his life and
work. Perhaps as a result, the theme of violence has been
discussed repeatedly in Pinter criticism.[2]

By the late sixties Esslin was still trying to sort out
connections between Pinter's personal act of conscientious
objection in 1948, when he was eighteen years old, and
political aspects of his drama (*Peopled Wound*, 24-27;
Pinter: The Playwright, 36-39). In 1971, when Mel
Gussow raised similar questions about his political
(ir)relevance, Pinter replied by criticizing the "totally
meaningless, hypocritical" language of "politicians":
"Politicians just don't interest me. What, if you like,
interests me, is the suffering for which they are responsible.
It doesn't interest me--it horrifies me!" He offered
comments on Vietnam, South Africa, and China as
evidence that he is "very conscious of what's happening in
the world. I'm not by any means blind or deaf to the world
around me. . . . I'm right up to the minute. I read the
papers. I have very strong objections to all sorts of things"
("Conversation," 133-34). Yet these objections still did not
enter his plays directly.

Anderson compares Pinter with Arnold Wesker and
Edward Bond in terms of their similar lack of popularity in
England ("This," 447). In 1979 Pinter alluded to the "very,
very strong *young* wave of political playwrights" currently
popular in England to help explain what he saw as his poor
critical reception there (Gussow, "I Started," 7). The next
year Pinter told Barber that he found himself in the "odd
position" for a writer of being "really quite unpopular" in
his own country, when he is apparently of interest
elsewhere. "I have a suspicion," he said, "that fashion at
the moment is with the young political Left. I'm never
going to be a young political Left. I'm afraid it's a bit too
late!" As Pinter also told Gross, "my last three full-length

plays [*Old Times, No Man's Land,* and *Betrayal*] have hardly been performed at all in this country, outside London" (27). About this time (1980) Pinter produced and published *The Hothouse,* a "heavily satirical" play which he had "discarded" as worthless earlier (Bensky, 28-29). Though Pinter described his decision to produce *The Hothouse* "rather quietly--at the Hampstead Theatre Club" in terms of having "a bit of fun" (Gussow, "I Started," 5), later remarks suggest that (for a variety of reasons perhaps) Pinter was also now ready to produce more overtly political work.³

At the University of East Anglia in 1981, ending his brief talk, Pinter directly addressed the difficulty that he was encountering as a "nonpolitical" writer: "I think it must be very much easier for other people, particularly people, writers who write from a very political point of view and are able to incorporate their politics in one way or another into their work. I do happen to have strong political views but they simply do not come into my work as far as I can see." Asked whether this avoidance of politics as a subject in his plays was "deliberate," Pinter said, "Of course not. It simply doesn't work out that way," adding: "I am myself a convinced nuclear unilateralist but I don't see there is any--there is no way I can write a play about it. It's simply something that would never occur to me, I suppose, any of these considerations. . . . I am sure that some writers do--can very easily and properly sit down and write plays from a political kind of ideology. I am unable to do that." Yet, as another audience member suggested in East Anglia, after having "obviously achieved what [he] set out to," Pinter can now "use the success . . . to help" dramatize sociopolitical and ethical issues.

Pinter began to "help" first by reassessing publicly the political implications of the work that he had suppressed earlier and then by writing and producing new plays. Talking about the 1982 American premiere of *The Hothouse,* he told William Gale that whereas *The Hothouse* "would have been taken as a fantasy, as something remote and surrealistic" when it was written in 1958, "I felt that was not the case then, and I *know* it is not the case now. In 1982 it cannot be denied that it fits in with the facts of life today. The real political hypocrisy and brutality are now blatant. We cannot be fooled by them any longer" (A-16). Pinter's most recent dramas--*One for the Road*, *Precisely*, and *Mountain Language*--present today's political "facts of life" more starkly. *One for the Road*, written in 1983 and first produced and directed by Pinter in 1984, dramatizes political torture. *Precisely*, a dramatic sketch that Pinter read before an audience at New York University upon accepting the Elmer Holmes Bobst Award in Arts and Letters in December 1984, satirizes nuclear war bureaucracy. *Mountain Language*, first published and produced in 1988, dramatizes institutionalized abuses of sociopolitical prisoners and their distrust of their guards' perhaps feigned ultimate tolerance, satirizing effects of censorship curtailing individual freedoms.

Pinter's more recent perceptions of the political relevance of his early work further counterbalances the critical commonplace that it lacks such relevance. In "A Play and Its Politics," a conversation between Pinter and Nicholas Hern in 1985 published in the Grove Press edition of *One for the Road* the next year, Pinter explicitly discusses the change in his attitude toward authoritarianism between his early plays, (e.g., *The Birthday Party*, *The Hothouse*, and *The Dumb Waiter*), all written in 1957-60, and *One for the Road* and *Precisely*. Though he actively considered "the abuse of authority" in writing the earlier plays, he says, they "use metaphor to a great extent, whereas in *One for the Road* the deed is much more specific and direct": "I don't really see *One for the Road* as a metaphor. For anything. It describes a state of affairs in which there are victims of torture. You have the torturer, you have the victims. And you can see that two of the victims have been physically tortured" (8). *One for the Road* is "brutally real: my earlier plays were perhaps metaphors for states of affairs in various respects. This is not a metaphor about anything--it's just a brutal series of facts" (back cover). As when discussing the germination of his earlier plays in other interviews, in "A Play and Its Politics" Pinter further explains the impetus for such violent acts of "actual physical brutality" as rape and murder in *One for the Road*. As well as citing the general context of torture "quite commonly" practiced in "at least ninety countries now" throughout the world, both "Communist and non-Communist," he recounts the more particular circumstances stimulating him to write it: his knowledge of torture and inhumane prison practices in Turkey and his anger at the insensitivity of two young Turkish women toward their own country's violation of human rights. His own active membership in Campaign for Nuclear Disarmament led to his awareness that members of a counterpart organization in Turkey (the Turkish Peace Association) have been inhumanely treated (12-14).

This "new direction" in Pinter's playwriting grows out of Pinter's long-standing engagement in some social activities against human rights abuses. As early as 1974 Pinter wrote a letter to the London *Times* to draw attention to the plight of Soviet internee Vladimir Bukovsky. Pinter told Gross, in 1980, "While we're talking now . . . people are locked up in prisons all over the place, being tortured in one way or another. I'm quite rattled with these kinds of images, with the sense that these things are ever-present" (25). Several months after his 1981 visit to the University of East Anglia, in the summer of 1982, with his wife, Lady Antonia Fraser, Pinter helped to coordinate "The Night of the Day of the Imprisoned Writer," described as "a charity occasion to benefit the all-too-many writers of the world who are now in prison" (Owen, 24). Pinter's claim for the "very positive effect" that this International PEN benefit could achieve seems deflated by his account of a previous benefit for the imprisoned Czech writer Vaclav Havel: "On my 50th birthday last year [10 October 1980] the National Theatre were kind enough to put on a play of mine [*Landscape*] for one night and the proceeds from that were for Havel's family. The awful thing is that now, a year later, nothing has changed for him" (Owen, 25). Despite this recognition, Pinter persisted in his efforts.[4]

Pinter represented International PEN again on behalf of imprisoned writers in March 1985, when, as vice presidents of English and American PEN, Pinter and Arthur Miller visited prisons in Turkey. On 23 March 1985 the two writers held a joint news conference in Istanbul to protest Turkish human rights abuses. During the five-day visit to Turkey, they talked with over "100 Turkish intellectuals, with former prison inmates, politicians and diplomats," expressing International PEN's concern with "'the dignity of its members throughout the world'" (Gursel; cf. Kamm). At the opening ceremonies of the 48th International PEN Congress in New York, on 12 January 1986, it was reported that "almost 450 writers on nearly every continent are known to be confined" (McDowell).

In a postscript to the interview with Hern, written after he returned from Turkey, Pinter points to support that the United States gives military regimes like Turkey (24). While he clearly protests human rights violations in *One for the Road*, those abused in the play comprise a family (a man, his wife, and their young son) whose national and social identity is not specified. Going beyond the imprisoned writer, the play embraces all prisoners of conscience and others whose rights are being violated by "the State" throughout the world. The play "could take place in totalitarian countries in Eastern Europe or South America," but, Dukore argues, "the many approving references to religion ironically exclude Communist countries, where the interrogator would be unlikely to call himself a religious man, to declare that God is on the side of the state not the dissidents, or to claim that the state's business is to cleanse the world for God" (132-33). To me Nicholas's religious references seem fanatical (not merely "approving"), as associated these days with Middle Eastern countries; yet, I would stress that the setting could still be almost anywhere in the world today, where, unfortunately, such religious, ideological, and other "anti-intellectual" fanaticism is all too widespread.

Vis-à-vis his own recent experiences and concerns as a social activist, it appears Pinter's perspective on the political themes of his earlier plays has sharpened. In the February 1985 interview with Hern, comparing those plays with *One for the Road*, Pinter alludes to a "run-through" of a television production of *The Dumb Waiter*: "It was quite obvious to the actors that the chap who is upstairs and is never seen is a figure of authority. Gus questions this authority and rebels against it and therefore is squashed at the end, or is about to be squashed. The political metaphor was very clear to the actors and directors of the first production in 1960. It was not, however, clear to the critics at the time . . . that it was actually *about* anything" (7).[5] *"The Birthday Party,"* Pinter tells Hern, "which I wrote more or less at the same time, in 1957, again has a central figure who is squeezed by certain authoritarian forces"; and *"The Hothouse*--which actually followed quite shortly, the next year, I think--is essentially about the abuse of authority" (8). (Pinter told Bensky that he wrote *The Hothouse* after *The Caretaker* [28], but his note to the published text confirms his statement to Hern.) When Hern suggests that, retrospectively, the early plays would appear to reflect Pinter's "unease about the Hungarian Revolution and the Soviet annexation of East Europe," Pinter qualifies this view somewhat: "Except that one doesn't normally write about today, but yesterday--or even the day before yesterday" (9). His own "political act" of conscientious objection resulted from being "terribly disturbed as a young man by the Cold War. And McCarthyism. . . . A profound hypocrisy. 'They' the monsters, 'we' the good. In 1948 the Russian suppression of Eastern Europe was an obvious and brutal fact, but I felt very strongly then and feel as strongly now that we have an obligation to subject our own actions and attitudes to an equivalent critical and moral scrutiny."

Even though *One for the Road* did not represent "a sudden crystallisation of [Pinter's] political sensibility" as Hern first thought, since Pinter had been a conscientious objector as a teenager and thus "involved in political acts from early on," nevertheless, "in 1958," critics saw Pinter's plays "as having no relation to the outside world at all"; his plays were, Pinter recalls, "dismissed as absurd rubbish" by most critics (10). "[F]or many people," Hern speculates, "it must have seemed that you've been operating on this political level invisibility" (11). Pinter recapitulates his political attitude: "I wouldn't say that my political awareness during those years was dead. Far from it. But I came to view politicians and political structures and political acts with something I can best describe as detached contempt. To engage in politics seemed to me futile. And so, for twenty years or so, in my writing I simply continued investigations into other areas" (12).

As Gussow has observed more recently, "In retrospect . . . [Pinter] can identify the political content in his plays, which he can trace back to 'The Birthday Party' and 'The Dumbwaiter.' Linking 'The Birthday Party' to 'One for the Road' and 'Mountain Language,' he said they all dealt with 'the destruction of an individual.'" The idea for the "knock" on Stanley's door in *The Birthday Party*, Pinter said, "came from my knowledge of the Gestapo. The character of the old man, Petey, says one of the most important lines I've ever written. As Stanley is taken away, Petey says, 'Stan, don't let them tell you what to do.' I've lived that line all my damn life. Never more than now" ("Pinter's Plays," C22; cf. Dukore, 143-46). Whereas, retrospectively, Pinter presents his most recent plays as a more overt development of a generally underestimated aspect of his earlier ones in "A Play and Its Politics," in another more recent interview Pinter further explains the change that *One for the Road* signifies more emphatically: "It certainly represents a permanent change in me as a citizen of this country . . . a man living in this world. It's been happening for a very long time. In other words, I've become more and more political over the last 10 years--more politically engaged. And now I'm profoundly engaged" (Drake, 6).

Whether or not this "change" will indeed prove "permanent" remains to be seen. So far what Gussow calls

Pinter's "politicization" ("Pinter's Plays," C17) has raised "anxious murmurings from his devotees that, by taking on the mantle of Amnesty International, he may lose the touch of genius with which he illumines the despair and the power games of less obviously charged situations" (Carne). In assessing this "new phase in Pinter's oeuvre, a departure into the realm of political debate, even propaganda," Esslin still asks, "To what genre do Pinter's anti-torture tracts belong?" To consider *Mountain Language* "straightforward *documentary drama*" is problematic because "the aestheticism . . . the beautiful way in which it is done, undercuts the documentary quality. Real torture is much more messy, much more sordid" ("Mountain Language," 76, 78).[6]

Pinter's Shift to Political Drama:
An Alternative Critical View

As if anticipating these concerns, in *British and Irish Political Drama in the Twentieth Century*, David Ian Rabey observes: "The merging of social drama into political drama is an easy transition and may cause problems of classification (as in the work of Osborne and Wesker)" (2). Rabey makes no mention of Pinter. Though *British and Irish Political Drama in the Twentieth Century* was probably in press at the time that Pinter published *One for the Road* and *Precisely*, even on the basis of these short works and *Mountain Language*, Rabey still might not have included Pinter, given this definition of the aims and styles of the genre:

> "*Political* drama" emphasizes the directness of its address to problematic social matters, and its attempt to interpret these problems in political terms. Political drama communicates its sense of these problems' avoidability, with implicit or explicit condemnation of the political circumstances that have allowed them to rise and continue to exist

(just as Brecht identifies *The Rise of Arturo Ui* as
Resistable).   In perceiving social problems as
avoidable, political drama is necessarily diverging
from the worldview that the agents of the status quo
would seek to impose for the continued smooth
running of society in its present form.   (1-2)

Whereas Rabey takes "*social* drama as that which purports
to act as an impartial report on social relations, or to focus
on specific social abuses, without stepping over into an
attack on the fundamentals of the society in question," he
takes "*political* drama as that which views specific social
abuses as symptomatic of a deeper illness, namely injustice
and anomalies at the heart of society's basic power
structure" (2).   Whereas it might seem that *One
for the Road*, *Precisely*, and *Mountain Language* could be
classified as political drama, Pinter's attitude toward social
change, as he describes it to Hern, does not fit "Leftist"
concepts of the attitude and kinds of change that a political
dramatist advocates.

Pinter does not seem to perceive social problems of
the kind he dramatizes as "avoidable."   When Hern asks
"whether a play like *One for the Road* can really have any
effect," Pinter explains: "[R]eason is not going to do
anything.   Me writing *One for the Road*, documentaries,
articles, lucid analyses, Averell Harriman writing in the
New York Times, voices raised here and there, people
walking down the road and demonstrating.   Finally it's
hopeless.   There's nothing one can achieve.   Because the
modes of thinking of those in power are worn out,
threadbare, atrophied.   Their minds are a brick wall" ("A
Play," 20).   Whereas Pinter recognizes hegemonic
paradigms governing institutional abuses--"the modes of
thinking of those in power"--he gives no indication that
solving the problem must involve a change in what Rabey
identifies as the "basic . . . structure" of power; indeed, he
denies that *any* solution is even plausible.   "But," he adds,
"still one can't stop attempting to try to think and see things
as clearly as possible."

In her interview with Pinter, Drake observes that
Pinter "feels artists don't influence politics much." "The
only thing that will influence politics," Pinter said,
"certainly in this country [America], and in my own
country, is the voters. I do take the point that if I say
something someone might listen. At the same time, I don't
talk as an artist; I talk as a man. Everyone has a quite
essential obligation to subject the society in which we live
to moral scrutiny" (6). Pinter defines his own position
quite clearly: "My own view is that the appalling danger
that the world is in at the moment has to do with a schism
that has actually been manufactured. I'm referring to Them
and Us. To inhabit rigid and atrophied postures like these
has led to the present danger." The McCarthyite
distinctions between political-economic systems
(Communists and non-Communists) that he objects to in
"A Play and Its Politics"; national alliances (Eastern Bloc
and Western Bloc); classes (bourgeois and working class,
or, more generally, the Haves and the Have-nots); and even
political ideologies (Left and Right): Pinter rejects all such
polarizing binary oppositions. "I was 15 when the war was
over, so that one emerged out of that and lurched through
adolescence into manhood as it were, with the weight of all
that and the further reverberations--such as The Bomb and
the Iron Curtain. McCarthyism here, repression in Eastern
Europe. There seemed to be no end to it. But there is an
end to it. There's an end all right. My view, incidentally,
is that that end is going to come. . . . I think it's inevitable,
yes." Ironically, he concludes, with (mock?) upper-class
panache: "And on that note I shall have a glass of
champagne."

In contrast, Günther Klotz defines the
"internationalism" of "recent progressive British drama" to
include such recurrent themes as "the combined efforts of
monopolies, governments and military commanders to keep
themselves in power and to enlarge their control by
enforcing maximum profits" and "socialist reality" (36, 39).
There are "a new strategy of anti-imperialist drama and a
new type of production as well as reception in the British

theatre, a new type of play which offers something constructive for people to identify with, the feeling of a prospective integration of the individual in a new common cause which is not an abstract idea but, in some parts of the world, tangible reality" (39-40). This is not the same "tangible reality" that Pinter has been describing and dramatizing.

For Pinter, altering his earlier emphasis on reality as relative and unverifiable: "All we're talking about, finally is what is real? What is real? There's only one reality, you know. You can interpret reality in various ways. But there's only one. And if that reality is thousands of people being tortured to death at this very moment and hundreds of thousands of megatons of nuclear bombs standing there waiting to go off at this very moment, then that's it and that's that. It has to be faced" ("A Play," 21). Thus intending to confront his audience with this "one reality," Pinter has been critical of their unwillingness to face it, despite his own awareness of "that great danger, this great irritant to an audience" of "agit-prop" ("A Play," 18). Pinter has not suggested any "constructive" measures for his audience to take against the atrocities dramatized in *One for the Road* and *Mountain Language* or those implied in *Precisely*. He may feel, as he has said about spectators' responses to his other plays, that any response is their own individual responsibility.

Several people walked out midway through performances of *One for the Road* that I attended in New York City and Portland, Oregon (see *Other Places* and *No Holds Barred*). Apparently, some could not tolerate the physical and verbal abuse on stage. Portland's Sumus Theatre management received complaints about the play's language, not the political issues it raised. Since the performance of *One for the Road* that I saw in Portland was a benefit for Amnesty International, it was preceded by a short speech about the aims of this organization, delivered by its local president, Arden Benson, who encouraged the audience to sign petitions in behalf of individual political prisoners, directing us to such petitions, as well as leaflets, in the lobby. In this way the theater management provided opportunities for purposive political action that Pinter's play does not directly prescribe, though they are activities likely to merit his approval, since Pinter himself is a member of Amnesty International (Drake, 6).

Rabey further distinguishes "the comparative aims and styles of political *dramas* (plays) and political *theatre*" by citing Sandy Craig's "working definition," which attributes the difference to a playwright's stance toward the audience:

> the important feature which distinguishes political plays from political theatre is this: *political plays* seek to appeal to, and influence, the middle class, in particular that section of the middle class which is influential in moulding 'public opinion.' The implication of this is that society can be reformed and liberalized, where necessary, by the shock troops of the middle class--and, of course, such people are influential in campaigns for reform. But further, political plays in bourgeois theatre implicitly realize that the middle class remains the progressive class within society. *Political theatre*, on the other hand, as embodied in the various political theatre companies, aims--with varying degrees of success--to appeal to, and be an expression of, the working class. Its underlying belief is that the working class is the progressive class within society. (Rabey 6, quoting Craig, 30-31; emphasis added)

Political theater tries "to produce plays that arouse a wider and deeper awareness of the necessity and of the possibility to change the present society," Günther Klotz also observes. "In its struggle against imperialism and against the set-up of the commercialized institutions and media of communication, the progressive drama had to change from the social criticism of the breakthrough [e.g., Osborne's *Look Back in Anger*] to a theatre looking for alternatives. . . . No longer can a progressive drama be effective if it continues to imitate life in a naturalistic way, in serving the old liberal aims of education and entertainment, or moralizing and edifying. What is required is a drama as medium of social movement" (40).

Though Pinter himself comes originally from a working-class background (his father was a tailor), he has, through his own professional success and his second marriage to Lady Antonia Fraser, risen through the middle class into the upper class of English society. Though his first few plays featured working-class characters loosely modeled on people encountered during his experiences as a struggling actor, these dramas were presented first to university audiences. After *The Caretaker* Pinter became more upscale, appealing to upper middle-class audiences. Some of his later characters could *attend* what Rabey calls "the legitimate, established theatre" (ix). If Pinter's political plays do not count as political theater, it is also because his customary audiences--"bourgeois" or "elitist"-- are not politically progressive.

The distinguishing "political" issue involved in "cultural analysis on the left" is "how to acknowledge and comprehend the tremendous capacity of patriarchal and capitalist institutions to regenerate themselves not only in their material foundations and structures but in the hearts and minds of people, while never losing sight or despairing of the power of popular organization and struggle to resist and transform them" (Batsleer et al., 5). Joining the "professional" classes (as an actor, writer, and director), Pinter has worked within our "patriarchal and capitalist" cultural institutions (what Klotz calls "the commercialized institutions and media of communication"--theater, radio, film, television, and print) and become a phenomenal commercial success. This success is sometimes cited as a symptom of Pinter's "cop-out"; he has become a symbol of the "mainstream," the kind of theater to which "alternative theatre" is an alternative.[7] Yet "whilst the tradition of academic Marxism which is now a familiar feature of literary criticism provides an ideology, a vocabulary and enough internal disputes for the committed critic of political theatre, the alternatives to *that* alternative are less clearly formulated and the continuities between one group and another largely uncharted" (Anderson, "This," 452). Unlike most other Leftist critics, who regard Pinter as a mainstream, commercial playwright and would term him *"boulevard,""*"West-End," or "Broadway bound," Klaus Köhler argues that Pinter's position is "the position of a bourgeois dramatist at variance with the sacrosanct beliefs of his class[;] the direction of his criticism is clearly antibourgeois. Rather than invite compliance with an untouchable status quo[,] [Pinter] discredits the illusion of possible harmony and integrity under imperialist power structures." With their "individual activities of consciousness warped by the ideologic strategies of the 'Welfare State,' [Pinter's characters] are unable to take stock of themselves and the world around them." Their alienation and "estrangement" result from "a repressive canon of bourgeois ethics and politics." But there is an important difference between Pinter's "distancing effects" and Brecht's contention that "'the present-day world can only be described to present-day people if it is described as capable of transformation.'" With other "congenial late bourgeois writers," Köhler argues, Pinter "shares . . . an unresolved dualism of rejection and doubts as to the alterability of what is rejected" (324-25).

Köhler concludes "The Establishment and the Absurd" (published before Pinter's *One for the Road* and the interview on its politics) by citing Pinter's repeated expressions of "his indifference to political issues" (326). But in both his plays and his public pronouncements Pinter has never been unequivocally indifferent to politics (Cf. Dukore). Köhler's more specific contention that "[c]rucial problems of the present-day class struggles in Britain are absent from [Pinter's] plays" is even qualified by rereading *The Caretaker* from the perspective of Sahai, for whom it dramatizes consequences of urbanization for the lower and would-be middle classes. Yet, as Köhler recognizes, "[Pinter] has also stressed the general social significance of his theatre" (326). Pinter presents "model situations from a micro-sociological perspective. Beyond all ambiguities they set forth a perpetual fight of opposites, not so much between the privileged and the unprivileged as among the representatives and camp-followers of the bourgeois regime today." From this perspective, "[b]y exposing [his characters'] fruitless navel inspection, self-laceration and incapacity for purposeful action[,] [Pinter] analyses the social and moral make-up of a class destined to perish by its own contradictions." But despite this "[t]renchant debunking," Pinter still refuses "to envisage any constructive commitment," Köhler concludes, and "this basic inconsistency . . . narrows the extent and impact of Pinter's critique." This opinion of Pinter's social and political range suggests a current strategy of some cultural criticism "on the Left": to devalue any author who does not espouse a Marxist and/or feminist ideology. Pinter is being "rewritten" by critics sympathetic to Marxism and feminism. To become successful "social strategists" themselves, these critics rewrite Pinter so as to enact their own scenarios for social change.[8]

A position somewhat different from Köhler's informs C. W. E. Bigsby's "Politics of Anxiety: Contemporary Socialist Theatre in England." Melmoth defines Bigsby's perspective succinctly: "the truly subversive dramatist is relativistic and anarchistic rather than programmatic, a farceur rather than a commentator or, as Bigsby puts it, 'not Arden but Orton, not McGrath but Pinter'" (Melmoth, 954). As neither Bigsby nor Melmoth was able to take into account *One for the Road, Precisely*, and *Mountain Language*, I wonder how these plays might modify their views. In all three plays Pinter suggests no particular solution to problems of culturally institutionalized oppression that they dramatize; but he does implicate his audience in these problems viscerally. Finding solutions (if there are any) is up to us--audiences and voters--and our governmental officials (elected or not). Pinter may have placed little stock in our ability to solve such social and political problems, but at least he has given

us the opportunity to "try to think and see things as clearly
as possible" too, to subject "reality" to intense "moral
scrutiny."

While accepting Pinter's viewpoint that *One for the
Road* is "not metaphorical in the same way that *The Dumb
Waiter* and *The Birthday Party* are," Judith Roof points out
that "the concreteness of the portrayal of abuse also
conveys larger ideological metaphors (the family, the
father). Its realism, thus, is not only a realism of detail and
behavior, but also a rendering of the context, of the ideas in
whose name horrors are perpetuated" (11). If, in *One for
the Road*, "[t]he central place of the subversive stare . . .
suggests that an unauthorized watching--a kind of seditious
theatre--is a way of opposing political oppression" (17), so
the final silence of the Elderly Woman in *Mountain
Language*--an unauthorized *refusal* to speak--subverts
linguistic oppression by "the State."[9]   Though Pinter
suggests that an impetus for *Mountain Language* was his
visit with Arthur Miller to Turkey, the play was advertised
falsely as "a 'parable about torture and the fate of the
Kurdish people'"; while Pinter accepts that it is about
torture, he denies both that it concerns "'the fate of the
Kurdish people'" and that it is "'a parable'" (Pinter,
"'Mountain Language'"; cf. Gussow, "Pinter's Plays,"
C17).   From Pinter's own "point of view, it is about
suppression of language, and the loss of freedom of
expression . . . [and] therefore . . . as relevant in England as
it is in Turkey" (C17).

"While the 'clear vision' Pinter proposes may make
a more intelligent populace," Roof argues further, "it too is
complicit in the maintenance of the power relations it
dissects. Awareness must be accompanied by a look back
at the forces which conspire to construct us all within a
dominant ideology which obscures problems in the interest
of maintaining status quo" (17).   Yet in "[u]rging a
different way to see"--and different ways to hear and to feel
as well, I would add--like Beckett's *Catastrophe*, Pinter's
political plays do "propose a theatrical model for that
seeing different from the analytical disengagement of

Brecht's alienation-effect. Committing theatre to political action in a most direct way, Pinter and Beckett involve both stage and audience in an enactment of the oppression theatre embodies and exposes."

Pinter's Future as a Political Dramatist

We do not know how Pinter's own beliefs in the political prospects of vast social change will develop. We do not know, as he himself has said that he does not know, how long he will continue to write political plays, or anything else ("A Play," 18-19). "I won't, I'm sure, continue to write plays about politics," he has insisted, "unless an authentic image comes into my mind which demands to be written. But I've no such plans and I can't write out of ideological *desire*. That, almost invariably, is artificial. Dry. Manufactured. In other words, I've no idea what I'm going to write and I don't anticipate that I shall continue to write political plays as such. I don't know what my future is as a writer" (Drake, 6). But while he may not know his "future as a writer," Pinter does predict his "future . . . as a man," and that is: "To continue to ask some very straight questions about the society in which we live, without fear or favor. In other words, I don't give a damn how many people I offend."10

"My attitude toward my own playwriting has changed," Pinter told Gussow. "The whole idea of a narrative, of a broad canvas stretching over a period of two hours--I think I've gone away from that forever. I can't see that I could ever encompass it again. I was always termed, what is the word? 'minimalist.' . . . Maybe I am. Who knows? But I hope that to be minimal is to be precise and focused. I feel that what I've illuminated is quite broad-- and deep--shadows stretching away." Reporting his answer to a Sussex University student's question about whether he could ally his current interests with "characters as [he] used to write them, people called Meg and Max"--"I don't think I can any longer"--he reserved this opening: "I don't want to cut myself off from all experiences likely to come" ("Pinter's Plays," C22).

On 3 October 1989, after his reading at the 92nd Street Y, when asked by Gussow if he had reconsidered the change in his attitude, Pinter said: "It is not a matter for me to reconsider. Nothing would give me greater pleasure than to write any play, of whatever length. I don't think length is in any way so important anyway, but one thing about the act of writing is that it is an act of--essentially an act of freedom, as I understand it, so it's great to write any way, if you can do it. I just find it more and more difficult." "I'm only concerned at the moment with *accurate* and *precise* images of what is the case," he added. In response to Gussow's opening statement that Pinter has "always been a political playwright" and his question about whether Pinter could trace "a serious interest" in the world of politics" from *The Birthday Party* through *Mountain Language*, Pinter replied:

> In the early days, which was thirty years ago, I was a political playwright of a kind. But I then took a break from being so for about seventeen years. And I wrote a lot of plays between 1970 and 1985 which can't be said to be political plays--things like *Old Times*, *Betrayal*, *Landscape*, and *Silence*, which were concerned with memory and youth and loss and so on . . . they didn't take place and didn't concern themselves with social or political structure, whereas the earlier plays did. . . . My early work was I think full of games and jokes and so on, but I think the distinction I would make between those plays then and these plays now is that I'm afraid that for me the joke is over. I can't see any more jokes. I can't play any more games. So I therefore find that I'm writing shorter and shorter pieces which are more and more brutal and more and more overtly naked, you see.

Though admitting that the theater may "affect the world in which we live" only a "little," Pinter explained: "But that little is something, and I respect the power, the correspondence between theater and audience. . . . I always have hated propaganda plays . . . agit-prop. . . . But I still feel that there is room, there is a role somewhere, for a work that is not following, pursuing, the normal narrative procedure of the drama, and it's to be found, and I'm trying to find it." Criticizing the "debased language" pervading American and English governmental statements about Central America, Pinter stated: "I just want to make the facts *absolutely clear*, and it's as I see myself not only as an actor and an entertainer, but . . . I'm also a citizen of the world in which I live, and I take responsibility for that, I really *insist* upon taking responsibility and *understand* my responsibility quite precisely as *actually* trying to find out what *the truth is*. And what actually happens. And so [what] I've found is that we're really at the bottom of a *blanket* of lies which unfortunately we are either too indifferent or too frightened to question."[11]

If Pinter does keep on writing plays--however minimalist, serious, and factually truthful--critics cannot rule out further developments that might alter assessments of what Köhler terms "the extent and impact of Pinter's critique" (326). Pinter may continue to widen his breadth while further deepening his insight into human social relations and global politics.

Signaling such a development perhaps, Pinter has written some new screen adaptations dealing with a variety of sociopolitically relevant subjects: *Reunion* (based on Fred Uhlmann's novel about Stuttgart in the 1930s and 1980s), *The Heat of the Day* (based on Elizabeth Bowen's novel about wartime London), and *The Handmaid's Tale* (based on Margaret Atwood's novel about a Christian fundamentalist regime in America).[12] *Reunion* is "a story of friendship between two boys--one a German aristocrat, the other a German Jew, beginning in 1932 and ending a half century later, when the Jewish man comes to terms with his belief that his friend has let him down"; the film's

American director, Jerry Schatzberg describes "the relationship" between them as the project's appeal (Van Gelder, "Togetherness"). According to writer-director Paul Schrader, Pinter has also written a screenplay adapting Ian McEwan's *Comfort of Strangers*, a novel "set in Venice-- about a vacationing young British couple whose lives are sort of taken over by a local couple," reminiscent of *The Servant* (1963); "full of innuendo and subtext," it is reportedly "quite close to the kind of thing Pinter writes for himself. Though it's an adaptation, it has the same themes and cadences of his original work, that element of dominance in relationships between men and women that is very Pinteresque" (Van Gelder, "Pinteresque Pinter"), that is, in the broadest sense, very political.

On 3 October 1989, when Pinter related his current project of writing a screenplay of Kafka's *The Trial* to people's distorted memories of it "as a political book" reminiscent of Arthur Koestler, he explained: "I simply wouldn't be interested in writing a screenplay of *Darkness at Noon* because it's so specifically of its time and place"; whereas "the nightmare of [Kafka's] world is precisely in its ordinariness, and that is what I think is so frightening." But, though chairman of the Arts for Nicaragua Fund in Great Britain, Pinter says that writing "a specific play about such a[n immediate political] situation" as Nicaragua "is not something I could possibly do."   Yet, like many of Pinter's past remarks, this one should not be taken as "final and definitive": what Pinter foresees now that he could not "possibly do" does not rule out what he may actually do in the future.

NOTES

1.   For a context of some of Pinter's current activities, see Atlas.

2. See Bensky, 30-31; Bosworth; and Gross, 25. For a more recent discussion of violence in Pinter's work, especially *Hothouse*, see Mengel.

3. See Pinter, "Author's Note," in *Hothouse*; cf. Bensky, 28-29. See also Gillen, "Nowhere," 86-87 and 96 n.5; cf. Knowles, "Hothouse," 134.

4. As a result of such efforts on his behalf, Havel's situation improved both politically and financially. Though Havel was released after the benefit in which the Pinters were involved, early in 1989 he was incarcerated again, becoming the focus of intense worldwide protests for his release, which finally occurred on 17 May. As a result of the remarkable national uprising in December 1989 ("the Velvet Revolution"), Havel became president of Czechoslovakia and was nominated for the Nobel Peace Prize (for the second time) on 28 January 1990. In February "[t]he Pinters [will] visit Havel to share his triumph" (Angelo, 66).

5. Concerning the premiere of *The Dumb Waiter* on American television in 1987, cf. Pinter's telephone remarks to Farber about the play's topical relevance: "I think it also has a serious subject. I always considered it a political play, though it's not overt. But it is a play about dissidence. It's a play about questioning and criticizing powers that remain complaisant and sure of themselves and somewhere upstairs. I think that's still a timely subject."

6. For other reviews of the London premiere, see *London Theatre Record*. See also Gussow, "Pinter's Plays."

7. James regards "alternative theatre" as "political theatre" (in Craig's sense, as quoted above). Cf. Anderson, "This," 450, 456 n.11.

8. On "the notion of the critic as social strategist," as exemplified by Terry Eagleton, see King, 60-61.

9. Cf. Gillen, "From Chapter Ten," 4.

10. Williams finds it "impossible to believe [Pinter's] assurances [on *Saturday Review* (BBC-2)] that 'I'm no longer interested in myself as a playwright.' There was something willed, media-ridden, even schizoid about [Pinter's] assessment that 'I've got an awful lot under my belt. It's no great loss.'" Cf. Pinter's remark to Gussow: "I understand your interest in me as a playwright. But I'm more interested in myself as a citizen" ("Pinter's Plays," C17). On Pinter's role as a "citizen," see Knowles's forthcoming article.

11. Cf. Pinter, "Language and Lies" and the refutation by Nyholm.

12. The parenthetical descriptions are all quotations from "Harold Pinter: Growth of an Angry Playwright." See also Canby; and Gussow, "Pinter's Plays," C17. Pinter has also adapted Joseph Conrad's anti-war novel *Victory* for the screen.

WORKS CITED

Anderson, Michael. "Harold Pinter: Journey to the Interior." Chap. 4 in *Anger and Detachment: A Study of Arden, Osborne and Pinter*. London: Pitman, 1976.

_____. "This, That and the Other: The Critic and the Alternative Theatre." *Modern Drama* 24 (1981): 445-57.

Angelo, Bonnie. "Profile: Not Quite Your Usual Historian." *Time*, 15 Jan. 1990, 66-68.

Atlas, James. "Thatcher Puts a Lid On: Censorship in Britain." *New York Times Mag.*, 5 Mar. 1989.

Barber, John. "Precise Words of Pinter." London *Daily Telegraph*, 30 June 1980, 11.

Batsleer, Janet, and Tony Davies, Rebecca O'Rourke, and Chris Weedon. *Rewriting English: The Politics of Gender and Class.* London and New York: Methuen, 1985.

Bensky, Lawrence M. "The Art of the Theater III: Harold Pinter: An Interview." *Paris Rev.* 10 (Fall 1966): 12-37. (Excerpted in "Pinter: 'Violence Is Natural.'" *New York Times*, 1 Jan. 1967, Sec. 2: 1, 3.)

Bigsby, C. W. E. "The Politics of Anxiety: Contemporary Socialist Theatre in England." In *Modern British Dramatists: New Perspectives*, ed. and intro. John Russell Brown, 161-76. Englewood Cliffs, N.J.: Prentice-Hall, 1984.

Bosworth, Patricia. "Why Doesn't He Write More?" *New York Times*, 27 Oct. 1968, Sec. 2: 3.

Canby, Vincent. "Critic's Notebook: Old Favorites Are No More at Cannes." *New York Times*, 18 May 1989, Sec. C: 23, 29.

Carlson, Marvin. *Theories of the Theatre: A Historical and Critical Survey, from the Greeks to the Present.* Ithaca and London: Cornell Univ. Press, 1984.

Carne, Rosalind. "Theatre: Space Probe." *New Statesman,* 23 Mar. 1984, 31.

Craig, Sandy. "Unmasking the Lie: Political Theatre." In *Dreams and Deconstructions: Alternative Theatre in Britain,* ed. Sandy Craig, 20-48. Ambergate, Derbyshire, Eng.: Amber Lane, 1980.

Drake, Sylvie. "Acting Is Just like 'Old Times' for Pinter." *Los Angeles Times,* 29 Oct. 1985, Sec. 6: 1, 6.

Dukore, Bernard F. *Harold Pinter.* Grove Press Modern Dramatists. New York: Grove, 1982. 2d ed. Macmillan Modern Dramatists. London: Macmillan, 1988.

Esslin, Martin. "Mountain Language Opens in London." Rev. of National Theatre (Lyttelton) production of *Mountain Language. Pinter Rev.* 2 (1988): 76-78.

_____. *The Peopled Wound: The Work of Harold Pinter.* Garden City, N.Y.: Doubleday, 1970. 4th ed. Repr. as *Pinter: The Playwright.* London and New York: Methuen, 1982. Corrected repr. 1984.

_____. *The Theatre of the Absurd.* Garden City, N.Y.: Doubleday, 1961. Rev. ed. London: Pelican, 1968. Repr. Garden City, N.Y.: Doubleday, Anchor Books, 1969.

Farber, Stephen. "Topical Relevance." Telephone interview with Harold Pinter. *New York Times,* 10 May 1987, Sec. 2: 25.

Gale, William K. "Pinter Believes Trinity Rep. Will Do 'Damn Well' in Staging His 'Hothouse.'" *Providence Jour.*, 12 Feb. 1982, A1, 16.

Gillen, Francis. "From Chapter Ten of *The Dwarfs* to *Mountain Language*: The Continuity of Harold Pinter." *Pinter Rev.* 2 (1988): 1-4.

_____. "'Nowhere to Go': Society and the Individual in Harold Pinter's *The Hothouse*." *Twentieth Century Literature* 29, no. 1 (1983): 86-96.

Gross, Miriam. "Pinter on Pinter." London *Observer Rev.*, 5 Oct. 1980, 25, 27.

Gursel, Mustafa. "Turkey Censors Blast on Rights by Two Authors: Miller, Pinter Say Torture a Fact in Turkey." *Washington Post*, 24 Mar. 1985, A27.

Gussow, Mel. "A Conversation [Pause] with Harold Pinter." *New York Times Mag.*, 5 Dec. 1971.

_____. "Harold Pinter: 'I Started with Two People in a Pub.'" *New York Times*, 30 Dec. 1979, Sec. 2: 5, 7.

_____. "Pinter's Plays Following Him out of Enigma and into Politics." *New York Times*, 6 Dec. 1988, Sec. C: 17, 22.

"Harold Pinter: Growth of an Angry Playwright." London *Observer*, Oct. 1988, 13.

Henkle, Roger B. "From Pooter to Pinter: Domestic Comedy and Vulnerability." *Critical Quart.* 16 (Summer 1974): 174-89.

James, Alby. "Alternative versus Mainstream." *Gambit* 9, no. 36 (1980): 7-9.

Kamm, Henry. "Two Playwrights Deplore Turkish Rights Record." *New York Times*, 28 Mar. 1985, A17.

King, Noel. "Rewriting Richardson." *Jour. of the Midwest Modern Language Association* 18 (Spring 1985): 42-61.

Klotz, Günther. "Internationalism and Present British Drama." *Zeitschrift für Anglistik un Amerikanistik* 27 (1979): 35-42.

Knowles, Ronald. "'The Hothouse' and the Epiphany of Harold Pinter." *Jour. of Beckett Studies* 10 (1985): 134-44.

Köhler, Klaus. "The Establishment and the Absurd: Trends, Ideologies and Techniques in Non-Realistic Drama from Beckett to Pinter (Part II)." *Zeitschrift für Anglistik und Amerikanistik* (Leipzig, E. Ger.) 32, no. 4 (1984): 315-29.

London Theatre Record 21 (1988): 1467-71.

McDowell, Edwin. "PEN Talks on Freedom of the Word." *New York Times*, 16 Jan. 1986, Sec. 3: C17.

Melmoth, John. "Theatre: Subversives and Hooligans." *Times Literary Supplement*, 30 Aug. 1985, 953-54.

Mengel, Ewald. "The 'Closed Society': Structural Violence in the English Drama to the Present." Photocopy.

No Holds Barred. Precisely. By Harold Pinter. Stage production directed by Robin Stone. With Douglas Mace and Megan Taylor. *The Dumb Waiter.* By Harold Pinter. Stage production directed by Keith Scales. With Gary Brickner-Schulz and Ken Colburn. *One for the Road.* By Harold Pinter.

Stage production directed by Gary O'Brien. With Daniel Kalapsa, Douglas Mace, Keith Scales, and Megan Taylor. MetroNorthwest Productions, Sumus Theatre, Portland, Ore., 16 and 28 Aug. 1986. Performance of *One for the Road* on 28 Aug. dedicated to Amnesty International.

Nyholm, Per. "Language and Nicaragua." Letter to the editor. *Index on Censorship* 17, no. 7 (1988): 6.

Other Places. Three Plays by Harold Pinter. Stage production directed by Alan Schneider. *Victoria Station.* With Henderson Forsythe and Kevin Conway. *One for the Road.* With Caroline Lagerfelt, David George Polyak, George Hosmer, and Kevin Conway. *A Kind of Alaska.* With Caroline Lagerfelt, Dianne Wiest, and Henderson Forsythe. Manhattan Theatre Club, New York, 18 May 1984. (From 3 Apr. to 20 May 1984.)

Owen, Michael. "Harold Pinter and His Lady and a Great Erotic Experience." London *Standard*, 11 Sept. 1981, 24-25.

Pinter, Harold. *Complete Works.* 4 vols. New York: Grove, 1976-81.

_____. *The Hothouse.* Incl. "Author's Note." New York: Grove, 1980.

_____. "Language and Lies." *Index on Censorship* 17, no. 6 (1988): 2.

_____. Letter to the Editor. London *Times*, 22 Mar. 1974, 17.

_____. "'Mountain Language.'" Letter to the Editor. *Times Literary Supplement*, 7-13 Oct. 1988, 1109.

_____. *Mountain Language*. New York: Grove, 1989.

_____. *One for the Road*. New York: Grove, 1986.

_____. "A Play and Its Politics: A Conversation between Harold Pinter and Nicholas Hern" and "Postscript." In *One for the Road*, 5-24.

_____. *Precisely*. *Harper's*, May 1985, 37.

_____. Readings of an excerpt from *The Hothouse* and of *One for the Road* and discussion with Mel Gussow, reading selected questions from the audience. The Poetry Center of the 92nd Street Y, New York, 3 Oct. 1989.

_____. Talk presented at the Univ. of East Anglia, East Anglia, Eng., 29 Oct. 1981.

_____. "Writing for Myself." Comp. Richard Findlater. *Twentieth Century* 169 (Feb. 1961): 172-75. (Repr. in Pinter, *Complete Works* 2: 9-12.)

Rabey, David Ian. *British and Irish Political Drama in the Twentieth Century: Implicating the Audience*. New York: St. Martin's, 1986.

Roof, Judith. "Staging the Ideology behind the Power: Pinter's *One for the Road* and Beckett's *Catastrophe*." *Pinter Rev.* 2 (1988): 8-18.

Sahai, Surendra. "Pinter's *The Caretaker*: A Treatise on Urbanization." *Indian Jour. of English Studies* 19 (1979): 69-79.

Taylor, John Russell. *Anger and After: A Guide to the New British Drama*. London: Methuen, 1962. 3d ed. London: Methuen, 1969.

Thompson, Harry. "Harold Pinter Replies." *New Theatre Mag.* 2 (Jan. 1961): 8-10.

Van Gelder, Lawrence. "At the Movies: Pinteresque Pinter." *New York Times*, 28 July 1989, B4.

_____. "At the Movies: Togetherness." *New York Times*, 22 Jan. 1988, C6.

Williams, Hugo. "Mumbo Gumbo." Rev. of *Saturday Review* (BBC2). *New Statesman*, 4 Oct. 1985, 36.

"YES! IN THE SEA OF LIFE ENISLED": HAROLD PINTER'S *OTHER PLACES*

Ewald Mengel

Introduction

Harold Pinter's *Other Places* opened at the National Theatre on 14 October 1982 in London, under the direction of Peter Hall.[1]   *Other Places* is a trilogy that combines three short plays of a different character: *A Kind of Alaska* dramatises the awakening of a patient after twenty-nine years of comatose or trance-like sleep; in *Victoria Station*, the controller of a radio-taxi station tries in vain to persuade one of his drivers to pick up a customer; in *Family Voices*, a son, a mother and a father express their feelings after the son has gone away from home.

On the surface, the title *Other Places* refers to the three different settings of the plays.   Secondly, the characters of the individual plays live, either in reality or in their minds, in "other places," so that communication between them has become difficult or problematic.   The title of this paper, in quoting the first line of Matthew Arnold's "To Marguerite," alludes to a deeper, symbolic meaning of *Other Places*. The common underlying theme of all three plays is the isolation and loneliness of man in modern mass society, a theme that Pinter has already dealt with in some of his earlier plays, for example in *Landscape* or in *Silence*.

161

In the following, I shall first interpret the plays individually. My focus will be on the question of how Pinter succeeds in dealing with such a basically lyrical theme in dramatic form. In conclusion, I shall try to describe the relevance of *Other Places* with reference to Pinter's other plays, and chart his development as a dramatist.

A Kind of Alaska

A Kind of Alaska may be compared to a modern version of *Sleeping Beauty*. Pinter's "Sleeping Beauty" is called Deborah; the part of "Prince Charming" is played by Hornby, the doctor; Deborah's sister Pauline, who has no counterpart in the fairy tale, completes the cast.

As Pinter has admitted in a foreword to *A Kind of Alaska*, something which is quite unusual for him, the play was inspired by Oliver Sacks's *Awakenings*:2

A Kind of Alaska was inspired by *Awakenings* by Oliver Sacks M.D., first published in 1973 by Gerald Duckworth and Co.

In the winter of 1916-1917, there spread over Europe, and subsequently over the rest of the world, an extraordinary epidemic illness which presented itself in innumerable forms--as delirium, mania, trances, coma, sleep, insomnia, restlessness, and states of Parkinsonism. It was eventually identified by the great physician Constantin von Economo and named by him *encephalitis lethargica*, or sleeping sickness.

Over the next ten years almost five million people fell victim to the disease of whom more than a third died. Of the survivors some escaped almost unscathed, but the majority moved into states of deepening illness. The worst-affected sank into singular states of 'sleep'--conscious of their surroundings but motionless, speechless, and without hope or will, confined to asylums or other institutions. Fifty years later, with the development of the remarkable drug L-DOPA, they erupted into life once more. (3)

At first sight, this foreword seems to have a fictional quality: the many forms of the illness, the claim that it cost millions of people their lives, the peculiar name of the physician, Constantin von Economo, and the miraculous drug L-DOPA seem to owe their existence to the imagination of the author. A closer investigation reveals, however, that Pinter is remaining true to the facts. Everything he claims with reference to Sacks is accurate. What seems to have fascinated him is that the facts to be represented fall already into the pattern of a fantastic story, and that there was no need to invent something additional. All he had to do was to bring reality into a shape that could be used for dramatic purposes.

The full extent to which Pinter was inspired by *Awakenings* is revealed by a reading of the book. The neuophysiologist-chemist's account pays attention not only to the medical, but also to the psychological, philosophical and ontological implications of this ominous illness. *Awakenings* consists of a number of case studies in which the consequences of the sleeping sickness and its effect on the mind and the body of the patients is described. The majority of these cases concern female patients who were treated by Oliver Sacks with the drug L-DOPA between 1969 and 1972, when he was Director of the closed asylum of Mount Carmel near New York. Almost all of these patients had had an attack of *encephalitis lethargica* shortly after the epidemic had started in 1916. Subsequently, they had developed grave psychosomatic behavioural disturbances, so that they had to be hospitalised. The symptoms of sleeping sickness described by Sacks vary. They are similar to those of Parkinsonism, and comprise insomnia, different forms of tics or involuntary and repeated movements, spasms, respiratory crises, hyperkinesis, echolalia, serious neuroses, and catatonic trances in which the patients sometimes remain for hours or even days.

Sacks reports how patients who had been suffering very badly from *encephalitis lethargica* and who were treated with L-DOPA, a drug discovered by a physician named Cotzias early in the sixties, began to recover consciousness and part of their normal physical abilities. Some improved so much that they became able to lead a fairly normal life. Others, however, became even worse after a short period of recovery, and the treatment with the drug had to be discontinued, the patients falling back once again into their usual state of coma or unconsciousness. In most cases, Sacks claims, it was possible to stabilise the patients by a skillful dosing of the drug, so that the overall effect was more positive than negative. All of these patients went through three successive stages: first, there was the moment of their awakening; secondly, after some weeks, their awakening was followed by a crisis during which the symptoms of their illness grew worse; thirdly, this crisis overcome, they entered a phase of accommodation during which they learned to live with their disease and control its more negative effects.

What can be shown is that Deborah's return to the world also has three stages, only that Pinter has compressed what in reality takes weeks and months into just a few minutes. Of course, *A Kind of Alaska* is not a case study, but rather a skillfully structured one-act play written for aesthetic purposes. Pinter obviously realised that the moment of awakening to the world after years and years of trance or semi-consciousness would have an enormous dramatic quality, and be particularly suitable for being turned into a play. Consequently, what interests us in *A Kind of Alaska* is the process of awakening itself and the patient's re-encounter with reality. Also, we are curious to know in what regions the patient's mind has travelled, and what feelings and memories are connected with her state. The form of Pinter's play is expressive of this double interest. The action taking place in the present has a progressive and teleological structure. After her awakening, Deborah is confronted with reality. What follows is a short moment of crisis. Having overcome this crisis, Deborah enters the phase of accommodation, during which she begins to adjust to the new situation. In contrast to this present-related action, the characters' memories have the function of embedding the past into the present. Pauline's and Hornby's memories basically have expositional functions. They elucidate Deborah's fate and the history of her family, forming a narrative context that gives meaning to the past and to the present for both Deborah and the audience. Deborah's memories are lyrical in character. Her childhood memories serve to define her self, her identity, in a subjective way. The memories connected with her illness conjure up the phantasmagoric "no man's land" Alaska, in which her consciousness has travelled in the meantime.

With regard to the interaction of the characters, Pinter's play acquires its dramatic character through a discrepancy of awareness between Hornby and Pauline, on the one hand, and the patient Deborah on the other, through the juxtaposition of two conflicting interpretations of reality, a subjective and an objective one. The audience is presented with two mutually exclusive views, but from the beginning it is obvious that Deborah's physical appearance, which indicates her age, proves her wrong, whereas it supports Hornby's and Pauline's interpretation of reality.

At the beginning of the play, Deborah, who looks like a woman in her forties, is sitting in a bed covered with white sheets and is staring ahead. The "kiss of life," the injection with the drug L-DOPA, has obviously just taken place, and Deborah begins to speak. Her first words, "Something is happening" (5), are indicative of a beginning process of self-reflection, although she still ignores Hornby's questions "Do you know me?" "Do you recognize me?" "Can you hear me?" (5). Her counter-question, "Are you speaking?" (6), is her first goal-oriented, purposeful act of communication. It shows that she is beginning to rediscover reality, but has no firm grasp on it as yet, her thoughts still dwelling in "a kind of Alaska."

Gradually, however, the presence of Hornby seeps into her consciousness. She begins to notice him, a fact which is underlined by the stage direction: "She looks at him for the first time" (7). However, this explanation that she has slept for a long time and is now awake does not make sense to her. It becomes clear that, in her mind, she is still living in the world of her childhood, in the world as it was before she fell ill. She remembers the games she played with her father, recalls her mother, her sisters Pauline and Estelle, and her friend Jack, and believes herself to be fifteen or sixteen years old. Her language is partly that of a young girl, and in her memories she mixes earlier and later stages of her childhood. It seems that, for her, time came to a standstill years ago.

A similar phenomenon is noticed by Oliver Sacks with regard to his patient Rose R.:

> But I also have the feeling that she feels her "past" as her present, and that perhaps it has never felt "past" for her. Is it possible that Miss R. has never, in fact, moved on from the "past"? Could she still be "in" 1926 forty-three years later? Is 1926 now?[3]

Deborah's subjective construction of reality comes into conflict with another reality that is objectively defined by her age and by her outer appearance. This does not mean, however, that Deborah's definition of reality is less true, or less authentic than what Hornby or the audience hold to be correct. Deborah's subjective and Hornby's objective views are both valid, because they refer to different realities.

An especially dramatic moment in the course of Deborah's "awakening" is reached when she is confronted with her sister Pauline. On the one hand, Pauline is connected with the past; on the other hand, she is also part of the present. For Deborah, therefore, Pauline visibly demonstrates the flow of time, the process of ageing. This process has also changed Deborah, and when she regains consciousness, her own body feels alien to her, and Pauline appears as a stranger. One of Pauline's functions is to confine and complete Hornby's story. In this way, his story gains an objective validity. Hornby and Pauline contradict each other only once: whereas Pauline claims that her father and mother are taking a cruise in the Indian Ocean, Hornby tells Deborah that her mother has died, and that her father has turned blind. For a moment, it seems that Pinter is making use of a technique of mystification that is characteristic of his earlier plays and that leaves the audience in the dark about the truth. The apparent contradiction may be resolved, however, when the situation is considered in which Hornby's and Pauline's conflicting stories are brought forward. Obviously, it is Pauline's intention to spare her sister the full truth, for she is afraid that Deborah, who has just regained consciousness, cannot take the impact of it. Pauline's story emphasises that her family is doing well, at the same time explaining their absence. Hornby's version comes a bit later in the course of Deborah's "awakening." It is part of a longer explanation which is caused by Deborah's reaction to Pauline's story-- "This woman is mad" (33). By being completely open to her and giving her an unpleasant piece of information, Hornby wants to make her face reality.

It is Pauline's function to tell Deborah--and the audience--what really happened in the past. Among other things Pauline recalls the moment when Deborah was overtaken by her illness:

No it was you--
PAULINE looks at HORNBY. He looks back at her, impassive.
PAULINE turns back to DEBORAH.
It was you. You were standing with a vase of flowers in your hands. you were about to put it down on the table. But you didn't put it down. You stood still, with the vase in your hands, as if

you were . . . fixed. I was with you, in the room. I
looked into your eyes.
Pause
I said, "Debbie?"
Pause
I said, "Debbie?"
Pause
But you remained . . . quite . . . still. I touched you.
I said: "Debbie?" Your eyes were open. You were
looking nowhere. Then you suddenly looked at me
and saw me and smiled at me and put the vase down
on the table.
Pause
But at the end of dinner, we were all laughing and
talking, and Daddy was making jokes and making
us laugh, and you said you couldn't see him
properly because of the flowers in the middle of the
table, where you had put them, and you stood and
picked up the vase and you took it towards that little
sidetable by the window, walnut, and Mummy was
laughing and even Estelle was laughing and then we
suddenly looked at you and you had stopped. You
were standing with the vase by the sidetable, you
were about to put it down, your arm was stretched
towards it but you had stopped.
Pause
We went to you. We spoke to you. Mummy
touched you. She spoke to you.
Pause
Then Daddy tried to take the vase from you. He
could not . . . wrench it from your hands. He could
not . . . move you from the spot. Like . . . marble.
Pause
You were sixteen. (29ff)

Pauline's tale is reminiscent of that passage in *Sleeping
Beauty* where the cook wants to box the boy on the ear, but
is overtaken by sleep at that very moment. As was
mentioned above, this motif was inspired not so much by

the fairy tale, but rather by Oliver Sacks's *Awakenings*. What Pauline describes is a typical symptom of the sleeping sickness. According to Sacks, however, this symptom is typical of an advanced stage of *encephalitis lethargica*, and does not appear right at the beginning. By thus deviating from reality, Pinter achieves a dramatic effect, for Deborah's illness acquires a mythical quality. Again, Pinter, for dramatic purposes, has condensed and accelerated a process that in reality takes weeks and months.

Whereas Pauline narrates what happened to Deborah in the past from the perspective of an eye-witness, Deborah's memories elucidate her illness from a personal point of view. She compares her experiences with those of the protagonist of *Alice in Wonderland*: "I've been dancing in very narrow spaces. Kept stubbing my toes and bumping my head. Like Alice . . . " (24). Deborah's statement is indicative of an active consciousness behind a seemingly inactive and lifeless front. A similar conclusion is suggested by the following passage, in which the audience can witness Deborah's illness *in actu* and from an inner point of view:

DEBORAH

Now what was I going to say?
She begins to flick her cheek, as if brushing something from it.
Now what--? Oh dear, oh no. Oh dear.
Pause
Oh dear.
The flicking of her cheek grows faster.
Yes, I think they're closing in. They're closing in. They're closing the walls in. Yes.
She bows her head, flicking faster, her fingers now moving about her face.
Oh . . . we.. . . . oooohhhhh . . . oh no . . . oh no . . .
During the course of this speech her body becomes hunchbacked.

Something panting, something panting. Can't see.
Oh, the light is going. The light is going. They're
shutting up shop. They're closing my face. Chains
and padlocks. Bolting me up. Stinking. The smell.
Oh my goodness, oh dear, oh my goodness, oh dear,
I'm so young. It's a vice. I'm in a vice. It's at the
back of my neck. Ah. Eyes stuck. Only see the
shadow of the tip of my nose. Shadow of the tip of
my nose. Eyes stuck.
She stops flicking abruptly, sits still. Her body
straightens. She looks up. She looks at her fingers,
examines them. (37ff)

Like Sacks's patients, Pinter's Deborah has to live through
a crisis during which the symptoms of her illness become
worse, only Pinter has compressed a process into a few
minutes that in reality lasts several weeks. Deborah's
flicking is an imitation of the spastic tics which Sacks
describes in *Awakenings*. The same applies to the fact that
her eyes seem to be frozen to a certain object ("Eyes
stuck"), imitating an occulatory crisis. The many
repetitions of words and sentences are characteristic of
patients suffering from echolalia, and patients with
hunchbacked bodies are shown in some of the photos in
Sacks's book.

What is perhaps even more important than these
physical similarities is the fact that Deborah's feelings also
correspond to those of Sacks's patients. In the passage
quoted above, her utterances refer to both an objective and
a subjective reality. Her feeling of being "closed in,"
against which she fights in vain, refers to both the "closed
institution" in which she had to live, and to the illness that
is taking possession of her. From the beginning of his
career as a dramatist, Pinter has shown a special
predilection for "closed institutions" and the effects they
have on their patients' psyches. Deborah's remarks--
"Chains and padlocks. Bolting me up. Stinking. The
smell"--may be taken to refer to the undignified
circumstances under which patients in closed asylums

sometimes have to exist. Her feeling that the walls are closing in on her, or that she is helplessly stuck in a vise, is characteristic of how patients subjectively experience their illness. The "objective correlative" for this experience can be seen in the catatonic trances into which patients suffering from *encephalitis lethargica* fall every now and then. The stronger the patients exert their willpower not to be overcome by their illness, the more they develop an inner resistance against their own willing, so that they have the feeling of being squashed by two opposing forces. What looks like a freezing of their movements, a ceasing of all their life-entertaining functions, is in reality a severe inner conflict the patients fight out with themselves:

> Patients so affected find that as soon as they "will" or intend or attempt a movement, a "counter-will" or "resistance" rises up to meet them. They find themselves embattled, and even immobilized, in a form of physiological conflict--force against counter-force, will against counter-will, command against countermand.[4]

Immediately after her crisis, Deborah is ready for the first time to accept her situation as it is, although she still refuses to face the full truth. This is shown by the ending of the play:

DEBORAH

I must be quite old. I wonder what I look like. But it's of no consequence. I certainly have no intention of looking into a mirror.
Pause
No.
She looks at HORNBY.
You say I have been asleep. You say I am now awake. You say I have not awoken from the dead. You say I was not dreaming then and am not

dreaming now. You say I have always been alive
and am alive now. You say I am a woman.
She looks at PAULINE, then back to HORNBY.
She is a widow. She doesn't go to her ballet classes
any more. Mummy and Daddy and Estelle are on a
world cruise. They've stopped off in Bangkok. It'll
be my birthday soon. I think I have the matter in
proportion.
Pause
Thank you. (39ff)

Deborah's refusal to look into the mirror amounts to an
evasion of reality. Her automatic way of speaking shows
that she has not quite accepted Pauline's and Hornby's
definitions of reality, although she is acknowledging them
now. One gets the impression that she is not convinced of
what she is saying, and is just recapitulating something she
has learned by heart. Especially relevant in this context is
the fact that she prefers Pauline's version of the "truth," at
the same time ignoring Hornby's, which is much more
unpleasant. Again, this is indicative of her evasion of
reality. When she therefore finally claims: "I think I have
the matter in proportion," this does not sound very
convincing. The new "reality" to which she begins to
adjust herself is still illusory in character, so that her final
words "Thank you" appear in an ironic light.
    Pinter's Hornby, about whom nothing has been said
so far, is another of those ambivalent "caretaker-figures" in
whom positive and negative qualities coincide. Although
Hornby succeeds in calling his patient back to life, the final
outcome of his medical manipulation is doubtful. Because
the play ends with Deborah's accommodation to reality, the
further physical and psychological consequences of her
"awakening" do not become clear, but what Pinter's play
suggests is that Deborah is also a guinea pig and victim of a
medical science whose methods and results can be
dehumanising. Whereas it is Sacks's intention in
Awakenings to celebrate the success of his psycho-
pharmacological experiments, the dramatist Pinter is much

more skeptical about the "rebirth" of his Deborah. The reason for this is that both have different concepts of reality. For Pinter, the empirical world is as shifting, ambivalent, and unreal as the phantasmagoric "Alaska" which Deborah has left behind. Conversely, Deborah's "no-man's land" is for him a concrete reality. Deborah's "awakening" therefore produces a conflict between two different kinds of reality, which, although they exclude each other, are both valid and authentic. The result is a mutual relativisation of both concepts of reality, the subjective and psychological on the one hand, and the objective and empirical on the other, so that a final answer to the question of what the "actual" reality consists of can no longer be given.

Victoria Station

Victoria Station, which comes second in *Other Places*, is much shorter than *A Kind of Alaska* and reminds one of Pinter's early revue sketches. In many respects it is a very funny play, but its underlying theme is also the isolation, anonymity and loneliness of man in modern mass society.

The two characters of the play, the controller and the driver, are not introduced by their names. Man is reduced to his role, his function, or number. The controller's vain attempts to convince his driver via radio to pick up a customer form the action of this play.

The isolation of the two characters from each other and from their environment is already underlined by the play's setting. The controller is sitting alone in his office. His only connection with the driver and with the outside world is his radio equipment. The driver is sitting alone in his car (although he claims later in the play that he has company). His exact location within London remains uncertain.

From the start, communication between the driver and the controller prove to be problematic. At first, Pinter leaves it open whether this is due to a bad radio connection, or whether it is the fault of the driver, who ignores the controller's question "274? Where are you?" (45), then asks "What?" (45). The comedy of the dialogue throughout the play is produced by the fact that the driver refuses to act according to his role, and disappoints the controller's--and the audience's--role expectations. What develops is one of Pinter's well-known battles for positions, the purpose of which is to decide who can dominate whom.[5]

Pinter's driver employs various strategies in order to achieve this goal. He asks puzzling questions ("Who are you?" 46), parries questions with counter-questions, pretends ignorance, or just keeps silent, which may be understood as a passive form of resistance.

In the course of the play's action, the driver's statements become more and more unlikely. When he claims that he is "cruising about" (47), he still sounds plausible because "cruising about" is something that taxi drivers searching for customers usually do. But when he claims that he does not know Victoria Station, we no longer have confidence in him, for this seems rather unlikely. Additionally, he increasingly contradicts himself. When he claims that he has parked his cab "underneath Crystal Palace" (55), from where he can see the building, this is an obvious lie, for Crystal Palace was destroyed by fire in 1936. As a result, the statements he makes from now on become questionable. He affirms that he has a wife and children, for example, but one is no longer inclined to believe him. A bit later he asserts that he has a passenger on board. Although he initially uses the personal pronoun "he" ("He doesn't want to go anywhere," 57), he finally states that the passenger is a woman, that he has fallen in love with her, and that they plan to get married--this in spite of his previous claim to be a married man with children.

As is the case of many other Pinter characters, the truth of most of what the driver says cannot be finally verified. The driver's behaviour, however, allows us to draw conclusions with regard to his mental and psychological constitution. By refusing to act in accordance with the controller's role-expectations, he succeeds in breaking out of the routine-like form of communication and starting a more or less private conversation which guarantees him the controller's attention. This is also emphasised by the fact that the driver takes the initiative as soon as the controller tries to talk to somebody else: "It's me, 274. Please. Don't leave me" (54). Interpretations which merely insist that Pinter's taxi driver has gone mad stop short of the truth, because they do not reveal anything about the motives underlying his behaviour.6 What Pinter wants to emphasise, with the help of his taxi driver, is the location and anonymity of the individual in modern mass society, and his desire for attention and recognition.

For his part, the controller employs various tactical manoeuvres in order to make his obstinate driver change his mind. He appeals to his reason and understanding, explains the circumstances and promises him a remunerative job. When he realises the fruitlessness of his attempts, he gets more and more excited and resorts to veiled and open threats and insults.

Accustomed to having his orders carried out without much ado, he is presented with a great problem by the peculiar behaviour of his driver. Since his only connection with the outer world is his radio, he cannot rely on his own senses, but is dependent on the information given by his driver. Soon he is forced to realise that the driver's statements are unreliable and incomplete. To the same extent to which the driver refuses to function according to his role, that is, to drive, the controller loses control of the situation. At first he tries to be patient, but then his latent aggressiveness erupts:

CONTROLLER

Do you have a driving wheel in front of you?

Pause
Because I haven't, 274. I'm just talking into this
machine, trying to make some sense out of our
lives. That's my function. God gave me this job.
He asked me to do this job, personally. I'm your
local monk, 274. I'm a monk. You follow? I lead
a restricted life. I haven't got a choke and a gear
lever in front of me. I haven't got a cooling system
and four wheels. I'm not sitting here with wing
mirrors and a jack in the boot. And if I did have a
jack in the boot I'd stick it right up your arse. (50)

Passages like this one suggest that frustration is partly
responsible for the controller's verbal bellicosity. The
driver's refusal to obey is only a random event that triggers
it off. The real cause of this frustration has something to do
with his job. The controller's work is characteristic of
modern mass society. Although communication with
others is part of his task, he leads an isolated life in the
anonymity of his office. The role he has to fill is relatively
undemanding, so that he cannot realise himself or find
fulfillment in his job. It becomes clear that it is not only the
driver with the number 274 but also the controller who is
suffering from alienation. In this way, Pinter shows that it
is not the position of the individual within the social system,
but rather the system as such which is to be held responsible
for the alienation of people from each other and from
themselves.

When the controller forgets himself and his role for
a moment and drops his mask, this is caused by the
deficient role behaviour of the driver: "You're beginning
to obsess me. I think I'm going to die. I'm alone in this
miserable freezing fucking office and nobody loves me.
Listen, pukeface--" (58). These words are characterised by
self-pity and sentimentality on the one hand, and violence
on the other, a mixture which gives him a complex and
ambivalent character.

In the following passage, the controller exchanges
the role of boss for that of friend and colleague:

CONTROLLER

You know what I've always dreamed of doing? I've always had this dream of having a holiday in sunny Barbados. I'm thinking of taking this holiday at the end of this year, 274. I'd like you to come with me. To Barbados. Just the two of us. I'll take you snorkelling. We can swim together in the blue Caribbean.
Pause
In the meantime, though, why don't you just pop back to the office now and I'll make you a nice cup of tea? You can tell me something about your background, about your ambitions and aspirations. You can tell me all about your little hobbies and pastimes. Come over and have a nice cup of tea, 274. (59)

It is generally characteristic of Pinter's plays that a friendly invitation often contains a hidden menace. This also applies to the above passage. The text shows a characteristic ambivalence that makes it difficult to describe what is really going on. The idea of the two men spending their holiday together snorkelling in Barbados has hints of homosexuality. The real intentions of the controller are revealed by the last sentence. He still wants to reassert his authority and get the driver, who is not functioning properly, back under his control. What is really going on, therefore, is a battle for positions, its purpose being the undermining of the position occupied by the partner in the interaction in order to dominate in the end.

As it turns out, the tactical manoeuvres of the controller are unsuccessful. The obstinate driver refuses to come to the office; on the contrary, at the end, the controller offers to visit the driver in his car. Who comes to whom is always very important in a Pinter play. Whether they will meet at all remains uncertain, however, for the actual position of the driver is unknown, so that the controller's intention--"I'll be right with you" (62)--cannot be realised. The play's effect is partly due to the fact that it is impossible to verify the truth of what the characters say. This suggests that Pinter initially must have intended *Victoria Station* to be a radio play. For the listener of a radio play, the characters gain reality only by their voices, something that makes it even more difficult to verify their statements. As far as the driver is concerned, the listener is in the same position as the controller, who has to depend on the driver for information. On the stage, however, the characters are physically present. When the driver, who is sitting in his car, claims that he is cruising about, this statement is contradicted by the fact that he does not move. The same applies to his claim that he has a passenger on board. The theatregoer knows that this is not true, because there is nobody in the car besides himself. That the driver is a liar, therefore, is much clearer on the stage than on the radio, where reality is much more ambivalent. This additional information which the audience gets because of the setting is not contributive to the overall effect of the play. It becomes clear, then, that a reality that is ambivalent or undefined and the impossibility of verification are important ingredients of Pinter's dramaturgy.7

Family Voices

Pinter's *Family Voices*, the third play of *Other Places*,8 was written for the radio and first broadcast on BBC Radio 3 on 22 January 1981. The theatre version was first performed in a "platform performance" under the direction of Peter Hall by the National Theatre on 13 February 1981. In the theatre version, the three characters still bear the name VOICE 1, VOICE 2, and VOICE 3, but in a stage direction Pinter has defined them by mentioning their age and their sex. Their relationship is revealed by what they say. They are father, mother and son, and in

their monologues they give expression to their feelings
after the son has left the family home. All three characters
are separated from each other. Whereas the mother has
remained at home, the son is now living in a big city, and
the father, who plays a minor role, even speaks out of his
grave.

Pinter has already dealt with the theme of the
family in some of his earlier plays. The mother-son
relationship has especially interested him. Early examples
of this are Meg and Stanley in *The Birthday Party*, or
Albert and his mother in *A Night Out*. The repressiveness
of a dominating mother-figure, who threatens the ego-
identity of her son, and the son's incapability of becoming
emotionally independent and forming a family of his own,
are characteristic of these relationships. Pinter's son-
figures are therefore torn between the conflicting impulses
of coming home and leaving home, and there is no solution
to this dilemma.

The impossibility of a satisfying emotional
relationship between mother and son is also characteristic
of *Family Voices*. The play dramatises "the agonized
isolation of the individual 'living pretty much alone' at the
same time that he lives in the midst of family, in this case a
newfound family and his original one."[9]

Although Pinter's characters do not communicate
with each other directly because of their local separation,
their monologues are all addressed in their minds to a
specific partner: that is, they are dialogic in character.[10]
The monologues of father and mother are addressed to the
son, whereas those of the son exclusively address his
mother. The behaviour of all three *dramatis personae* is
characterised by a high degree of self-monitoring;[11] they
are extremely careful of what they say, hide their actual
feelings behind false claims and masks, and invent stylised
self-images. Their statements are "other-determined," insofar as they can be related to the assumed expectancies of
their imaginary partners. Behind their pretensions,
however, is hidden a completely different emotional
reality: "And there is a total contradiction between what is

said and what is felt. So in order to show reality, one has to show the mask and the distorted vision."[12] The longer one listens to them, the clearer their contradictions become. Their masks begin to crumble, and their true faces show through. Their high self-monitoring partly breaks down, but only to be substituted by new attempts at self-stylisation and role-playing.

Family Voices begins with a monologue from the son, who has a room in a house inhabited by strange people who leave a more than dubious impression.[13] The imaginary letters he addresses to his mother inform us that the family he lives with and whom he gets to know by and by is called Withers. It consists of a "Mrs. Withers," who is seventy years old, a certain "Lady Withers," and a girl who answers to the name of Jane, aged fifteen. In addition, there is a bald-headed old man, who is also called Withers but has no contact with the others, and Riley, who confesses to be homosexual, but also claims to be deeply religious.

The intercourse of these people with each other and with the son is characterised by a peculiar and puzzling mixture of intimacy and indifference. Although the son gets to know all the people in the house as time goes by, he can define neither their actual identities nor their relationships. Riley claims to be a policeman but rarely leaves the house to go to work. Lady Withers is at night visited by strange, anonymous people whose dealings remain unknown. She wants him to call her "Lally." Jane puts her feet into his lap. He is visited by Riley in the bathroom while he is sitting naked in the tub. Last but not least, the Withers have given him the pet name "Bobo" and thereby a new identity.

At the beginning of the play, the son claims to be happy with his new situation--"I am having a very nice time" (67); "I like walking in this enormous city, all my myself. It's fun to know no-one at all" (68); "I get on very well with my landlady, Mrs. Withers" (69)--but, because of the frequency with which they turn up, these affirmations sound forced and uneasy. His monologues are characterised by a high degree of self-monitoring because his intention is to convince his imaginary addressee--that is, his mother--that he is leading a totally happy and fulfilled life.

The climax of this development--some time passes between the individual monologues--is reached when he finally claims in a very emotional speech that he has found a new family and a new home: "Oh mother, I have found my home, my family. Little did I ever dream I could know such happiness" (77).

After his encounter with Mr. Withers ("Mother, mother, I've had the most unpleasant, the most mystifying encounter, with the man who calls himself Mr. Withers . . . " 77) and with Riley ("And who is Riley?" 80) at the latest he begins to have some doubts. Even if he still says: "But if you find me bewildered, anxious, confused, uncertain and afraid, you also find me content. My life possesses shape. The house has a very warm atmosphere . . . " (80), his assertions turn out to be desperate attempts at convincing his mother and himself of their truth. In reality, just the opposite is the case. He has to admit this at the end, when he declares his intention to return home, thus accepting defeat:

> I'm coming back to you, mother, to hold you in my arms. (82)
>
> I am coming home. (82)
>
> I am on my way back to you. I am about to make the journey back to you. What will you say to me? (83)

Although the son is still self-monitoring his utterances at this point, because he is not completely open and honest but is hiding his doubts with regard to his possible return, he can no longer maintain his initial pose of independence and contentment. He also implicitly acknowledges his emotional needs. Whether he will actually return home, however, remains completely open.

The character of the mother develops in the opposite direction. At the beginning, she admits her need for love and attention. Her questions directed to the son-- "Darling. Where are you? . . . Why do you never write?" "Do you ever think of me?" "Have you made friends with anyone?" (69)--show that she misses him and wants him near her. Her letters (which are never written) inform us that her husband has died, and that she is alone in the house. Her monologues create the impression of total loneliness and isolation, of life lived in a kind of "no man's land," which reminds one of Deborah's "Alaska":

> I hear your father's step on the stair. I hear his cough. But his step and his cough fade. He does not open the door.
> Sometimes I think I have always been sitting like this. I sometimes think I have always been sitting like this, alone by an indifferent fire, curtains closed, night, winter.
> You see, I have my thoughts too. Thoughts no-one else knows I have, thoughts none of my family ever knew I had. But I write of them to you now, wherever you are. (76)

Out of the loneliness and senselessness of her life grow frustrations, which by and by come to the surface and give her monologues a different tone. At the end of the play, she even shows her hatred towards her son openly, although she is still asking him to come home. It becomes clear that her feelings toward him are ambivalent, and that the longing for him which she expressed at the beginning was only part of the truth. As she emphasises at the end, she has even put the police on his track: "You will be found, my boy, and no mercy will be shown to you" (82). With her last words in the play, she breaks with him completely: "I'll tell you what, my darling, I've given you up as a very bad job. Tell me one last thing. Do you think the word love means anything?" (82). The voice of the father, which comes out of the grave, makes itself heard towards the end of the play. His "ghostly" appearance underlines that *Family Voices* is not a realistic representation of an empirical reality, but that Pinter is interested in the secret inner life and the psychology of his characters, forming a drama out of imaginary wishes and thoughts that are never spoken and do not reach their addressee.

Psychologically speaking, Pinter's procedure takes account of the fact that somebody's inner thoughts and feelings do not necessarily correspond to what he or she actually says, that important things remain unsaid because courage is lacking, and that the intention to tell them to somebody is realised too late, or never at all, as is the case with the father.

Although the mother claims that, on his deathbed, the father has condemned the son, the father still sends "Lots of love" (81) from the grave and tries to give him courage for his future life. One cannot say with certainty how serious he is, and whether he has changed his mind about his son. But even if he is serious, the son will never know what his father had to say. The chance to improve their relationship has gone forever. Only the listening audience gets an insight into the thoughts of the dead father and can realise that he wanted to say so many things to his son. The image of the father who addresses his son *post mortem* from the grave effectively emphasises the actual isolation of the characters and the silence that surrounds them.

All in all, the father is a less important character in the context of the play, whereas the relation between the mother and son is the play's focal point. If the changing positions of mother and son are related to each other, there is something like a dramatic development, which is chiastic in structure. Whereas the son at the beginning emphasises his satisfaction with the situation and pretends to be thrilled with his new family, he grows increasingly uneasy in the future course of the play, and finally admits his desire to return home. His development is therefore characterised by the fact that in his thoughts he is drawing ever nearer to his mother. The development of the latter, however, points in exactly the opposite direction. Whereas she admits at the beginning that she is missing her son, thereby showing her emotional dependency, anger and frustration break out at the end. The irony of this double development, therefore, lies in the fact that the mother is rejecting her son exactly at the moment when he is trying to draw closer to her. The characters themselves are not aware of this process, for their letters are never written or sent, or the partners do not hear the words addressed to them in their imagination. In contrast to the characters, the audience is in a privileged position, for it is informed about both characters and can relate their development to each other. Therefore, the conclusion has to be drawn that the actual drama takes place in the minds of the audience. Seen from their point of view, the dramatic character of the mental and emotional processes is created by the fact that for a moment there seems to be a chance of a satisfactory communication between mother and son, which is then given away. Pinter's *Family Voices* is a drama of the mind in a double sense of the phrase. On the one hand, the form Pinter has chosen for his play allows him to elucidate mental processes which take place in the imagination of the characters and make them visible and audible. On the other hand, the dramatic process is transposed into the minds of the audience, for here the mental and emotional development of the isolated characters can be related to each other, and the above mentioned chiastic, dramatic structure evolves. All in all, this is a new and innovative form of drama for Pinter, since plays like *Landscape* and *Silence*, which resemble *Family Voices* in many respects, are still comparatively lyrical and static. In *Family Voices*, therefore, Pinter succeeds in creating a form of dramatic monologue that is suitable to both the basically lyrical character of the theme of isolation and the genre of drama which relies on action and interaction as its most important constituents.

Conclusion

It is certainly not easy to describe the development that Pinter has gone through over the past ten years,[14] but, in my opinion, there are two clear trends that can be recognised. As Pinter's critics have observed, *Betrayal* (1979) was an uncommon play for him insofar as he no longer employed the techniques of mystification that were characteristic of his previous plays.[15] The alienation of reality is achieved not by a deficit of information on the part of the audience, but by a surplus of information in comparison to the characters on stage. This is effected by a reversal of chronology. Pinter begins with a portrayal of the present, then blends back into the past. Whereas the characters are of course blind to what the future has in store for them, the audience knows where it will end. This is a kind of parallel to *A Kind of Alaska* and to *Family Voices*. Here too the audience knows how the characters are doing, whereas the latter lack this information. The first effect which is achieved by this distribution of information is that the action on the stage appears less mysterious, more probable and therefore more "realistic" than that of Pinter's earlier plays. Secondly--and this applies to both *Betrayal* and *Family Voices*--the actual drama takes place in the minds of the audience, so that there is a shift of focus from the mimetic towards the receptional pole of Pinter's dramaturgy.

The other trend concerns the relation between fictional and empirical reality. Pinter's *The Hothouse* (1980) must be mentioned in this connection. *The Hothouse* was actually written as early as 1958, but then put aside. It was first staged more or less unchanged in 1980. Pinter himself has explained the late date of publication by pointing out that, in 1980, the play appeared much more modern than in 1958, when we didn't know anything about the Russian psychiatric hospitals, did we? Now we do. But then, it might have been dismissed as fantasy. No, I certainly had no special knowledge of such things. Of course I knew Koestler's *Darkness at Noon* and so on, but in 1958 I don't think there was general knowledge that these things were being refined, as they are to this day. Not that I consider this play to be a grim piece of work, I don't think it is. An odd mixture of "laughter and chill" if you like.[16]

In the light of those revelations Pinter is talking about, *The Hothouse*, which in 1958 might have been read as a fantastic satire on society, becomes disconcertingly realistic. Pinter shows himself especially satisfied about the fact that the disclosed political reality *a posteriori* confirms the fictional reality of his play, or, to put it the other way round, that the fictional reality of *The Hothouse* had always been more than a mere invention, and what at first seemed to be a fantastic creation of the brain existed in reality.

If this is conceded, an interesting parallel between *The Hothouse* and *A Kind of Alaska* can be discovered. In Oliver Sacks's *Awakenings* Pinter found the "objective correlative" for the fictional "kind of Alaska" which already plays an important role in plays like *Old Times* (1971) and *No Man's Land* (1975). Although reality in *A Kind of Alaska* still seems strange, mysterious and even a bit absurd, this impression is not created by a willful alienation of reality but rather, paradoxically, by its imitation. Basically, Pinter's dramaturgy in *A Kind of Alaska* is still founded on a kind of realism that is characteristic of some of his earlier plays, for example, *The Caretaker* or *The Homecoming*. That this realism did not exclude interesting innovative experiments and could be developed, Pinter has shown in his later plays.

NOTES

1. All quotations are based on the Methuen paperback edition (London, 1982), to which the page numbers in parentheses in the text also refer.

2. Harmondsworth, 1976.

3. *Ibid.*, p. 110.

4. *Ibid.*, p. 24.

5. About this motif compare, among others, Rüdiger Imhof, *Harold Pinters Dramentechnik. Gestalterische Mittel im Kontext des Gesamtwerks*, p. 19 and *passim*; Ewald Mengel, *Harold Pinters Dramen im Spiegel der soziologischen Rollentheorie* (Frankfurt, 1978), 36ff.

6. This is overlooked by Fenton and Barber in their reviews. See James Fenton, "The Miniature Masterpiece of Harold Pinter," *The Sunday Times*, October 17, 1982; John Barber, "The Disturbing Pinter," *The Daily Telegraph*, October 15, 1982.

7. But see also my observations on Pinter's development as a dramatist in the conclusion of this article.

8. On the first night of *Other Places* in the National Theatre, however, *Family Voices* came first, whereas *A Kind of Alaska* concluded Pinter's trilogy.

9. Katherine H. Burkman, "*Family Voices* and the Voices of the Family in Pinter's Plays," in *Harold Pinter: Critical Approaches*, ed. Steven H. Gale (London: 1985), 164-170, here 164.

10.   About this and other Pinter monologues in general see Paul Goetsch, "Die Tendenz zum Monologischen im modernen Drama: Beckett und Pinter," in *Das Hörspiel im Englischunterricht*, ed. Horst Groene (Padenborn, 1980), 73-98.

11.   About the concept of self-monitoring, see Mark Snyder, "Cognitive, Behavioral, and Interpersonal Consequences of Self-Monitoring," in *Perceptions of Emotion in Self and Others* [Advances in the Study of Communication and Affect, 5] (New York/London, 1979), 181-201.

12.   Daniel Salem, "The Impact of Pinter's Work," *Ariel*, 17 (1986), 71-83.

13.   In this respect, Pinter's *Family Voices* is also reminiscent of the early play *The Room*.

14.   This is emphasised by Joachim Möller, "Neueres zu Harold Pinter (1975-85): Kritik als Kaleidoskop," *LWU*, 19 (1986), 142-155, here 155.

15.   About *Betrayal* see also Ewald Mengel, "Unterschiedliche Formen der Bewußtseinsdiskrepanz und ihre dramatische Funktion in Harold Pinters *Betrayal*," *GRM*, 32 (1982), 333-44.

16.   Quoted by Arnold Hinchliffe, "After *No Man's Land*: A Progress Report," in *Harold Pinter*, ed. S. Gale, 153-163, here 157.

"TO LAY BARE": PINTER, SHAKESPEARE, AND *THE DWARFS*

Francis Gillen

In one chapter in the last third of Harold Pinter's unpublished novel, *The Dwarfs*, Pete and Mark, two of the three male characters whose friendship is detailed in this work, are sitting in a bar discussing Shakespeare. That such a conversation might take place in a novel written by a young Pinter is not surprising, for he began writing the novel in 1950, working on it sporadically for about six years, before leaving it uncompleted and then, in 1960, turning a small part of it into the play *The Dwarfs*. During those years he toured Ireland (1951-52), playing Shakespeare in the company of the great Shakespearean Anew McMaster before performing, from 1953-57, in the touring provincial company of another great Shakespearean Sir Donald Wolfit.[1] What is of interest is the way the discussion of Shakespeare provides some noteworthy parallels with the plays Pinter was to write, and it is those parallels and the light they shed on Pinter's own work that I intend to explore. I do not wish to suggest that Pinter consciously set out to write with a Shakespearean or any other kind of model, nor that Pinter's plays may be "explained" by looking at the parallels. What a reading of both the chapter and some of the plays does suggest, however, is that in discussing Shakespeare, Pinter's novelistic characters use terms similar to those which both Pinter and his critics have used in describing the playwright's own work. When Pete says of Othello, Macbeth, and Lear, for example, that "the trouble with

189

these people is that they refuse to recognize their own territorial limitations,"² one cannot help thinking of Pinter's rooms and territorial battles that take place in them. Therefore, while I do not propose these parallels as in any sense providing a full reading of what occurs in Pinter's plays, I believe they offer the possibility of significant new insight. The discussion of Shakespeare begins with both Mark and Pete expressing their dismay over those who would pin onto Shakespeare's plays easy moral tags which support their own view of the world. They would, Mark argues in words that echo in *The Hothouse*, "give him a name and number."

On the contrary, they argue, Shakespeare's admiration and sympathy are not so much attracted by what is seen as good or evil in a narrow, socially moral sense-- what they call "garden" morality--as by that which is outside of ordinary morality and which creates demands outside of its considerations. To quote from the novel:

> . . . Mark said, I mean, look what he does. Look at the way he behaves. He never uses a communication cord or a life belt, and what's more, never infers he's got one handy for your use or his. No.
> How can moral judgments be applied when you consider how many directions he travels at once? Hasn't he got enough troubles? Look at what he gets up to. He meets himself coming back, he sinks in at the knees, forgets the drift, runs away with himself, falls back on geometry, turns down blind alleys, stews in his own juice, and he nearly always ends up by losing all hands. But the fabric, mate, never breaks. The tightrope is never at less than an even stretch. He keeps in business, that's what. And if he started making moral judgments he'd go bankrupt like the others.
> -- The point about Shakespeare, Pete said, thumping the table, is that he didn't measure the

man against the idea and give you hot tips on the outcome.
-- He wasn't a betting man.
-- He laid bare, that's all. I defy any man who said he saw good and evil as abstractions. He didn't.

The frequency with which Harold Pinter has insisted that his own plays do not "measure the man against the idea" suggests that his thinking about Shakespeare may have in some way helped shape his conception of characters in his own plays. "I've never started a play from any kind of abstract idea or theory and never envisaged my own characters as messengers of death, doom, heaven or the milky way or, in other words, as allegorical representations of any particular force, whatever that may mean," he told an audience at the National Student Drama Festival in Bristol in 1962. "We don't carry labels on our chests, and even though they are continually fixed to us by others, they convince nobody" (*Plays: One* 10-11). Similarly, when he was awarded the 1970 German Shakespeare Prize, he again expressed his distrust of theory and lack of concern with general statements. "When a writer sets out a blueprint for his characters, and keeps them rigidly to it, where they do not at any time upset his applecart, where he has mastered them, he has also killed them, or rather terminated their birth, and he has a dead play on his hands" (*Plays: Four* xii). As he had Pete and Mark say of Shakespeare, he would allow his characters autonomy and would simply "lay bare."

In neither the discussion of Shakespeare in the novel, nor Pinter's own plays, however, does such autonomy preclude the observance, after the fact, of discernable patterns in the created work. If we take the four Shakespeare plays Pete and Mark discuss, we note patterns which are similar to Pinter's early plays:

1.   All the tragic heroes must deal with ambiguous signs whose objective veracity is beyond verification: Hamlet with the reality of his father's ghost;

Macbeth with the witches' portents and predictions; Othello with the evidence Iago presents him of Desdemona's infidelity; Lear with his daughters' statements and promises.
2. Each acts upon what is essentially a private vision, an individual reading of the signs not in accord with what the novel calls "garden" or "social" morality. Hamlet takes justice upon himself; Macbeth begins the slaughter to attain and then preserve the throne; Othello executes Desdemona; Lear gives his land to Goneril and Regan and disinherits Cordelia. As Pinter writes in the novel:

> The trouble with these people is that they refuse to recognize their own territorial limitations. Their feelings are in excess of the facts. All they're doing is living beyond their means. And when they have to act, not upon their notions but upon their beliefs, they are found to be lacking.

3. When forced to account for their actions, they are inarticulate. Pete argues:

> The necessity of action smothers their virtue. They cease to be morally-thinking creatures. Lear, Macbeth, and Othello are all forced, in one way or another, to account for what they do and they all fail to do it. Lear and Macbeth don't even attempt to.

4. While their private misreading of the signs and their own passionate intensity gave them what they believed was the ability to act as they did, they remained at the same time a part of an objective order which ultimately calls them into account. The novel reads:

> Their unique qualities gave them, if you like, the power of dispensation over others. So they thought. . . . Where these geezers slip is that they try to overcome a machine of which they remain, whether they like it or not, a part.

This pattern, discussed in the novel in terms of Shakespeare's plays, is likewise apparent in Pinter's three early, full-length plays, *The Birthday Party, The Caretaker,* and *The Homecoming.* Before discussing them, however, let me make one important distinction. The orders with which Pinter's characters collide are obviously not Shakespeare's world order; they are personal, orders which may or may not even be real. This is part of both the humor and terror of Pinter's plays, their particular tragicomic nature which Bernard Dukore has described so well in *Where Laughter Stops: Pinter's Tragicomedy.* But they are, nonetheless, within this contemporary context, no less destructive.

In *The Birthday Party* it is at least in part Stanley's easy victories over Meg which cause him to misjudge his own strength in dealing with Goldberg and McCann and to misread the signs of their intentions. In other words, he does not, in the language Pete and Mark use of Shakespeare's characters, recognize his own territorial limitations. Within that safe territory, he teases Meg about the cereal, complains about the tea and the pigsty-like condition of the home in which he has been a guest, easily embarrasses Meg with words like "succulent," and brutally threatens her with the idea that the men she mentions as coming to her house are bringing with them a wheelbarrow to cart her away. No wonder then that his initial response to Goldberg and McCann reflects to some extent a false bravado. It is Stanley who initiates the questioning of McCann, using language almost as circuitous as that which Goldberg will later use:

> I've got a small private income, you see. I think I'll give it up. Don't like being away from home. I used to live very quietly--played records, that's about all. Everything delivered to the door. Then I started a little private business, in a small way, and it compelled me to come down here--kept me longer than I expected. You never get used to living in someone else's house. Don't you agree? I

lived so quietly. You can only appreciate what
you've had when things change. That's what they
say isn't it? Cigarette? (50)

It is also he who threatens Goldberg:

You don't bother me. To me, you're nothing but a
dirty joke. But I have a responsibility toward the
people in this house. They've been down here too
long. They've lost their sense of smell. I haven't.
And nobody's going to take advantage of them
while I'm here. (55)

He refuses to sit when told, instead tricks McCann into
sitting, and after the questioning which is often referred to
as breaking him, he kicks Goldberg in the stomach.
Accustomed to being superior in both language and force,
he does not yet realize he has moved into a new game and
to a new territory in which, as the rest of the play
demonstrates, Goldberg and McCann provide superior
versions of his verbal agility and force. If, at the pivotal
moment of the play McCann takes away Stanley's glasses,
there is also a sense in which Stanley has quite deliberately,
in his *hubris*, blinded himself.

Such *hubris* caused by early victories is also present
in Pinter's most Shakespearean play, *The Caretaker*. Here
the tramp Davies, outcast and desperately in need of
shelter, has difficulty reading the signs and promises of the
two brothers Aston and Mick, both of whom appear to offer
him a permanent position as caretaker on quite differing
terms. The flashy Mick bombards him with an outpouring
of duties, promises and potentialities for the house; Aston
treats him kindly but tells him almost nothing. Ultimately
feeling superior to Aston when Aston confides that he has
undergone shock treatment at a mental institution,
believing Mick's promises, and failing to realize the
continuing bond between the two brothers, he denounces
Aston to Mick, declaring that "He's no friend of mine. You
don't know where you are with him. I mean, with a bloke

like you, you know where you are" (*Plays: Two* 70).
Misreading Mick as "straightforward" (70), he rejects
Aston's simple request to keep open a window in the room
they share so that Aston will not be bothered by Davies'
stink, and he turns on his benefactor,

> I've seen better days than you have man. Nobody
> ever got me inside one of them places, anyway. I'm
> a sane man. . . .[3] Just you keep your place, that's
> all. Because I can tell you, your brother's got his
> eye on you. He knows all about you. I got a friend
> there, don't you worry about that. I got a true pal
> there. (76)

Rejected by Mick when he presses what he mistakenly read
as friendship, Davies attempts to return, almost on any
terms, to Aston, but he clearly has lost his place.

The terms used to discuss Shakespeare's world in
The Dwarfs would also apply to a number of characters and
situations in *The Homecoming*. Teddy, the philosopher
who is at ease in those abstractions which deny the whole
physical side of his nature, returns home believing in his
superiority to the milieu he has left. "There's no point in
my sending you my works," he tells his family, "You'd be
lost. . . . I'm the one who can see. . . . You're just objects"
(*Plays: Three* 78). What he fails to understand is that he
remains part of that family, that he cannot be separated
from the physical side of the world, and this is most clearly
demonstrated when he accepts the family's conditions for
keeping and maintaining Ruth as a working whore and
even agrees to be their American representative. His
family--Max the butcher, Lenny the pimp, and Joey the
boxer--feel secure in the absolutely masculine world they
have created, one in which they have either appropriated or
excluded the feminine, the *anima*. They grow confident
because of what appear easy victories over Teddy and
Ruth--and so do not realize that the Ruth they have taken
into the house, on what they believe to be their terms, may

well be the mysterious *anima* they have excluded, the one who will dictate terms to them.

The three early full-length plays I have discussed by no means exhaust the possible or useful parallels with the discussion of Shakespeare in *The Dwarfs*. Gus in *The Dumb Waiter*, Bill in *The Collection*, and Disson in *Tea Party* are all clearly operating beyond their territorial limits. While Gus seems least responsible for his fate, Bill chooses to ignore his real position as part of Harry's collection, and the exclusivity of friendship as Harry sees it, and there is an element of *hubris* in Disson's assumption that all reality, including the relationship between a brother and sister, may be reduced to the physical world of bidets and touching which he understands. Because both Deeley and Anna in *Old Times* assume an untested superiority of Kate, they regard as equally superior their versions of the past, until both founder against Kate's unmovable will to see all their stories dead. Somewhat like Davies, the vagrant Spooner in *No Man's Land* relies on what he believes to be his unlimited ability to "do any graph of experience you wish, to suit your taste or mine" (*Plays: Four* 82). His pride in his verbal agility blinds him, however, to the power of the preexisting arrangement between Hirst and Foster and Briggs, as well as Hirst's alcohol-induced amnesia and his host's reluctance to admit no other but his own comforting grasp of a past which seems a final hold on reality. Similarly in some ways *Betrayal* might almost be described as a contemporary, non-tragic *Othello*, in which Jerry's blindly false assumptions of a inviolable friendship with an "honest" Robert prove to be a false basis for his actions and assumptions.

None of this provides any radically new reading of any of the plays, nor is it my intention to do so. It does provide, however, the possibility for seeing not only a possible source, but greater depth, more interiority in the characters. Because of the theatrical and intellectual climate at the time they were first produced, Pinter's early plays were frequently brought together under the rubric of comedies of menace, emphasizing some outside threat, or a wholly irrational, incomprehensible world. While I certainly do not mean to deny an outside threat or the presence of absurdity in the plays I have discussed, the parallels with Pinter's own discussion of Shakespeare help balance this emphasis on the external. The characters in these Pinter plays are at least to some extent responsible for their own fates. Deluded by false evidence of their own invincibility, they act, like Shakespeare's tragic heroes, with some degree of *hubris* upon what is essentially a private vision which is no longer justified by the facts of the situation. Goldberg and McCann are no easy foes like Meg; Davies has no genuine relationship with Mick that affords him a position to be superior to Aston; Teddy is not superior to his family, merely fragmented in a different way; the easy victories of the other members of that family may, but probably do not, prefigure future victories. Moreover, since they are acting upon illusion, when called upon to justify their acts, they have no basis, and that lack of basis may be one of the roots of Pinter's silences. Except for his incomprehensible scream, Stanley is silent in the third act of *The Birthday Party* and Davies' pathetic, nervous talk at the conclusion of *The Caretaker* embodies that other kind of silence which Pinter describes as talk which covers nakedness. Finally, all do remain part of the machines, the orders, which their subjective visions would deny: Stanley of the victory of greater force and cleverness; Davies and Teddy of family bonds they would not see or would deny; Max, Lenny, and Joey of a world that contains the *anima* as well as the *animus* they previously regarded as solely triumphant in their home.[4]

Similarly the parallels with Shakespeare help balance our conception of the theatricality of Pinter's characters and their language. Pinter's characters are undoubtedly creating themselves as they go along, and their language is most often non-referential as Austin Quigley has demonstrated convincingly in *The Pinter Problem*.[5] But they are not, on the other hand, infinitely or unlimitedly theatrical. They do remain parts of a machine, a reality which is finally less malleable than their early linguistic manipulations would suggest. Some of the most telling moments in Pinter's plays occur when language collides with what it can no longer shape nor change: when Stanley knows he cannot manipulate Goldberg and McCann; when Davies encounters Aston's final, stolid silence ("Aston remains still, his back to him, at the window" 87); when Teddy speaks not as the philosopher, but as a member of the family unit, a physical reality his abstractions may ignore but not escape.

Though the young Pinter may not have realized it, the analysis of Shakespeare in the novel may well have provided one pattern for the plays in which he, like Shakespeare, would lay bare a much more tattered, but none the less significant, humankind.

NOTES

1. This part of Pinter's life is described in detail in the early chapters of *Pinter: The Player's Playwright* by David T. Thompson. While Thompson provides possible sources for some of the techniques of Pinter's plays, there is surprisingly little overview of any Shakespearean influence.

2. I am quoting here from the notes I took while reading the unpublished manuscript of *The Dwarfs*. All subsequent quotations from the unpublished novel are from this source. I am grateful to Harold Pinter for allowing me access to the manuscript.

3. Since Pinter frequently uses three dots in the dialogue he writes, I have followed here and elsewhere in the essay the practice now used by many who write on Pinter of using four dots to indicate my own ellipses.

4. Among "the machines" of which Pinter's characters remain an unchanging part and with which they therefore collide are: the physical world which they as academicians ignore (Teddy; Edward in *A Slight Ache*); family (*The Caretaker, The Homecoming, Tea Party*); organizational orders either real or perceived (*The Birthday Party, The Dumb Waiter, The Hothouse*); friendship (*The Collection, Old Times, Betrayal*); and the *anima* (*A Slight Ache, Tea Party, The Homecoming, Old Times*).

5. Quigley writes: "The point to be grasped about the verbal activity in a Pinter play is that language is not so much a means of referring to structure in personal relationships as a means of creating it" (66).

WORKS CITED

Dukore, Bernard F. *Where Laughter Stops: Pinter's Tragicomedy*. Columbia and London: University of Missouri Press, 1976.

Pinter, Harold. *Plays: One*. London: Eyre Methuen, 1976.

———. *Plays: Two*. London: Eyre Methuen, 1977.

———. *Plays: Three*. London: Eyre Methuen, 1978.

———. *Plays: Four*. London: Eyre Methuen, 1981.

Quigley, Austin E. *The Pinter Problem*. Princeton and London: Princeton University Press, 1975.

Thompson, David T. *Pinter: The Player's Playwright*. New York: Schocken, 1985.

MIND-LESS MEN:
PINTER'S DUMB WAITERS

Robert Gordon

It is the underlying assumption of all traditional literary criticism--and all traditional literature--that characters are *really like* something. Characters have characteristics, for one, and our job as interpreters is to ferret out essences. We ask of Hamlet (and Hamlet of himself): is he an embittered humanist who cannot act justly in an unjust world; a spineless, overgrown pube who is afraid to die; a psychotic whose thoughts and actions are incoherent and irrational; a little boy paralyzed by oedipal attraction to his mother; or is he all of these, or none, or something else? We debate the question, quote act and scene, cite what we can of Shakespeare's experience, put the play in historical perspective, and quite possibly, engage vitriol in our exchanges. Thus we plumb the depths of Hamlet's character. Somewhere in there, in the great masses of data we collect and analyze like unknown alloys, Hamlet *is*. His essence is theoretically attainable, and the questions we ask about him are soluble.

As democrats, we may say that "there is no right answer." We do not doubt, however, that we ask the right question. We attribute Hamlet's ambiguity to his depth and complexity as a character, and ultimately say that Shakespeare's hero is "for the ages" and therefore sensibly complex and open to shifting interpretation. But even if we admit that Hamlet circa 1600 was entirely different from Bergman's Hamlet, we still say that in either case, the Hamlet being depicted *was* a certain way. Hamlet's essence may be newly defined tomorrow, and then Hamlet tomorrow will have a new essence. Essence he will have.

How exactly we define that basic self is a different issue.[1] (People have been arguing it for two millennia.) At the advent of philosophy, the Greeks spoke of soma and psyche: body and soul. Soma became carrion for vultures and worms to devour, but psyche continued. The psyche was what people were all about. Christians adopted the dichotomy when they preached the salvation of the soul: what mattered in the next world was not how pretty you were or how much money you had, but the state of your innermost self--whether you were at heart, really and truly, a good person or a bad one. We have had a fixation on the soul ever since.

Christians conceived of the soul in necessarily unscientific terms: they made a leap of faith to believe that some inner part of man was more important than all the money in the world. It was Descartes who recast man's dualism in the "scientific" terms which most of us heedlessly accept today. The body and mind are separate, he said: the body is physical and external, the mind "mental" and internal. My mind constitutes my true self: my essence and soul, perhaps. But only I can know my mind: it is a "windowless chamber" to which I have "privileged access." This chamber is my consciousness, and in it are my moral values, as it were: the things I really believe. ("One should not tell a lie: I love Jane; the Democratic Party acts in the best interests of the United States.") The contents of this inner self constitute my consciousness, and this is my essence. It is essentially mind and mine alone.

Hamlet's essence is that windowless chamber. Our quest as interpreters is to discern its contents; so much is in it, after all: feelings, preferences, pangs, detestations, yearnings, desires, fears, hopes, ideals, values, beliefs. When we analyze a character, we are guessing what he is "really thinking" in that little room, his consciousness. *That* is what *it* is all about.

In the postmodern manner, Pinter dumps most of this. His "absurdist" theater rejects traditional principles of soul and person. Pinter's exaggeration and, as it were, absurdism, place this rejection in bold relief.

Shakespeare's Hamlet always appears in some sort of costume. Clothes express the man, one tends to say, and when the man has substance, his clothes should as well. So too a realist like Ibsen dresses his characters meticulously. In Pinter's *The Dumb Waiter*, Gus and Ben wear "shirts, trousers and braces." Their clothes express only their sameness with any imagined "average businessman" and with each other. They are businessmen, and their general formality means that they're down to business, and nothing more. In their appearance, Gus and Ben reveal neither individuality nor conviction or style--a hint of their behavior in the rest of the play.

"KAW!" Ben begins. Is it Moral Outrage? "A man of eighty-seven wanted to cross the road. But there was a lot of traffic, see? He couldn't see how he was going to squeeze through. So he crawled under a lorry. . . . The lorry started and ran over him."

BEN:	It's enough to make you want to puke, isn't it?
GUS:	Who advised him to do a thing like that?
BEN:	A man of eighty-seven crawling under a lorry?
GUS:	It's unbelievable.
BEN:	It's down here in black and white.
GUS:	Incredible.

Perhaps there was an earthquake that day, or a war began or ended. Perhaps Ben's mother died. Certainly, there was some other "more notable" horror elsewhere in Ben's newspaper. But Ben was outraged by this one. He has no special affinity for eighty-seven-year-olds, one assumes; it happened to occur to him to be outraged by this event. His eyes passed over the page, probably, and happened to stop where they did--perhaps because a bit of dust, swept up when Gus walked in, dropped under Ben's eyelid. Then he was angered, perhaps because he remembered having almost been hit by a lorry once, or because an eighty-two-year-old had struck his eye on the bus, or because his head had been turned right instead of left because he had twisted his neck last week mowing the lawn.

To be fair, Gus is upset by the story, too, but only because Ben is. Gus owes it to Ben to remain interested in what he says. An inkling of his sensibility comes in his question: "Who advised him to do a thing like that?" Gus has engaged a vital guiding principle: that people do things because they are told.

Such is moral horror in the (post-) modern world, and so with pleasure. Gus fixates on the crockery, going on and on about it--he's "quite taken with the crockery." He is not an expert in porcelain; it just happens to catch his eye. So he rambles on about it, enjoying it, maybe.

In short, Gus and Ben have no long-standing, deeply felt commitments to anything. They believe nothing in particular. They take pleasure in nothing in particular. Or:

> BEN: You know what your trouble is?
> GUS: What?
> BEN: You haven't got any interests. . . . I've got my woodwork. I've got my model boats. Have you ever seen me idle? I'm never idle. I know how to occupy my time.

The nature of pleasure is occupying time with whatever's around. Woodwork and model boats do not reflect any real beliefs or genuine desires: interests are like the pacifiers which angry mothers stick in little babies' mouths. One doubts that infants really prefer the pacifiers to crying anyway.

Only in this apparently senseless sensibility can *The Dumb Waiter* be understood. Pinter has banished the morally aware mind from his characters; Gus and Ben are extreme realizations of Gilbert Ryle's man, as he defines them in a book like *The Concept of Mind*.2   To aim to understand these two as Plato and Hamlet sought to know themselves would be absurd, for Gus and Ben have neither inscribed nor had inscribed any commandments within any windowless chambers in their heads. They neither seek to obey nor do obey any coherent ethical principles or emotional attachments.   Gus and Ben seem more like animals to us who revere the ghosts in our machines. But to those for whom Hamlet's and our introspection is a moronic effort to find a mythical mind, Gus and Ben are the first honest men.

In fact, Gus and Ben are post-ghost, or so they are supposed to be. Ben certainly is, as we shall see. Without the moral values and coherent desires which we proudly ascribe to ourselves, Ben aims to please others. He feels shame when he doesn't and joy when he does. His moral existence is outside him: in the room and the people up the dumb waiter. He fulfills or fails himself exactly to the degree that he satisfies the requirements of his world. This gives him exactly the sensibility which anthropologists ascribe to pre-literate man, and which people like Ryle seek to prove is quite close to our own. If we look at Ben as a sort of "true man," then his behavior and his conflict with Gus will make perfect sense.

Gus and Ben are hit men.   They are waiting to receive orders from a mythical Wilson about whom to hit. As they wait, they become increasingly nervous and fearful. They need something to do, something to occupy themselves. Without that, they are left to contemplate themselves and their worlds. Shakespeare had a lot in mind in both these areas of human activity, but Pinter has very little. So Gus and Ben become more nervous. Their room has no window. It is dark. Their world has no window. It is dark, too. Ben and Gus are stuck with each other and their task, and that's it.

It occurs to Gus to remember an event earlier that day--when Ben had stopped the car and waited "for something" before entering the hideout hotel room. Like Vladimir and Estragon, Ben and Gus are always waiting. Godot may never come for Beckett's men, but the things for which Ben and Gus wait do arrive--and that's part of the problem. At any rate, Gus ascertains: "You mean someone had to get out before we got in? [He examines the bedclothes.] I thought these sheets didn't look too bright. I thought they ponged a bit."

The getting in and out and the turn to the sheets raise two interrelated issues: sex and word play. Through punning, murder comes to substitute for sex and prostitution--they get in and money for it. This motif repeats later when Gus comments on the girls he's killed: "They don't seem to hold together like men, women. A looser texture, like. Didn't she spread, eh?" Ben, the more mature man, is always polishing his revolver and tells Gus to do the same; he rubs it on the sheets, which pong, whatever that means.

All this implies that murdering has replaced real sex and passion for these men, that they've become metaphorical whores and vicarious masturbators. They are capable of vague homosexuality, as when Ben puts his mouth to the speaking tube toward the end of the play, but mainly, the play is devoid of real sexual (or any other sort of) passion, and punning here and there has replaced it.

The kind of societal criticism which Pinter may or may not be implying is really standard romantic fare. Indeed, through much of *The Dumb Waiter*, it is Pinter's medium and not his message which so radically differs from tradition. He often criticizes aspects of our lives which romantics have already thoroughly assaulted.

An example of Pinter's marvelous use of words comes early:

GUS:	Have you noticed the time that tank takes to fill?

BEN:	What tank?

> GUS: In the lavatory.
> BEN: No does it? . . .
> GUS: What do you think's the matter with it?
> BEN: Nothing.
> GUS: Nothing?
> BEN: It's got a deficient ballcock, that's all.
> GUS: A deficient what?
> BEN: Ballcock.
> GUS: No, really?
> BEN: That's what I should say.
> GUS: Go on! That didn't occur to me.
> *[Gus wanders to his bed and presses the mattress.]*

Gus, the kid who doesn't even polish his revolver, also doesn't know what is wrong with the toilet. The toilet is a metaphor for Gus's sexual development. It doesn't flush until the end, just before Gus and Ben are going to make the hit. The murder/sex theme climaxes, particularly interestingly since the hit seems to be on Gus. Ben "adjusts his jacket to diminish the bulge of the revolver. The lavatory flushes off left." As Gus emerges stripped and about to be shot, he seems to have attained the maturity he lacked throughout the rest of the play because he flushed the toilet. Hence the tragic aspect of Ben's still having to shoot Gus.

"Ballcock" tips off the toilet-sex metaphor. This word alone underlies an entire metaphor, motif, theme, and plot. Pinter may not have meant for it to do so, but in the play he's written, he provides powerful examples of the vast power of words to mold the post-modern reality. Witness:

> GUS: Light what?
> BEN: The kettle.
> GUS: You mean the gas.
> BEN: Who does?
> GUS: You do.

BEN: *[his eyes narrowing]* What do you mean, I mean the gas?

GUS   Well, that's what you mean, don't you. The gas.

BEN: *[powerfully]* If I say go and light the kettle I mean go and light the kettle.

GUS: How can you light a kettle?

BEN: It's a figure of speech! . . . .

The episode ends with "Ben: *[grabbing him with two hands by the throat, at arm's length]* 'THE KETTLE, YOU FOOL'"

If we view Pinter as a moralist, then his word play says that nothing really matters, or that Gus and Ben can find nothing that really matters, so instead they've been reduced to arguing about trivial matters in order to salvage some sense of purpose and caring. This is what the modern world reduces us to.

But Pinter is saying more: this is what the modern world *is*. It's all about words. Walter Ong argues that the invention of writing caused a fundamental alienation of man from reality because words ceased to be immediately participatory.[3] For an illiterate, there can't be any words without the *act* of speaking, whereas a modern's writing presents words where speech and activity are absent. In short, words have moved out there; they are no longer always a part of what we're doing anymore. The Homeric Greeks had epithets which strung together adjectives and nouns into a descriptive whole--like, say, "rose-fingered dawn." Pinter's characters and we no longer have the luxury of finding "put" and "kettle" or "light" and "gas" invariably stuck together, because since people have been writing, we've been able to break words up and stick them back together again as we please.

It is therefore understandable that Ben and Gus fixate on word choice: it is perhaps a symptom of their grappling with reality. Couple this with the way in which language influences our view of reality[4]: that is, the way our choice of words not only reflects but in turn influences our view of a situation. Pinter titles the play *The Dumb Waiter.* Is that the box that brings messages from above? Or is it Gus, who's going to get hit? Is it even Ben, who's scurrying around serving people upstairs who couldn't care less about him? The choice of title unquestionably influences our views, or at least raises questions about them. What if the play were called *The Little Elevator?* That title has the same literal meaning as "the dumb waiter," but think how limited its implications. Ben's and Gus's arguing about "lighting" and "putting" is not as idle as it seems: the words they eventually choose are not an entirely moot point. Add, finally, the distinct lack of firmly defined moral fiber in either man: having been reduced to twinges and inclinations, Gus and Ben should indeed take an interest in the words they choose, because those words constitute the fullness of their characters. Since they have no private selves, actions like choosing words are all that is left to them.

Having said all that, the bickering remains a little trite, but not so silly as before. Nor is a psychological interpretation based on the use of the word ballcock quite so silly. Words can take on great force in a world without clearly defined moral values, and in a play without an obvious lesson.

Other themes which emerge seem to fall under the purview of traditional romantic criticism of society. The two men frequently fail to make emotional contact with each other, perhaps because they are selfish or bound up in their own problems. They are bound to perform their job even though they hate it passionately--their dark and windowless workplace is a modern hell.

The dumb waiter ultimately intervenes. It comes from above, from the powers that be on which poor Ben and Gus wait. Ben continues to order Gus around; Ben is the leader, even as he constantly fears punishment by his superiors for what he does. Indeed, Gus's sin is caring too much about himself, not being a loyal employee. Ben will do what he's told, be the person he's supposed to be. The people upstairs ask for food, so Ben is the restaurateur.

But Gus constantly asks why, and, ultimately, hoards some of his food--that's his "dirty little game," part of the immaturity (i.e., selfishness) for which he must die. To the traditional modern mind, the irony is that Gus is the more human figure. To Pinter, though, that is part of the point. Gus constantly questions: "What do you think of that? Who's got it now? What do we do if it's a girl? Who moved in? Who sent those matches?" He has the active mind which is trying to understand the world. And he has the mind which is out for itself, which is perhaps growing into what we label moral values, or at least trying to find them. Gus is on the point of having what we would call a *self*, personal desires and beliefs included; or at least, he is thinking that he has a self, and acting as though he does. He seems to want to do things because he "believes" in them, or because he believes in himself. It is this very self which Hamlet thought he had, and which the post-modern sensibility has minimized or even banished as solipsism.[5] *The Dumb Waiter* can be viewed as a post-modern morality play, and the man who believes he has a consciousness must die.

Gus and Ben are told by the power above (literally) that the food they sent was no good. Ben copes with his failure to serve--apologizing, trying to make good. But Gus feels that he's been taken advantage of. He thinks that they must have a salad bowl upstairs. He thinks that there is a world which there is not: a sure sign of the pretentious modern consciousness (that perhaps still hungers after the good old windowless chamber).

In the play's final moments, the two enter a ritual of repeating commands to each other. Ben is the father to Gus the son. Ben knows that Gus will die. Does Ben want to kill Gus? Probably not, but he knows he has to, because that is his job--to please another. Ben goes into a ritual of repetition, ordained by his superior, because that's the only way that he can feel secure from the moral responsibility for killing his partner; he won't have to think, he can just act. He can maintain the banishment of any conception of self. The play's conclusion has a clear resemblance to

God's testing of Abraham's faith--Pinter's Biblical allusion for his morality play--when He asked Abraham to sacrifice his son Isaac in order to prove his belief. The obvious irony is that this god, the one just up the dumb waiter, has no intention of stopping the sacrifice. But Gus asks the same questions Isaac did of the analogous, wrong thing that he thinks is going on (Isaac thought a lamb would be sacrificed; Gus thinks Macaroni Pastitsio and Ormitha Macarounada are being cooked): "Well, what's he playing all these games for? That's what I want to know. What's he doing it for?" Like Isaac, Gus feels that he has paid his dues.

There is some high tension and fury as Gus's cries "We've proved ourselves" crescendo. The absurdity persists as the dumb waiter asks for scampi. Finally, Ben the father takes control and restores his own tranquil disinterest, which is the only way to survive. He returns to his paper, where he can get in touch with moral outrage in little pangs and twinges. The source of his moral outrage now? Nothing:

> BEN: Kaw!
> *[He picks up the paper and looks at it.]*
> Listen to this!
> *[Pause.]*
> What about that, eh?
> *[Pause.]*
> Kaw!
> *[Pause.]*
> Have you ever heard of such a thing?
> GUS: *[dully]* Go on!
> BEN: It's true.
> GUS: Get away.

Ben continues to partake of the ritual of outrage, devoid of content, as always. That is the only way to get by.

But Gus joins in. How come? He has begun to understand the way of the world, the way man cannot question, the way his own self-interest has no place. It jars him, but he survives, now grown. He flushes the toilet, a virgin no more. But as the curtain drops, Ben faces Gus, gun in hand, ready to destroy the now adult man. Pinter leaves the play in paradox. If Ben shoots Gus, then Ben shows his loyalty to the powers above but at the same time commits what seems to be an unjust act, thereby throwing this entire system into disarray. The man who would obey his world's dictates does the wrong thing. But if Ben doesn't shoot Gus, then he asserts a responsibility for his own actions which he really didn't have up to that point.

One makes what one will of Pinter's absurd dramatization of what I have called Gilbert Ryle's view of man. Ryle was, in his way, a humanist who sought to perpetuate a sense of free will and decency, simply stripped of self-important pretensions. Pinter goes further. He presents a vision of man which, if we accept it, is at least as horrifying to our sensibility as any Shakespearean tragedy. In this, and in the ambiguous and unfulfilling conclusion which Pinter contrives, *The Dumb Waiter* may ultimately protest the position to which the anti-ghost assigns man.

NOTES

1.   The discussion which follows was developed through a course in anthropology taught by Thomas De Zengotita during the spring of 1989, in which our readings and discussions included Jacques Monod, Peter Farb, Dorothy Lee, Victor Turner, Walter Ong, Bruno Snell, Ludwig Wittgenstein, and Gilbert Ryle.

2.   (London: Hutchinson, 1949). I am particularly indebted to Ryle for my discussion of the "ghost in the machine."

3. See "Transformations of the Word and Alienation," in Walter Ong, *Interfaces of the Word* (Ithaca, N.Y.: Cornell UP, 1977), pp. 17-49.

4. Dorothy Lee, "Lineal and Nonlineal Codifications of Reality," in *Explorations in Communication*, ed. Edmund Carpenter and Marshall McLuhan (Boston: Beacon Press, 1972), pp. 136-55.

5. Ryle, p. 60.

HAROLD PINTER IN NEW YORK*

Observed by Lois Gordon

Tonight, we'll see him in several simultaneous roles--as playwright, director, actor, and activist--performing the provocative work of Harold Pinter.

--Mel Gussow, introducing Pinter

"Stan, don't let them tell you
what to do
[*The Birthday Party*]."
--I've lived that line all my damned life, never more than now.

--Harold Pinter, to Mel Gussow

Back in November 1961, T. S. Eliot appeared at what was then called the "Lexington Avenue Y." He was the reigning laureate of contemporary letters, an artist secure of his place in literary history--a longtime master of his art and, on this night, of his audience. He confessed early *faux pas* ("Criticizing Milton as I did was just symptomatic of a young man hiding behind his typewriter") and recited *The Waste Land*. The audience was entirely forgiving of what he called his "youthful indiscretions" and utterly appreciative of his exalted presence and the fact that he was sharing his life with them.

* From *The Pinter Review* III (1989). Reprinted by permission.

On October 3, 1989, Harold Pinter appeared on the same stage, for at least the same number of sophisticated and spellbound devotees (including the likes of Arthur Schlesinger, Jr., and Diane Sawyer)--another literary figure assured of his place in the pantheon of great contemporary writers and, on this night, an elder statesman as well. Pinter was also in complete control of his art and the audience before him. Younger of course than Eliot (Pinter drew gasps of disbelief when he mentioned his upcoming sixtieth birthday), he is still handsome and possessed of that wonderfully resourceful, resonant voice. Unless appearances are entirely deceptive--as they often are in the Pinter universe--he looked abundantly healthy and prosperous. In a word, Pinter seemed to be riding the crest.

To name a few of his current projects, he was in New York to help restage the by-now canonical *The Birthday Party*, along with *Mountain Language* (1988). He will soon celebrate the twenty-fifth anniversary of *The Homecoming* (with a revival, directed again by Peter Hall, who will also be sixty), which, on the evening of his reading, was in production at Chicago's Steppenwolf Theatre. He is also working on a filmscript of *The Trial* ("I read [it] when I was a lad of eighteen . . . and it's been with me ever since. . .").

And last, but surely not least, accompanying and cheering him on in all these enterprises--and seated inconspicuously in the audience that night--is the beautiful and prodigiously talented Lady Antonia Fraser. Like T. S. Eliot thirty years ago (just about the time Pinter began writing), Harold Pinter has come into his own, and whatever his (admitted) anxieties in writing new plays, would seem to have the world at his feet. That night in New York, he could not have found an audience happier for him.

The program consisted of two parts: first, Pinter's reading of an extract from *The Hothouse* (from "My cake! We haven't cut the cake!" to "I AM AUTHORIZED") and the entire *One for the Road*. I had heard him perform the latter two years ago and was once again astonished by his

uncanny ability to convey different degrees of menace,
banality, and madness (all at the same time). Once again, I
wondered if anyone could act Pinter as well as Pinter.
After a brief intermission, Pinter sat opposite
Gussow and answered, with alternating wit and
seriousness, as well as consistent precision of phrase and
diction, Gussow's and the audience's questions (submitted
on cards). One suspects that most of these were Gussow's,
for they followed what seemed to be a well-orchestrated
sequence. Gussow's first (and rhetorical) question--had
Pinter's work come full circle from *The Birthday Party* to
Mountain Language in terms of his political interests--
clearly spelled out for the audience Pinter's motives in
selecting his readings; it also set the tone for the rest of the
evening. Pinter would be exploring two things tonight:
oppression and the individual, and the subversive function
of language.

He began by saying that "in the early days," he was
"a political writer of a kind," although "between 1970 and
1985," plays like *Old Times*, *Betrayal*, *Landscape*, and
Silence, were about "memory, youth, loss and so on."
However, in his early political work, such as *The Hothouse*,
his "power-crazy lunatic" was a "farcical character" as
well, both a "savage [and a] nut." The early plays, Pinter
continued, mixed social and political interests with humor.
He then added, with great emphasis: "The distinction . . .
between those plays [and now] is that I'm afraid for me the
joke is over, and therefore I can't play any more jokes, and
I can't play any more games. So I am therefore writing
shorter and shorter pieces which are more and more brutal
and more and more overtly naked, you see."

Two or three political statements, interspersed
within several charming or amusing remarks, followed.
These political comments were clearly Pinter's main
agenda, a complement to his earlier readings. In a deeply
felt and lengthy statement, he reiterated the issues of his
continuing concern:

I think we are extremely intimidated by the
countries in which we live. . . . Many live a life of
intimidation, . . . even if they don't know it. . . .
[There are] the millions who have no money, who
are dispossessed, practically disenfranchised by
governmental techniques and tactics. . . . This has
to do with a very successful pattern of lies which
the government actually tells to its citizens and . . .
is repeated [in some of] the media. So that you're
told that you're a happy man, . . . that everything is
fine, that you're doing very well, . . . that this is a
free country, . . . a democracy, . . . that other people
suffer various ills and various oppressions of which
we are free. And we say, yes, that must be the case.
Yes, it seems that is the case.

Pinter immediately turned to specific U.S. foreign
policy: "I see it most strongly embodied . . . in this
country's relationship with Central America, where
the actual facts simply do not correspond to the language
used by those facts or the language of the media and
certainly the administration of this country, and [these
are] echoed indeed . . . by the government of England."
And, he explained: "What language does is actually debase
itself . . . [And] the lie is simple, automatic, . . . persuasive,
[and] infinitely pervasive. . . . It pervades the tradition in
which we live, . . . our western democracies. . . . We are
told . . . for example, there is a totalitarian dungeon existing
in Nicaragua and democracies in El Salvador and
Guatemala. The real facts [as many know are that] in the
last fifteen years, nearly 300,000 people have died in
Guatemala, El Salvador, and Nicaragua, and this has
precisely . . . come about by the foreign policy of this
country. Now while this has been going on, our attention
has been drawn very successfully . . . to the other side, to
what used to be called the Iron Curtain, now breaking
down."
Pinter's role, he reaffirmed, is not only "as an actor
and entertainer" but also as "a citizen of the world in

which I live, [and I] insist upon taking responsibility . . . to actually find out what the truth is and what actually is happening, . . . to [investigate] the blanket of lies which unfortunately we are either too indifferent or too frightened to question."

At other moments during the evening he addressed Clause 28, Parliament's effort to make illegal any efforts to "promote" (whatever that means) homosexuality. He also defended his continued support (as well as that of English PEN, along with others in the English literary community and Article 19) of Salman Rushdie. He spoke of the genesis of *One for the Road* (inspired by the remarks of some Turkish women blindly condoning their country's violence, saying that those brutalized deserved torture because they were "probably Communists"). He discussed *The Trial.* ("The nightmare of that world is precisely in its ordinariness." A major difference between his and Orson Welles's version would be that "instead of Welles's . . . spasmodic, half-adjusted lines, images, and . . . effects," he will concentrate "on the important thing [of how the man] fights like hell all the way"). He also spoke of the way his writing has developed over the years. (Gussow had previously said that Pinter is entering a third phase, notable since *A Kind of Alaska*, now "treating the effect of science and politics on the individual," and writing about "power and powerlessness.") Pinter proceeded to add that although he can no longer write the traditional two-hour play, "whatever the length, . . . length is not important": "Nothing would give me greater pleasure than to write any play, whatever the length." He then explained: "One thing about the act of writing is that it is an act of necessity and freedom," and that under the circumstances, this is becoming increasingly difficult. He remains concerned primarily "with accurate and precise images of what is the case."

There were, throughout the evening, lighter questions and answers, but these were consistently brief. Some were one-liners, and others a mixture of tongue-in-cheek and affectionate banter. He spoke, for example, of having "*two* [sic]" major things "happen" to him at an early age: "girls, cinema, [and] sprinting"; he made a sheepish but unsuccessful attempt to recall a proposed commercial (which he was sure his wife would remember); he praised with deep sincerity the "abyss" of "uncertainty" which actors face daily; he was chipper about how he "laughs like hell" when he "tests" aloud his dialogue to himself; he was waggish about "the darkness and psychological terror" variously attributed to him and his work.

In a more mischievous vein, when asked if he had a special affinity with the several villainous roles he has played, such as Iago and his own Goldberg and Nicholas, his response was swift and unhesitating: "Yes . . . my better roles . . . were the sinister ones. . . . [This] started at a very early age [in my] hating the audience [*Loud laughter*], . . . an attitude I've preserved until this very day--with the exception of this audience, of course. [*Even louder laughter.*]" Another example of his ambiguous playfulness occurred after his remark "I believe in fun." He was about to take on what he called his "reverential" critics in "English departments [and] literary journals." The audience responded to the following with raucous laughter:

> I made a terrible mistake when I was young [from which] I've never really recovered, which is I wrote the word "pause" into my first play--a fatal error. [*Pause.*] People have been . . . obsessed with this pause. [*Pause.*] I meant it merely as a natural break in the proceedings, as a breath. [*Pause.*] It's come to be seen as something metaphysical.

Pinter's timing with Gussow, and Gussow's questions--virtually, a script--were perfect:

> What's the best thing you ever said in a pause?
> [Pinter paused.]

One felt at moments like a participant in a Pinter play. For example, Pinter's long comment above, on intimidation through language, followed what might be construed as a masterful interchange on the meanings and moods evoked by the word "intimidation": Gussow asked if there were a correlation between acting and writing, to which Pinter's succinct but emotionless response--in the midst of otherwise lengthy and enthusiastic replies--evoked a touch of menace: "I've no idea really." In fact, Gussow replied: "Oddly enough, [the card here] says: 'Sir, discuss intimidation.'" After some banter and a Pinter pause, Gussow continued: "Perhaps we've seen enough intimidation already." When he then proceeded to question if the theater can change the world, Pinter said, "I prefer to go back to the question of intimidation" and gave the long, political response cited earlier, an illustration, in fact, of how language--any language and in any capacity--can be manipulated for (personal or) political ends.

Pinter concluded the serious part of the evening in response to Gussow's repeated question regarding whether or not theater can change the world. "Just a little," he said, "but that little is something." He continued: "I respect the power of that correspondence between audience and theater." Despite his "hatred" of propaganda plays and disinterest in writing a play, say, about Nicaragua, "there is a role . . . for a kind of art which is not, in strict terms, pursuing the normal narrative decisions of the drama." In addition, in his conclusion, he repeated his personal imperative to actively pursue political action: "I make a damned nuisance about myself [and] that is the way I understand my role as a citizen of my country and the world." This was followed by a pithy summary of his concerns throughout the evening:

> How is power actually manifested through the state?
> How does it work?
> What is actually happening?

> And what, of course, does invariably happen
> when . . . rhetoric really rules the day?

There was no reception following the presentation
("Y" speakers frequently host a receiving line), but signed
books were available (a rare event for Pinter audiences) and
appropriated within minutes. Although worlds apart
politically from T. S. Eliot, like his predecessor, Pinter
received a standing ovation and the gratitude of an audience
which felt graced by the presence of one of the greatest
living English writers.

PHOTOS, FROM PAULINE FLANAGAN

Editor's Note: In 1968, Pinter published an essay titled *Mac* --a tribute to the late Anew McMaster, the great Shakespearean actor in whose company, the McMaster Company, Pinter acted during 1951-53. The company, which "Mac" formed in 1925, had played throughout the world, but in the years of Pinter's tenure, it traveled to the large and small cities of Ireland, performing Shakespeare and other classic and contemporary works. As one reporter put it, farmers left their fields and shopkeepers closed their stores in order to touch spirit with Oedipus, Macbeth, Hamlet, and Lear.

Mac, according to all reports, was an extraordinary teacher as well as actor and manager. When he died in 1962, this was, in Pinter's words, "the end of an era." Mac was "the last of the great actor-managers unconnected with film and television." Those who worked with him shared a deep sense of loss for, again citing Pinter, although "Ireland wasn't golden always, . . . it was golden sometimes and in 1950 it was, all in all, a golden age for me and [the] others."

Pauline Flanagan, a young actress from Sligo (both her parents had been mayor of Sligo), distinguished for her beauty and magical voice, joined the company at about the same time as Pinter. Praised repeatedly for her talent and broad repertory (she could act "the gamut from pantomime to Shakespeare"), she was often cast opposite both Mac and Pinter. As the programs below indicate, the company, a traveling, repertory troupe, would perform as many as nine plays over a one-week period. As a result, other than the time spent on stage and in travel, the ten or so young actors who joined Mac, of necessity, also spent a great deal of time together. As the photos indicate, there was an occasional trip to the beach, although most of the time was spent learning one's lines.

I am very grateful to Miss Flanagan for having allowed me to reproduce these photos, alongside her reminiscences about this "golden" time. The photos are also accompanied by citations from *Mac*.

"[Mac] was a great actor and we who worked with him were the luckiest people in the world and loved him."

--HP, *Mac*

"His wife, Marjorie, organised the tours, supervised all business arrangements, . . . ran the wardrobe, sewed. . . . Her spirit and belief constituted the backbone of the company. There would have been no company without her."

--HP, *Mac*

"[Mac's greatest roles were Oedipus,] Othello, and Lear. He understood and expressed totally the final tender clarity which is under the storm, the blindness, the anguish. For me his acting at these times embodied the idea of Yeats' line: 'They know that Hamlet and Lear are gay, Gaiety transfiguring all that dread'. Mac entered into this tragic gaiety naturally and inevitably."

--HP, *Mac*

"I remember [Mac's] delivery of this line: 'Methinks (bass) it should be now a huge (bass) eclipse (tenor) of sun and moon (baritone) and that th'affrighted glove (bass) Should yawn (very deep, the abyss) at alteration.' We all watched him from the wings."

--HP, *Mac*

"He offered me six pounds a week, said I could get the digs for twenty-five shillings at the most, told me how cheap cigarettes were and that I could play Horatio, Bassanio and Cassio. It was my first job proper on the stage."

--HP, *Mac*

Anew McMaster Company, 1951
Standing: Jack Aronson, Don Conlon, Will Hey, Jerry Breheny, Ronald Grierson,
Harold Pinter, Paddy Gardner. Seated: Pauline Flanagan, Anew McMaster,
Laurel Streeter, Mary Rose McMaster, Joe Nolan, Kenneth Haigh

"As Ken Haigh put it, 'When you start at the top with Mac, it's all down hill from there.'
We all joke about this when we meet. You see, we gained a great level of expertise
working with Mac. We worked very hard.... He taught us ... very gently.... He was
never mean, but he was demanding. It was constant work. You see, we learned by
'doing,' not going to class."   --PF

"Mrs. Mac taught us movement--how to hold a fan, flip a train, that one never exposes
an ankle and that one's hands are always held above the waist, so the blood runs down,
and the hands are always white,. . . . that kind of thing."   --PF

"The company centered in Dublin, Belfast, Londonderry, and Cork, but traveled to
places like Dundalk, Tralee, Enistymon (County Clare), Co. Kerry, Sligo, Castle Bar,
Ballina, Ballyshannon, Athlone, and Mullingar."   --PF

"We went from small to large parts, and Harold and I were the juvenile leads: Lord and
Lady Chilton, Bassanio and Portia, Lord and Lady Windermere. We were always cast
opposite one another."   --PF

"We learned our Shakespeare fairly fast,. You had to. Mac only did the Shakespeare and
Greek tragedies. He left the Wilde and mysteries to the younger company." --PF

McMaster as Othello, Pinter as Iago, 1952

"[Once the company raced to Limerick when there was a cinema strike; it was St. Patrick's night, and although *Othello* was scheduled for 9 p.m., the house was empty until 11:30. Everyone was drunk and rowdy.] We could not hear ourselves speak, could not hear our cues. The cast was alarmed.... We kept our hands on our swords. I was playing Iago at the time. . . . Don't worry, Mac said.... When he walked onto the stage for the 'Naked in bed, Iago, and not mean any harm' scene (his great body hunched, his voice low with grit), they silenced. He tore into the fit. He made the play his and the place his. By the time he had reached 'It is the very error of the moon; She comes more near the earth than she was wont, And makes men mad.' (the word 'mad' suddenly cauterized, ugly, shocking) the audience was quite still. And sober."

--HP, *Mac*

Pinter as Iago, Jack Aronson as Brabantio

In the *Merchant of Venice*, the role of Bassanio was "played with fine impetuousness by Harold Pinter. Barry Foster was a flashing Lorenzo . . . Pauline Flanagan was a commanding Portia," wrote the Waterford reporter.

"In the trial scene in *The Merchant of Venice* one night I said to him (as Bassanio) instead of 'For thy three thousand ducats here is six,' quite involuntarily, 'For thy three thousand *buckets* here is six'. He replied quietly and with emphasis: 'If every *bucket* in six thousand *buckets* were in six parts, and every part a *bucket* I would not draw them—I would have my bond'. I could not continue. . . . I turned upstage . . . But Mac stood, remorseless, grave, like an eagle, waiting for my reply."

--HP, *Mac*

". . . Going into Bandon or Cloughjordan would find the town empty, asleep, men sitting upright in dark bars, cow-pads, mud, smell of peat, wood, old clothes. We'd find digs; wash basin and jug, tea, black pudding, and off to the hall, set up a stage on trestle tables; a few rostrum, a few drapes, costumes out of the hampers, set up shop, and at night play, not always but mostly, to a packed house (where had they come from?) . . ."

--HP, *Mac*

Pinter as Horatio, Ken Haigh as Laertes

On tour in Galway, 1952
Barry Foster, Pauline Flanagan, Harold Pinter

Pinter holding a notebook and ink bottle, Galway, 1952

"On tour--Monday morning," Carrickmacross, Pinter, Flanagan,
unidentified, Streeter, Conlon, Haigh

"Harold was always writing. He kept a journal about growing up in London. He wrote about his group of friends and their experiences in London. One friend was Henry Woolf, and he joined Mac the following year. I think that generally, Harold's friends were not in the arts, particularly."   --PF

"Harold was a wonderful actor; he was brilliant as Jack in *The Importance*—funny and marvelous. He had an entrance in the second act when he came in with a black bordered handkerchief, after the funeral, and he had the audience convulsed."   --PF

"[Harold] was a very gripping actor; we learned together; we didn't know a great deal, but he was easy to play with. He had wonderful comic timing."

The Importance of Being Earnest

"It would have been a difficult task for any player to have bettered Pauline Flanagan's characterisation of Gwendoline Fairfax, the poised, sophisticated society beauty.... In the principal male parts of Algernon Montcrieff and John Worthing, Max Ettlinger and Harold Pinter were word and action perfect, turning in performances which would have pleased even the author himself."   (*The Munster Leader*)

"The success of the play depends almost entirely on its brilliant conversation--. . . and never have we heard Wilde's most unreasonable utterances spoken so reasonably as by Max Ettlinger (Algernon Moncrieff) and Harold Pinter (Jack Worthing, J.P.)."

(Unsigned review)

Pinter as Lord Windermere in *Lady Windermere's Fan*, 1951

Flanagan and Pinter in *Ten Little Indians*, 1950

"In Front of the Gypsies" 1952
Laurel Streeter, Penny Parry, Mary Rose McMaster, Jack Aronson

Enistymon, Co. Clare, 1952
Flanagan and Pinter (with notebooks)

"We did lines all time with each other. We were constantly putting new plays on. But it wasn't work; it was enjoyment, a time of very happy memories."   --PF

"There was always giggling and laughter."   --PF

"It appeared at the time that he would be an actor."   --PF

McMaster Company, Blarney Castle, 1952
Max Ettlinger, Will Hey, Pinter, Ken Haigh,
Penny Parry, Flanagan, unidentified

On tour in Galway, 1952
Pinter, Maurice Good, Gerry Breheny, Barry Foster, Flanagan

"Harold was very loyal. One fellow in the Mac company once got into trouble in London, and there was a court case. Harold said he'd pay his bail and be responsible for him."

--PF

"He kept a journal of growing up. I found him a very happy man who had had a happy childhood. He was also mad about Yeats, and I think Yeats was highly influential. Harold introduced me to Yeats's more difficult, late poems, the poems I wasn't familiar with, like the one about the tin can tied to a dog's tail. Yes, I think Yeats had a great influence on him. He read Eliot and read *The Waste Land* aloud. You can imagine: 'When Lil's husband got demobbed . . . --Good night, ladies, good night, sweet ladies . . . '"

--PF

Pinter at Ballybunion, 1952

Kilkenny, 1952
Back row: Paddy Gardiner, Haigh, Pinter
Middle: unidentified, Laurel Streeter, Flanagan
Front: Don Conlon

"He left the company at the end of a tour and then joined Donald Wolfit, the other 'last of the actor-managers'; Wolfit and Mac were interchangable in that way. There was one turn Wolfit did with a cape; when he gave the 'No, you are unnatural hags' speech in *Lear,* he did a turn with his cape that was 360 degrees. Harold studied it; technically it was brilliant."

--PF

Kilkenny, 1952
Pinter, Flanagan, Haigh, Jack Aronson

OPERA HOUSE, CORK

Telegrams: "Opera, Cork"   Manager: W. G. TWOMEY   Telephone 20022

MONDAY, 20th OCTOBER, 1952 at 8 p.m.

ANEW McMASTER

PRESENTS

"OTHELLO"

By WILLIAM SHAKESPEARE

Characters in order of appearance :

Duke of Venice	Eugene Wellesley
Senator	Barry Foster
Michael Cassio (a Lieutenant)	Max Ettlinger
Brabantio (a Senator, and father of Desdemona)	Jack Aronson
Othello (a Moor, General in the Venetian Army)	Anew McMaster
Iago (his sergeant)	Harold Pinter
Roderigo (a Venetian gentleman)	Joseph Nolan
Desdemona (Brabantio's daughter)	Mary-Rose McMaster
Messenger	Maurice Good
Montano (Governor of Cyprus)	William Hey
Emilia (Iago's wife)	Laurel Streeter
Bianca (a Courtesan, Cassio's mistress)	Pauline Flanagan
Lodovico	Jack Aronson

Soldiers, Natives of Cyprus, etc.

THE DRAMATIC EVENT OF THE SEASON!

PERSONAL APPEARANCE OF

ANEW McMASTER

AND HIS INTERNATIONAL COMPANY

AT KILKENNY THEATRE

Mon. Nov. 10th to Sun. Nov. 16th (inclusive)

ALL PRODUCTIONS NEWLY COSTUMED

Monday	TEN LITTLE NIGGERS
Tuesday	The IMPORTANCE OF BEING EARNEST
Wednesday Matinee	AS YOU LIKE IT
Wed. Night	AS YOU LIKE IT
Thursday Matinee	MACBETH
Thurs. Night	AN INSPECTOR CALLS
Friday	ŒDIPUS
Saturday	MACBETH
Sunday	DUET FOR TWO HANDS

Nightly at 8.30 o'clock. Booking at Hall daily from
11.30—2 o'clock, 3.30—5 o'clock.

Admission—3/6 (reserved), 2/6 and 1/6.

The Southern Star Ltd., Skibbereen.

Handbill, Killkenny, 1952-1953

Price 3d.   *Programme*

MR.

ANEW McMASTER

AS

OTHELLO

By WILLIAM SHAKESPEARE

OTHELLO

Characters in order of appearance

DUKE OF VENICE ... ... JOSEPH NOLAN

SENATOR ... ... KEN HAIGH

MICHAEL CASSIO (a Lieutenant) ... ... HAROLD PINTER

BRABANTIO ... ... JACK ARONSON
(a Senator, and father of Desdemona)

OTHELLO ... ... ANEW McMASTER
... (a Moor, General in the Venetian Army)

IAGO (his sergeant) ... ... JOHN MAYES

RODERIGO (a Venetian gentleman) ... DONALD CONLON

DESDEMONA ... ... MARY-ROSE McMASTER
(Brabantio's daughter)

MESSENGER ... ... JEROME BREHENY

MONTANO (Governor of Cypress) ... ... WILLIAM HEY

EMILIA (Iago's wife) ... ... LAUREL STREETER

BIANCA ... ... PAULINE FLANAGAN
(a Courtesan, Cassio's mistress)

LODOVICO ... ... JACK ARONSON

SOLDIERS, NATIVES OF CYPRESS, ETC.

PRICE 3d.

Programme

MR. ANEW McMASTER

AS "**HAMLET**"

By WILLIAM SHAKESPEARE

Hamlet
✳ ✳ ✳

CHARACTERS IN ORDER OF APPEARANCE

BERNARDO		TERENCE TWOMEY
FRANCISCO	SOLDIERS	WALTER PLINGE
MARCELLUS		JAMES BARRY
HORATIO (friend to Hamlet)		HAROLD PINTER
GHOST OF HAMLET'S FATHER ...		JACK ARONSON
CLAUDIUS (King of Denmark)		JOHN MAYES
GERTRUDE (Queen of Denmark) ...		SUSAN BOLEYN
HAMLET (her son)		ANEW McMASTER
POLONIUS (Lord Chamberlain)		JOSEPH NOLAN
LAERTES (his son)		KEN HAIGH
OPHELIA (his daughter)		MARY-ROSE McMASTER
ROSENCRANTZ		DONALD CONLON
GUILDENSTERN	COURTIERS	PATRICK
		GARDINER
FIRST ACTOR		WILLIAM HEY
SECOND ACTOR		JAMES BARRY
THIRD ACTOR		PAULINE FLANAGAN
A GENTLEWOMAN		MAUREEN PARRY
FIRST GRAVEDIGGER		JOSEPH NOLAN
A PRIEST		TERENCE TWOMEY
OSRIC (a courtier)		DONALD CONLON

THE HOUSE OF QUALITY AND GOOD SERVICE

JOHN DALY & CO. LTD. CORK
OFFICIAL CATERERS TO ALL BARS IN THIS THEATRE

OPERA HOUSE, CORK

Telegrams: "Opera, Cork." Manager: W. G. TWOMEY. Telephone 20222

Commencing Monday, September 21st, 1953. Nightly at 8.
Matinee Saturday at 2.30 p.m.

ANEW McMASTER
IN

"**KING LEAR**"
BY WILLIAM SHAKESPEARE

(Characters in order of appearance)

Edmund (bastard son of Gloucester)	Pat McGee
Earl of Kent	Ronald Grierson
Earl of Gloucester	Eugene Wellesley
Lear (King of Britain)	Anew McMaster
Goneril	Elizabeth Gott
Regan his daughters	Pauline Flanagan
Cordelia	Mary Rose McMaster
Duke of Cornwall (husband of Regan)	Joseph Nolan
Duke of Albany (husband of Goneril)	Nicholas Brady
Duke of Burgundy Suitors to	Eric Pattison
King of France Cordelia	John Riggs-Millar
Edgar (Gloucester's legitimate son)	Harold Pinter
Oswald (steward to Goneril)	John Riggs-Millar
Fool	Christopher McMaster
Doctor	Walter Plinge
A Captain	Eric Pattison

Soldiers, Pages, etc.

E. MAC SWEENY
Chemist
& PHOTOGRAPHIC DEALER
91 PATRICK STREET CORK

Ask for DALY'S DRY GINGER ALE in ALL Bars of THIS Theatre

Ask FOR TANORA SUPPLIED IN ALL Bars of THIS Theatre

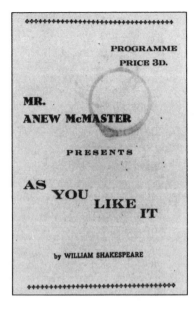

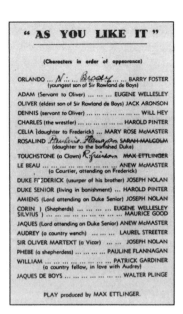

PRICE 3d.

Programme

ANEW
McMASTER

—IN—

THE TAMING
OF THE SHREW

By WILLIAM SHAKESPEARE

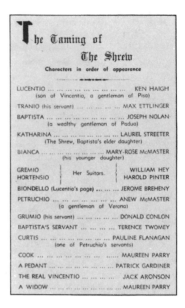

The Taming of
The Shrew

Characters in order of appearance

LUCENTIO ... ...   KEN HAIGH
(son of Vincentio, a gentleman of Pisa)

TRANIO (his servant) ... ...   MAX ETTLINGER

BAPTISTA ... ...   JOSEPH NOLAN
(a wealthy gentleman of Padua)

KATHARINA ... ...   LAUREL STREETER
(The Shrew, Baptista's elder daughter)

BIANCA ... ...   MARY-ROSE McMASTER
(his younger daughter)

GREMIO | Her Suitors. | WILLIAM HEY
HORTENSIO | | HAROLD PINTER

BIONDELLO (Lucentio's page) ... ...   JEROME BREHENY

PETRUCHIO ... ...   ANEW McMASTER
(a gentleman of Verona)

GRUMIO (his servant) ... ...   DONALD CONLON

BAPTISTA'S SERVANT ... ...   TERENCE TWOMEY

CURTIS ... ...   PAULINE FLANAGAN
(one of Petruchio's servants)

COOK ... ...   MAUREEN PARRY

A PEDANT ... ...   PATRICK GARDINER

THE REAL VINCENTIO ... ...   JACK ARONSON

A WIDOW ... ...   MAUREEN PARRY

"A sketch of the company we had backstage."   --PF

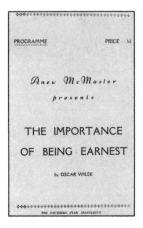

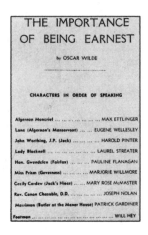

"He showed me London my first time there, and I met his parents. When Harold and I had toured, I had helped him get free digs. He reciprocated by inviting me to his house, although I stayed in a hotel. But I met Mr. and Mrs. Pinter my first time in London. They were very quiet, proud, very welcoming, and modest. They were not poor but very much middle class with a very nice house. I remember that they had a refrigerator. Harold and I were both very poor in those days, and we had been on the road. Harold looked in [the refrigerator] with great glee: "There's some chicken in there." Mrs. Pinter was a very good cook, and she always had it in there for us--plenty of chicken. Other times, we would buy minestrone soup for a shilling."   --PF

"Harold loved London. He loved living there--the parks, the movies, the 'cafs' [cafes]. He loved all that--the business of living in London. He introduced me to films that had never been in Ireland. The Marx Brothers. He loved them. He loved comedy and he loved the modern, experimental films. We saw Buñuel's *Los Olividados*. There was one scene, I recall, with a blind man--not your stereotypical blind man--but a nasty man, flailing with a stick. . . . Yes, he was very loyal and fond of his friends, like Jimmy and Moishe. Imagine that I remember their names after forty years. I met them one afternoon in the park, and they all played cricket. They remained friends."   --PF

"Although I was shy, I felt from the first day I met Harold that he was sure of himself--completely self-assured and very kind. And later he was wonderful with his baby. He and Vivien loved just watching him crawl. I saw them when they came to New York and stayed at the Navarro. Harold was a very caring father. Before that, when they were in London, they were doing fortnightly rep, so that there was always someone free to be at home with the baby: one rehearsing and the other playing."   --PF

"Harold and I didn't work together again until he directed *The Innocents*, which we rehearsed in London and played in New York."   --PF

An anecdote. . . . When *The Caretaker* was in rehearsal in Boston, one of the producers expressed his anticipation of having a hit show and added: "We'll just have to pare the first act down to the bare bones." Pinter replied: "Yes. Great. But there aren't any bones."

HAROLD PINTER'S ACHIEVEMENT AND MODERN DRAMA

Kimball King, with the assistance of Marti Greene[1]

Nearly thirty years ago I argued in an introduction to a volume on British playwrights that England's theater had undergone a second Renaissance after World War II. There are few eras of theater history as fertile as the last half of the twentieth century in Great Britain. The range and accomplishments of its playwrights, the majority of whom are still producing fine plays and inspiring younger colleagues, is unparalleled. Of course, excitement over British theater led to new interest in Irish and American drama as well. Not surprisingly, many of the Irish and American dramatists have used themes and techniques first made popular by their British counterparts. I would not presume to rank the accomplishments of late twentieth-century British playwrights, nor do I feel it would be appropriate to do so. However, Harold Pinter's guiding role in virtually all important aspects of modern drama cannot be overlooked. It could be said that Beckett's poetic minimalism, dense with meaning, and John Osborne's creative use of the stage to express his feelings of outrage and injustice, began a spirited uncovering of theatrical possibility. It remained for Pinter to alter expectations of drama permanently, however; and the language, action, and meaning of all performance art is inevitably measured against his achievements. Exposition and dialogue in such fine dramatists as, say, Eugene O'Neill or Arthur Miller, seem either contrived or turgid or both. Bertholt Brecht's ambitious political sagas with immense casts of ensemble actors still provide theatrical excitement and intellectual stimulation, but their grandiosity, and that of his many imitators, seems to belong to an earlier era. Pinter's audiences, like Brecht's, are encouraged to "think," but they are required also to observe subtleties of gesture, nuances of language, and minute details of staging. The intimacy of a Pinteresque stage space recalls Beckett's, of course, but it is also more instantly recognizable.

Pinter has brought a form of natural speech to the stage that has surpassed the most ambitious attempts of his predecessors. The dialogue of contemporary playwrights either imitates Pinter's or sounds prolix by comparison. But while Pinter captures the speech patterns of his characters with exactness, he "improves" upon everyday speech, creating humorous effects by the deliberate addition or omission of words or phrases, such as Lenny's referring in the *Homecoming* (1965) to "dear old Venice" (34) when he's never been there or Meg's denial that she's served sour milk on Stanley's cornflakes: "Petey ate his, didn't you Petey?" (*The Birthday Party* 1968, 15). Or characters answer questions in the reverse order in which they were asked. Thus, when Emma in *Betrayal* (1978) asks Jerry who had recently seen her daughter Charlotte why Charlotte hadn't told her, Jerry responds, "[S]he didn't see me. In the street" (18). Along with words selected to reflect believable conversation that is simultaneously amusing, if often unintentionally so, Pinter has greatly increased the importance of subtext. By physical gestures, by his famous pauses and silences and by the addition of a single adverb or adjective, the playwright reveals the insult or rebuke that lies beneath the surface banter, such as Lenny's accusation that Ruth and Teddy put pleasure before family in his remark that " . . . you went to Italy *first*, did you?" (29) or Jimmy's suggestion that Bill is a "kept" gay male in *The Collection* (1976) when he refers to him "A man's man" (31). And one cannot forget Jerry's recognition that his affair with Emma is over, when his comment on the weather, "It's pretty cold now," acknowledges the dissolution of their previously "heated" feelings (50).

Perhaps even more than the transformation of stage dialogue into conversations that might well be heard in everyday life (though carefully edited for maximum effect by the playwright) and the underscoring of feelings, often hostile or competitive, that lie beneath conversational pleasantries, Pinter's assault on the ancient conventions of dramatic irony is his most radical yet enduring contribution to the stage. Neither Oedipus nor Jocasta in Sophocles's *Oedipus Rex* nor King Claudius in Shakespeare's *Hamlet* dared lie to the audience. Horror spread through the Greek amphitheater when Oedipus cursed the sinner who brought the plague upon Thebes, and Elizabethan audiences knew that King Claudius was too filled with self-loathing to pray when his stepson did not; but who knows if Robert is telling the truth in Pinter's *Betrayal* when he claims to have cheated on Emma? Perhaps, he would rather be called a willing philanderer than an unwitting cuckold. Similarly, we wonder if Emma in the same play really believes Robert is the father of her little boy or if Sam's insistence in the *Homecoming* that Max's wife, Jessie, had an adulterous relationship with their friend, McGregor, may have been a malicious lie.

While Pinter's contributions to modern drama have major significance, it is nevertheless interesting to observe how scholars have assessed his oeuvre during his lifetime. Any single year might provide examples of original critical insights that have precedent. Still, each decade of the playwright's career seems to have focused on different arenas of interest. Even more compelling is the consistency with which certain works have received widespread recognition in every one of those decades. A glance at two sets of charts (see pp. 253-54) should provide a quick overview of Pinter scholarship. The charts are based on the MLA International Bibliography (1963-1999).

It is worth noting that out of fifteen plays Ms. Greene and I graphed on the enclosed chart, the three most frequently analyzed texts first appeared thirty-five to forty years ago and that ten of the plays were published before 1980. This could suggest a certain critical "lag" where scholars prefer to examine more "canonical" works and are hesitant to make forays into new areas of research. Although several plays written in the 1980s and one in the

1990s are included in my "list," between one third and one half of the articles and books written on the plays of the fifties, sixties, and seventies appeared during the 1990s as well. Clearly Pinter is now considered a "safe" topic for scholars who wish to be recognized as leading interpreters of modern drama.

There are both predictable and unexpected results of conducting a superficial survey of "popular" critical topics. For example, film criticism was in its infancy in the 1960s, and although the *The Go-Between* (1969), which premiered at the end of that decade, remains one of Pinter's more frequently discussed works, it has been mainly later films, such as *The French Lieutenant's Woman*, appearing in 1981, that seem to have gained the most attention from scholars of all of Pinter's screenplays. This can be partially accounted for by Pinter's postmodern treatment of John Fowles's novel and by the respect given to Fowles himself as a contemporary novelist. Then, too, academics, led by Steven Gale and Christopher Hudgins, have been examining Pinter's film archives in the past decade. Throughout academia movie criticism has become a respected field of scholarly research, surpassed only by studies of "language" as a most favored topic.

Surprisingly, the psychological analysis of Pinter's characters peaked in the 1980s when insight therapy throughout the world was receiving decreasing attention. The sixties, when Freudians still dominated the medical/psychological professions, produced remarkably few studies of Pinter's complex characters and so-called dysfunctional families. Perhaps, Lois Gordon's *Stratagems to Uncover Nakedness* (1969) and, one would assume, those books and articles inspired by it, exhausted the subject matter. Unexpectedly, critics who followed them ten to twenty years later spilled almost twice as much ink on similar topics. During the 1990s, however, divisions within the psychiatric profession itself over the value of insight therapy versus biomedical solutions to personality problems may have contributed to a drastic reduction in psychologically oriented research.

After looking at the graphs one can observe obvious scholarly trends. Now that all major colleges and universities contain divisions of film studies and the Modern Language Association devotes a number of panels at its annual meeting to cinematic topics, no one can be surprised by the increased currency of research on Pinter's movies. Next to studies of "language," a topic that includes both theoretical and pragmatic discussions of the artist's special patterns of phrasing and his precise selection of words, film criticism is at the top of the charts.

Nor is it surprising that the terminology of Absurdism was applied with great frequency to Pinter's work in the 1960s and that studies of his relationship to the Theatre of the Absurd should decline in subsequent years. Lacking any other adequate vocabulary to explain the bizarre situations and seemingly fragmented dialogue of his early works, scholars selected terminology that they had used to account for Ionesco's, Beckett's, and Genet's transformation of the stage. In some cases comparison with Absurdism accounted for behavior that was difficult to explain under the old rubrics of realism or naturalism. How convenient it often was to dismiss the actions of Max and his family in *The Homecoming* as purposeless and deliberately untrue!

Another logically popular early topic was that of literary influence. The 1960s not unexpectedly contained its share of materials suggesting Pinter's predecessors-- Shakespeare, Chekhov, Yeats, and Beckett among them. It is also important to note that the chart on these particular essays does not distinguish between influences on Pinter and Pinter's influence on the writers who followed him-- significantly, Orton, Churchill, Mamet, and Shepard, to name a few. Yet issues of influence have not waned; there are more studies of influence in the 1980s than there were in the 1960s. There are equally unpredictable results to the bibliographical survey. While academic interest in literary theory increased during the late seventies and early eighties, it reached its zenith in the 1990s. Many of the essays and book topics of the past ten years have involved the theoretical interpretation of earlier work, emphasizing the clues which language has provided to the followers of Wittgenstein, Lacan, Jameson, Foucault, Kristeva, and more. It is somewhat difficult to understand, however, why earlier Pinter plays like *The Homecoming* or *The Birthday Party* should be chosen more frequently as evidence for these language studies than his much more recent works. The small body of scholarship on women's roles and on women's issues in Pinter's plays has increased, as we might have imagined, but it still accounts for less than one third of the research done on the more abstract subject of language.

When scrutinizing critical materials for "natural speech," one may presumably wish to consult the largest topical group over the years, "language." However, in fairness, one should also peruse articles and books that include in their titles specific references to silence, menace, cruelty, or violence. Frequently, as Austin Quigley pointed out in *The Pinter Problem* (1975), language becomes the new weapon of competitors or adversaries and words are crafted to claim victory or to wound (6). The inability or refusal of a character to speak betrays his or her true feelings and is potentially more dangerous than words. Thus, the silent match seller in *A Slight Ache* merely waits for Edward to exhaust himself with pointless banter until he usurps his place. Verbal teasing may contain elements of menace. After Lenny describes his jabbing an old lady in the belly (probably his mother Jessie), Ruth begins calling him "Leonard," an appellation that terrifies him because it reminds him of his late mother when she scolded him in anger (35). Cruelty is often implicated by conversational ploys rather than by physical confrontation. For example, Rose cowers when Mr. and Mrs. Sands assert that they understand that apartment seven can be rented, because Rose lives there. Rose, an old lady, wonders if the strange landlord has some premonition of her impending death (118).

Finally, violence can be hinted at in a casual aside or described by characters in such a way that their words seem harsher and more explicit than specific actions that have taken place offstage. In classical drama, being told by the chorus or a minor character of the suicides of Jocasta or a Lady Macbeth is no less horrifying than being a witness to the actual event. Similarly, in *The Birthday Party*, McCann and Goldberg's boasting of the huge "boot" in the back of their car (a cargo area large enough to hold a man's body, one assumes) communicates the probable fate of Stanley to the audience. Contract killers Ben and Gus in *The Dumb Waiter* (1960) don't need to assassinate anyone in front of the audience; it's sufficient to listen to their commentary on their last "hit": "She wasn't much to look at I know, but still. It was a mess, though, wasn't it? Honest, I can't remember a mess like that one . . . who cleans up after we've gone?" (146-7).

The subtext lurking beneath the natural speech of Pinter's characters can imply sexual innuendo (when Stanley says his fried bread is "succulent," Meg replies that "you shouldn't say that word to a married woman" [27], incredulity (Lenny's exclamation of "[W]hat did you say?" when Ruth's monosyllabic answers to his question challenge all of his attempts to make "small talk" [29]), or anger, signaled in Max's response when Ruth spoils his story of material success and he exclaims, "[T]his is a lousy cigar!" (47). But the subtext of a statement can be cruel, such as Max's taunting of Sam for being homosexual. "[F]unny you never got married, isn't it?" (14), or merely patronizing, as when Jerry tells Emma that her gallery job is "marvelous for you" (51), implying that her occupation is not a serious one like being an editor, a writer's agent, or a physician, as Robert, he, and Judith are, respectively. Silence can of course imply subtextual meanings--the refusal to corroborate a story, for example. But again, one would look to discussions of language as a main source of examinations of subtext. Some writers on psychology also demonstrate the importance of subtext as a nonverbal means of communication, as one that explores latent feelings. Jimmy tells Stella in *The Collection* that she has "opened up a whole world" for him, both suggesting to her and taunting her with the notion that her false claims of adultery have brought him in contact with a wrongly accused gay male who has aroused his previously suppressed homoerotic feelings. The issues of reverse dramatic irony must of necessity remain unresolved. An audience may assume that Ruth and Teddy are actually married (for why have rumors of the union never reached his father and brothers before?), that they have no children (how many parents travel without photos of their offspring, and never refer to them by individual names?), and how convenient for the symmetry of *The Homecoming* that Teddy, like his father, should have three sons whose true paternity is in question!

Similarly, no one can be sure that Robert has actually had numerous affairs during his marriage to Emma in *Betrayal* or that Judith is a faithful wife and not the lover of another physician or even Robert. The paternity of Emma's boy Ned is questionable, for although she claims Robert is the boy's father, Jerry has just explained he would never leave his wife. Therefore, she tells him that she's pregnant by her husband. If she is being altruistic, she may not want to force Jerry into a second marriage against his will. However, if she's feeling vengeful, she may not want him to have the satisfaction of claiming Ned as his son. At the conclusion of *Old Times* (1970), it is difficult to know whether Deeley and Kate's relationship has ended, whether she rejects her old friend Anna, or whether any of their mutual past recollections are valid. Did Deeley actually meet Anna twenty years earlier? These unanswered and unanswerable questions reflect the ambivalence of human experience.

Did Hornby in *A Kind of Alaska* really marry Deborah's sister Pauline? He learns Pauline is now a widow. Did he and Pauline divorce and now her second husband is dead? Earlier, Hornby had advised Pauline to tell Deborah "both" truth and lies (27). Is that what he does also, or does Pinter believe that all memory is a mixture of actual and fantasized moments?

Scholars interested in new projects on Harold Pinter might do well to focus on plays other than *No Man's Land*,

Betrayal, Old Times, The Birthday Party, The Caretaker, or *The Homecoming*. Other plays and areas of study have thus far been underrepresented. More work can clearly be done on women's issues and on the psychology of characterizations in more recent plays. Pinter's political issues have become more significant in the past two decades, though it may be noted that, of the fourteen most frequently discussed works, only two, *Mountain Language* and *The Hothouse*, seem overtly political. At the Pinter at Seventy conference, for example, Susan Hollis Merritt discussed resonances of the Holocaust in the recent *Ashes to Ashes* (1998). More work undoubtedly needs to be directed at political overtones, especially the spectre of fascism as it appears during the Thatcher years. I have already noted that some critics have observed Pinter's influence on Churchill, Shepard, and Mamet; but it would be productive to pursue a study of these comparisons more fully. Churchill's now famous overlapping dialogue is, in part, a variation of Pinter's use of natural speech on the stage. Shepard's very naturalistic treatment of seemingly surreal incidents or characterizations, as well as his tendency to portray role reversals (shades of *A Slight Ache*) or needy dysfunctional families, suggest Pinter's example, as Ann Hall and others have noted. Shepard's Pulitzer prize-winning *Buried Child* has been compared to *The Homecoming*, but only as a passing suggestion. David Mamet's use of language derives from that of Pinter and the American playwright has acknowledged his debt to the British writer, but more specific analogies need to be drawn between Pinter's and Mamet's natural speech and subtext. The fact that the English author directed Mamet's *Oleanna* is interesting as well. Gender issues, along with methods of presenting stylistic techniques, might be considered here. I find the absence of religious experience interesting in Pinter's plays. Is he, like Jean-Paul Sartre, an atheistic existentialist? Contrarily, his imitator, Mamet, is steeped in Old Testament philosophy; the Jewishness of Mamet's characters is related to his ethical landscape. Where does Pinter stand on metaphysical issues?

Pinter, as stage actor, recently in *The Lover* at London's Donmar Warehouse, or as a movie star in an adaptation of Jane Austen's *Mansfield Park*, reveals talents that may possibly be related to the interpretation of his plays. In the case of Sam Shepard, mentioned above, there is a definite connection between Shepard's cinematic roles and the personality traits and values revealed in his major protagonists. There have been articles written on Pinter's poetry, published in *The Pinter Review*. It is understandable that specialists in drama and dramatic theater would focus on Pinter's plays--and he is still best known as a playwright. Nevertheless, a student of the writer's use of language (and there appear to be many), or anyone who examines his subtextual devices or imagery could profit from an in-depth study of his poetic works. If, for example, a critic finds the poetry "less interesting" in some sense than the drama, it might be worth noting which particular aspects of the writer's talent are better suited to the stage than to the more intimate revelations of poetry.

Future Pinter scholarship will have to take more account of the drafts in the Pinter archive. After the conference, for example, Francis Gillen researched the drafts of *Ashes to Ashes*, among others. Most of the questions about the play that Pinter finally wrote can be at least responded to by a study of the drafts, which clarify what Pinter intended at least at some point in the process of arriving at that final draft. Pinter had someone research Dinesen for the screenplay of *The Dreaming Child*. One box in the archive contains that research. How much was Pinter's outlook in writing the screenplay determined by that research? Next, one should consider *The Dwarfs*. Almost all of Pinter is there in that early novel, but almost no one writes about it (nor of the chapters in the archive that were not included in the published version).

All of these areas provide countless opportunities for ambitious admirers of Harold Pinter, and even the most thoroughly researched plays have been used as examples of a very limited number of issues. It is exciting to observe that Pinter, while transforming modern drama, also opened endless possibilities for deepening our understanding of his own complex achievement.

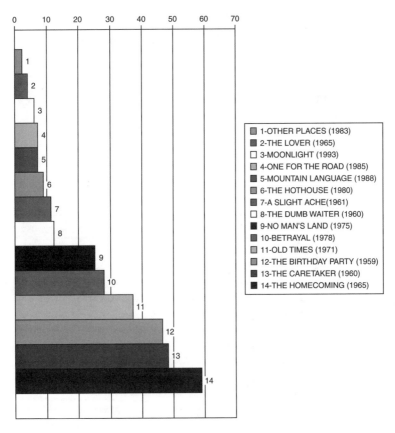

Fig. 1 Trends in Pinter Scholarship (III)--Frequency of Play Study: 1963-1999. (Published texts used by scholars appear above. The data were taken from the *MLA International Bibliography [1963-1999]*. The number of plays considered determined the graph parameters of 70.)

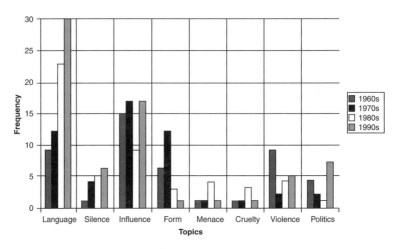

Fig. 2 Trends in Pinter Scholarship (I).

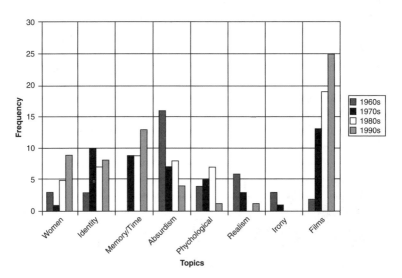

Fig. 3 Trends in Pinter Scholarship (II). (Published texts used by scholars appear above. The data were taken from the *MLA International Bibliography [1963-1999]*. The number of plays considered determined the graph parameters of 30.)

NOTE

1. Marti Greene is a graduate student in the English department at the University of North Carolina. She contributed more than fifty hours of research to this project and designed the graphs for this article. This essay is reprinted with the permission of *The Pinter Review*.

WORKS CITED

Burkman, Katherine and John Kundert-Gibbs. *Pinter at Sixty*. Bloomington: Indiana University Press, 1993.

Esslin, Martin. *The Peopled Wound: The World of Harold Pinter*. Garden, N.Y.: Doubleday, 1970.

Gale, Steven H., and Christopher C. Hudgins. "The Harold Pinter Archives II. A description of the filmscript materials in the archive in the British Library." *Pinter Review Annual Essays* (1995-96): 101-42.

Gardner, Stanton B., Jr. "Raiding the Inarticulate: Pinter and the Politics of Silence." *Cycnos* 12, no. 1 (1995): 31-36.

Gillen, Francis. "'Nowhere to go': Society and the Individual in Harold Pinter's *The Hothouse*." *Twentieth Century Literature: a Scholarly and Critical Journal* 29, no. 1: (spring 1983): 86-96.

Gordon, Lois. *Stratagems to Uncover Nakedness: The Drama of Harold Pinter*. Columbia: University of Missouri Press, 1969.

Hall, Ann C. *"A Kind of Alaska": Women in the Plays of O'Neill, Pinter, and Shepard.* Carbondale: Southern Illinois University Press, 1993.

Knowles, Ronald. *Understanding Harold Pinter.* Columbia: University of South Carolina Press, 1995.

Merritt, Susan Hollis. "The Harold Pinter Archive in the British Library." *The Pinter Review Annual Essays*, (1994): 14-55.

Page, Malcolm. *File on Pinter.* London: Methuen, 1993.

Pentice, Penelope. *The Pinter Ethic.* New York: Garland, 1994.

Pinter, Harold. *The Birthday Party and The Room.* New York: Grove Press, 1961.

——. 1965. *The Homecoming.* New York: Grove Press.

——. *Old Times.* 1971. New York: Grove Press.

——. *The Collection.* 1976. London: Methuen.

——. *The Dumb Waiter.* 1976. In *Pinter Plays: One.* London: Methuen.

——. *Betrayal.* 1978. New York: Grove Press.

——. *Other Places: Three Plays.* 1982. London: Methuen.

Quigley, Austin. *The Pinter Problem.* Princeton: Princeton University Press, 1975.

ACTING PINTER

Mel Gussow

Harold Pinter, along with Athol Fugard, Wallace Shawn, and others, is both a playwright and a professional actor. It was as an actor with a provincial repertory company (in 1957) that he discovered his talent for playwriting, with his first play, *The Room.* For many years after that, as he concentrated on writing, his acting was dormant, but he retained his love for the profession--and his admiration for actors. Increasingly in recent years he has been a performer both on stage and in films, while continuing to work as a director. There is a close connection between Pinter's writing and acting, both in the kind of roles he has chosen to do and in his approach to performance. As a writer, he is masterly at demonstrating the shifting balance of power that can rule one's daily life, and, in Peter Hall's phrase, the use of "words as weapons." Similarly, as an actor, he has an instinctive ability to convey the domination of one character over another and to pose a threat of violence.

Most of his acting has been, as he says, in plays "written by H. Pinter." He has appeared with Liv Ullmann in *Old Times*, with Paul Eddington in *No Man's Land*, and in *The Hothouse* and *The Collection.* There is at least one absolute: he would never improvise dialogue in his plays (or works by anyone else). As he explains, "You may have written the damn lines, but you didn't expect to say them when you wrote them. You suddenly find you have to say them every night"--and the actor has to respect the playwright. There have been those rare occasions, however, when he was acting in one of his own plays and wanted to rewrite dialogue. This happened when he was appearing in London as Roote, the keeper of the sanatorium

257

in *The Hothouse*. "I think I changed two words," he said, "after consulting with the director, and putting on my hat as the author." It was a case of bad grammatical construction, which he realized only when he was speaking the lines. When he was in *The Hothouse*, he could also sense the audience's shock. "Almost every night one hears a certain amount of actual gasps, gasps of shock, because of what is actually said. This play, as you know, takes place in an institution and you've got this crazy, brutal, violent tyrant at the center of it: me, the part I assume."

In one instance, his acting and writing had a direct bearing on each other. While he was acting in the London revival of *No Man's Land* he had "some kind of mystical awareness" that those who have died live on in our lives. That gave him the idea for *Moonlight*, which represented his return to writing after an absence of several years.

In contrast to other playwrights (Tom Stoppard, Michael Frayn), he has never written a play about the theater--and he has seldom written about his days as an actor, except in his nostalgic memory piece, *Mac*, which is about his several years working in the troupe led by Anew McMaster. McMaster was his teacher, director, and role model and his fellow actor. Among his many roles, Pinter played Iago to McMaster's Othello. In a photograph of that event, preserved in Pauline Flanagan's portfolio, Pinter is a dark, shadowy figure lurking behind McMaster, who is seated majestically. As Pinter said in *Mac*, McMaster "made the play his and the place his."

Many years later, Pinter was working on a film in Waterford, Ireland and revisited the Theatre Royal, the scene of their *Othello*. As he recalled, "I stood on the stage and I remember exactly the position I had stood when I played Iago to Mac's Othello, which was one of the great thrills of my life." He felt that at that moment he could have done both roles, the whole play, on the spot. One specific moment was deeply planted in his memory, when McMaster strangled him and said the line, "Villain, be sure thou prove my wife a whore." "It was the most incredibly dramatic gesture," Pinter said. "In fact I can still feel his hand round my throat!"

He admired McMaster's Othello, but not his Hamlet. In *Hamlet*, Pinter played Horatio--with Kenneth Haigh as Laertes. For one performance at a Thursday matinee, McMaster let Pinter ascend to the title role, and he subordinated himself in the role of the Gravedigger. When he was not on stage, McMaster watched the young actor perform. After the performance, Pinter asked, "How was it, Mac?" and McMaster answered, "Very good, but be a little more compassionate with your mother. You are very hard." Pinter accepted that criticism, with the explanation, "As a young man, I wasn't going to go in for this romanticism with my mother." He never got to play Hamlet again, but he did do other Shakespeare as well as Oscar Wilde: he played Jack Worthing in *The Importance of Being Earnest* and Lord Windermere in *Lady Windermere's Fan*. Later, briefly and with less satisfying results, he joined Donald Wolfit's company.

Looking back on his days in rep, he said, "I suppose Shakespeare's dominated my life the way he's dominated many people's lives. We don't recover from Shakespeare." He specialized in playing villains: murderers in *Macbeth*, as well as Iago. As he acknowledges, "My favorite roles were undoubtedly the sinister ones," and one attraction for him as a young actor was that it enabled him to "frighten the audience."

The first time I saw Pinter act, aside from his walk-ons in movies he wrote (*Accident*, *The Servant*, *Turtle Diary*), was at the 92nd Street Y in New York in October 1989. The occasion was twofold: Pinter acting from his own work followed by a conversation between the two of us onstage. He did a scene from *The Hothouse*, playing both Roote and his assistant, Lush, leading to Roote's attack on Lush and his shout, "I AM AUTHORIZED!" That was followed by the author's performance of *One for the Road* in its entirety. This was an evocative pairing of political plays, one early, one midway in his career, and it also demonstrated the range of Pinter's acting. His Roote was malevolently amusing. In *One for the Road*, he played all four characters: the torturer and his three victims, a married couple and their seven-year-old son, and seemed to take particular pleasure in the role of the torturer, originally played by Alan Bates, under Pinter's direction.

In our conversation, I asked him how it felt to enact his own plays. Does Pinter the playwright or Pinter the director watch Pinter the actor? He did not answer the question directly, but said, "I'm just aware of the peril that actors, to whom I take my hat off, go through every night. . . . There are no certainties in performing at all. You don't know what's going to happen next, although you try to plan. . . . You can slip down so many keyholes, abysses, in the course of that journey. It really is an adventure. To sustain it is an extraordinary feat."

Early in his career as an actor--and later--he has faced the actor's nightmare--stage fright--and he feels that it is endemic to the profession. "I think it's an essential part of the act of acting," he said. "I'm not alone in this. Almost every actor I know possesses this ingredient. Every night before I go on, before the play begins, standing in the wings, I feel a slight tension in the stomach. Not in the feet or the hands or anywhere else. A little quiver, a tremor, shall we say."

Some years later, again at the 92nd Street Y, he performed *Ashes to Ashes*, taking on both roles, that of the interrogator and his wife, playing the wife in a voice that was a shade higher, not emphasizing gender but focusing on the cat and mouse quality of the dialogue. It was the purest Pinter, a conversation with himself. Hearing Pinter read Pinter made one realize how persuasive a director he must be, both reading the play to his actors and listening to them read it back to him. For one thing, there is no greater guide to Pinter intonations, silences, and of course, pauses. When he reads or acts, he does not extend his pauses, as other actors are sometimes tempted to do, but uses them for most effective dramatic purpose. Except for those appearances at the Y, he has not yet acted in New York. As he says, seemingly without regret, "I've never been on the Great White whatever you call it."

At the same time, his career as an actor in films has been flourishing. He played a gangster in Jez Butterworth's *Mojo*, a role added to the film and a perfect fit for Pinter. In 1999, in Patricia Rozema's film of Jane Austen's *Mansfield Park*, he was Sir Thomas Bertram, his most sustained role in the movies. Watching him, larger than life, in period costume as the proud paterfamilias of Austen's imagination, one must acknowledge Pinter's acting roots and the fact that he apparently has not lost his taste or his talent for that art. "I know a hawk from a handsaw," he says conclusively, "and a costume from a pair of jeans. I like my cloak. This acting business isn't something I suddenly started doing again. I've done it all my life."

Mansfield Park was a particular challenge in that it was a period piece and it was based on a classic. Sir Thomas was the fulcrum of the story. He brings Fanny Price (Frances O'Connor) to Mansfield Park, supervises her life, and sets the tone for the family's cool, upper-class behavior. In a crucial scene, he criticizes Fanny for refusing to marry a rich, eligible suitor. As the camera swirls around them, he is relentless in his intensity: to him, Fanny's act is a dereliction of her duties as his ward. But she is adamant, and the confrontation is a standoff, superbly executed by both actors, in tandem.

In the movie, in contrast to the novel, Sir Thomas's activity as a slave trader in the West Indies was emphasized, confronting him with a moral crisis. When I suggested to Pinter that playing such a character might run counter to his own position in life as an outspoken defender of individual freedom, he responded as an actor. The morality of a character was not an issue; he was simply playing the part. Portraying Sir Thomas did not mean he approved of slave traders or of slavery, and he added that in *Mojo* he was a killer and "whatever else, I don't go around killing people." In the series of films of Samuel Beckett's plays, he played the Director in *Catastrophe*, directed by David Mamet. His autocratic character places a tortured prisoner (Sir John Gielgud) on public display. This was not Pinter's first performance in a work by Beckett. In 1976, he was in the radio play *Rough for Radio II*, playing the manipulative Animator opposite Billie Whitelaw and Patrick Magee.

As always, his most assured performances are as figures of authority, roles that call for at least an intimation of menace, which is why, of course, H. Pinter is such a natural to appear in works by H. Pinter.

"YOU'RE SPEAKING TO SOMEONE AND YOU SUDDENLY BECOME ANOTHER PERSON": STORYTELLING IN PINTER'S *MOONLIGHT* AND *ASHES TO ASHES*

Ann C. Hall

In a program note to a 1960 production of two of his earliest plays, *The Room* (1957) and *The Dumb Waiter* (1960), Harold Pinter defends his theatrical technique, saying:

> The desire for verification is understandable but cannot always be satisfied. There are no hard distinctions between what is real and what is unreal, nor between what is true and false. . . . A character on stage who can present no convincing argument or information as to his past experience, his present behavior or his aspirations, nor give a comprehensive analysis of his motives, is as legitimate as one who, alarmingly, can do all these things. The more acute the experience the less articulate the expression. (quoted in Esslin 1961, 206)

Despite Pinter's political activism of the past twenty years, and his claim that all his plays are "political," Pinter's most recent one-act, *Moonlight* (1993), and his full-length *Ashes to Ashes* (1996) illustrate that while his topics may have become more explicitly political through works such as *One for the Road* (1985), *Mountain Language* (1988), and *Party Time* (1991), his dramatic strategy is still as befuddling as ever.[1] Like the characters in *The Room* and *The Dumb Waiter*, the characters in

Moonlight and *Ashes to Ashes* do not offer a complete resume, a "comprehensive analysis" of their motives, or even a clear sense of time and place. Pinter, for example, sets *Ashes to Ashes* "Now," and the only distinction he makes between the two stage areas in *Moonlight* is that one is "well furnished" and one is "shabby." Clearly, Pinter is still firmly rooted in the Theatre of the Absurd movement, a movement that challenged the conventions of the "well-made play" and continues to challenge the facile solutions offered by traditional stage and film. Like the characters of many absurdists, Pinter's figures face crumbling social institutions, the loss of faith, and the absence of a stable identity, and like the characters in Samuel Beckett's plays, Pinter's characters perform and tell stories in the face of nothingness and existential crisis. In the seminal absurdist play, Samuel Beckett's *Waiting for Godot* (1952), for example, one character, Lucky, is admonished to think on cue. And in his *Endgame* (1958), as long as the two main characters, Hamm and Clov, continue to tell stories, the game is not ended. Pinter's recent plays function similarly. In *Moonlight*, for example, two sons toy with language, alter reality through fantasy, and create comic narratives to pass the time; one character even notes how ardently they all played "word games" as children (16). In *Ashes to Ashes*, a woman and man struggle through a narrative from the woman's past. Finally, although Pinter said "the more acute the experience, the less articulate the expression" in his early years as a playwright, these two recent plays demonstrate that language and power are closely related. Telling a story is not an innocent act; it is powerful. In *Moonlight*, humanity's ability to create realities through language is not entirely comforting. In *Ashes to Ashes*, the ability to tell one's story is the key to personal and social freedom. In both plays, though, Pinter illustrates that those who control language and speech have power--whether it be in the personal or political realm.

For many critics, *Moonlight* is about father-son relationships, a mythic power struggle.[2] Andy, the patriarch, is dying, while his two sons refuse to see him;

given his treatment of his wife, Bel, it is no surprise that his sons are reluctant to visit him on his deathbed. He is caustic, abusive, foul-mouthed, and the embodiment of conformity. He brags, for example, about his work as a civil servant:

> I'll tell you something about me. I sweated over a hot desk all my working life and nobody ever found a flaw in my working procedures. Nobody ever uncovered the slightest hint of negligence or misdemeanor. Never. I was an inspiration to others. . . . I inspired them to put their shoulders to the wheel and their noses to the grindstone and to keep faith at all costs with the structure which after all ensured the ordered government of all our lives. (17)

And while his wife, Bel, praises a mutual friend, Ralph, for his sensitivity, Andy praises the friend's career as a referee:

> You know why? Because referees are not obliged to answer questions. Referees are the law. They are the law in action. They have a whistle. They blow it. And that whistle is the articulation of God's justice. (68)

Through Andy, Pinter creates a father with a capital "F." According to Raymond Armstrong, Pinter started the play after he had worked on the screenplay of Kafka's *The Trial*. In addition to being one of the most important influences on Pinter, Kafka also had a very strained relationship with his overbearing father (1999, 115-71). Here, as in Pinter's other works, father figures may appear to be in control, but ultimately, they are exposed as weak, impotent, and vain: Petey in *The Birthday Party* (1958); Max and Teddy in *The Homecoming* (1965); and in a world with only patriarchs, Pinter ironically creates *No Man's Land* (1975).

At the same time, *Moonlight* also illustrates the manner in which people respond to extreme difficulties associated with existence. Andy faces death, and his sons face despair and possibly mental breakdowns.[3]   And all three use language to cope. For Andy, the only way to cope with impending death is rage. His sons, in their challenge, are more celebratory; they experiment with language, vocabulary, and the creation of narratives. Much of the play's humor comes from their linguistic fencing. In this way, the play offers alternative strategies for coping with loss, separation, and pain: Andy, who violently clings to the vestiges of his clearly diminishing authority, and the boys, who seem all too aware of their own impotence, "play" to pass the time.

To highlight the differences, the play, like Sam Shepard's *A Lie of the Mind* (1986), offers a split set, with Andy and his wife, Bel, on one side and his sons, Jake (also the name of Shepard's main character) and Fred on the other. And like the Shepard play, the physical relationship between the two sets is symbolic of the characters' emotional relationships: they may be close in proximity, but they are emotionally divorced. Though the family members stay apart, scenes are juxtaposed, and what often happens through the juxtaposition is an undercutting of the father's statements. While Andy struggles to recall the woman who came toward him at some point in his life, for example, Jake and Fred joke. Andy is dying, but no one will miss him.

In the midst of this patriarchal battle are three women, Maria, the ultimate other woman who has supposedly had an affair with Andy and Bel; Bel, Andy's wife; and the ghost-child, Bridget.[4] The suggestion that Maria has had an affair with both Andy and Bel, as well as the fact that she appears in scenes on both sides of the familial divide, might suggest that she has the power to reconcile the two sides, bridging both family and even gender. At the beginning of both scenes she appears in, however, she introduces herself with the same maternal information: "My three are all in terribly good form. Sarah's doing marvelously well and Lucien's thriving at the Consulate and as for Susannah, there's no stopping her" (16, 68). In both instances, it is difficult not to be reminded of the relationship between Sally Seton and Clarissa Dalloway in Virginia Woolf's *Mrs. Dalloway* (1925). Just as Sally Seton and Clarissa Dalloway have a strong attraction for one another, so do Maria and Bel. And just as Sally announces her male offspring with pride at the Dalloways' party, so, too, does Maria pride herself on her progeny, perhaps in the hope of recreating herself through the repetition of the maternal narrative. In this way, Maria, like Andy, seems to have succumbed to social pressures, and she now fits into the expected behavior of successful wife and mother.

Whether or not Maria and Bel actually consummated their affection is not clear. Andy asserts that they did, but Bel denies it, saying that the only one she has ever "had" and could still "have" is Andy (40). Be that as it may, the relationship between Bel and Maria was a strong one, and it is through her description of their bond that the play offers the most powerful statements concerning the effect language has on reality and identity:

> I spoke to her in a way I had never spoken to anyone before. Sometimes it happens, doesn't it? You're speaking to someone and you suddenly find that you're another person. (64)

Bel may have been betrayed by Andy with another woman, but she is no victim. When Andy makes an attempt at poetic language, after hurling abuses at her, calling spring blooms a "paraphernalia of flowers" (19), Bel sarcastically and then violently attacks his misuse of language, usage that was "mainly coarse, crude, vacuous, puerile, obscene, and brutal" (19). Andy may assert that he has been writing poems since before he was born, but it is Bel who understands the power of language. He, for example, says death is "like screaming with fright at the sight of a stranger only to find that you are looking in a mirror" (46), while she describes it as a "new horizon" (46).

The mirror image is an important one because it is in the role of mirror that women have been frequently cast within the patriarchal society. According to Virginia Woolf in *A Room of One's Own*,

> Women have served all these centuries as looking-glasses possessing the magic and delicious power of reflecting the figure of a man at twice its natural size. . . . Whatever may be their use in civilized societies, mirrors are essential to all violent and heroic action. . . . For if she begins to tell the truth, the figure in the looking-glass shrinks. (35-36)

Bel may stay with Andy, but she will no longer reflect, and her challenges to him may finally facilitate his diminishment.

The couple's discussions about Bridget and her offspring illustrate the shift in Bel's participation in Andy's narrative. Ironically, Andy, the dying, abusive father, is the first to bring up the topic of grandchildren. Since the boys do not have them, we must infer that he means Bridget's children. He, however, creates them in order to make his death more important: the children "will cry or they won't, a sorrow too deep for tears, but they're only babies, what can they know of death?" (47). Bel does not challenge his creation of these children but instead reassures him saying, "[T]he really little ones I think do know something about death, they know more about death than we do. We've forgotten death but they haven't forgotten it . . . and the moment before their life began they were of course dead" (47). Bel's narrative is clearly constructive; life and death are connected. There is no separation. Later, however, when Maria and Ralph come to visit the dying Ralph, Maria asks about Bridget and assumes that she must be a mother. Andy asserts that he has three grandchildren, but Bel only says, "By the way, he's not well. Have you noticed?" (71). In much the same way George and Martha in Edward Albee's *Who's Afraid of Virginia Woolf?* (1962) construct a son, it appears that Andy and Bel have constructed a fantasy life regarding Bridget. Only in the later scene, Bel will no longer support Andy's narrative.

If Bel posits a connection between life and death, Bridget clearly illustrates the partnership between the living and the dead. As a spirit, she watches over her parents while they are sleeping, and later in the middle of the play, she describes her surroundings as a lush jungle that makes her invisible to others. The play includes a scene in which Jake, Fred, and she are younger, and she attempts to keep the two boys together. Here, her cohesive powers do not work; the boys are separated by a social engagement. The concluding image is much more horrifying. In it, she describes a story "someone said to me" and attributes it to one of her parents (79). In this narrative, she has been told that if she dresses in her old clothes and waits until the moon goes down, she will be able to attend a party:

> When I got to the house it was bathed in moonlight. The house, the glade, the lane, were all bathed in moonlight. But the inside of the house was dark and all the windows were dark. There was no sound. (*Pause.*) I stood there in the moonlight and waited for the moon to go down. (80)

Given Bel's descriptions of death, as well as Bridget's own lush description earlier, this narrative comes as a surprise. It is placed at the end of the play, after we hear that Andy has died. The boys appear free, but as Armstrong notes, they are also trapped, walking around their room, and unable to break free (171). Bridget has been lied to--there is no one in the house. She is alone, waiting, in the moonlight. Given the self-absorption of her parents throughout the play, it is not difficult to conclude that her parents, in fact, told her this lie, only to have her disappointed by the results. And given Pinter's statements about socially constructed explanations, it is not improbable to read this final scene as an indictment regarding the myths our culture tells us about death and other life questions. Pinter, for example, recently remarked that his mysterious characters Goldberg and Mecca in *The Birthday Party* represented "how religious forces ruin our lives" (Gussow 71). The play supports such a conclusion when Jake tells Fred that scientists have perfected a "light meter," which can find and locate light:

> JAKE: Then they place it in a little box. They wrap it up and tie a ribbon round it and you get it tax free, as a reward for all your labour and faith and all the concern and care for others you have demonstrated so eloquently for so long. . . . It will serve as your own personal light eternal. . . . This is what we can do for you.
> FRED: Who?
> JAKE: Society. (54-55)

Not only does this scene follow Andy's admission regarding his fear of the darkness of death, it is difficult not to pair it with the conclusion. Through received information, Bridget expects a party, but when she arrives, there is nothing but an empty house and moonlight, perhaps a child's worst nightmare--separated from parents, alone, and abandoned. Andy, too, has been a good, well-behaved civil servant, so he is hoping for some reward, some comfort in the face of death, but Jake and Fred indicate that all that is available is a manufactured point of light, nothing more. Given the conclusion of this play, it is difficult not to conclude that Pinter is once again cautioning us to beware of society's bedtime stories. At the same time, Bel has reassured Andy earlier that children understand death better than adults do, that they would know how to find him, and given the fact that Bridget is waiting in the moonlight, there may be a hint that she and Andy will be united.

Ashes to Ashes also highlights storytelling and its implications. The play begins with Rebecca, apparently a middle-class, educated, married woman, telling a story about her participation in a sadomasochistic relationship.

Her listener Devlin, an educated, middle-class man, seems inordinately interested in her story. And for many critics of this play, through the course of the Rebecca's narrative, he, attracted by the sheer power expressed through the male lover in her story, becomes abusive in the very same way the lover in the narrative abuses Rebecca (Billington 1996). Through this reading, narrative's power is also illustrated, but this solution does not account for many of the details in the play. Some critics, such as Benedict Nightingale, conclude that Rebecca is also attracted to male power and enjoys her masochistic role in the abusive relationship. And while this may be frequently true of domestic abuse cases, such a conclusion does not take Rebecca's development as a narrator into account.

As was the case in *Moonlight*, this play's setting is undefined. The play is set "Now," and the couple, like the characters in *Moonlight*, give us little information by way of biographical sketches. The couple could be anywhere, in any country. According to Pinter, he wrote the play after reading Gitta Sereny's *Albert Speer: His Battle With Truth* and directing Ronald Harwood's *Taking Sides*, a play that examines the life and culpability of conductor Wilhelm Furtwängler during Nazi Germany (Billington, 1996, 365-74). In both works, the relationship between art and politics is highlighted: passionate about their art, both men fall prey to the promises of Nazi German, promises that include the opportunity to use their talents. When one reads the Sereny book what is so striking is the ordinariness of Speer's life with Hitler, and as Billington notes, the "play also conclusively proves that for Pinter the 'personal' and the 'political' are not separate, vacuum-sealed categories" (Billington 1996, 375). The lack of specific details further blurs these distinctions. According to Susan Hollis Merritt, who reviewed and read the play's drafts, Pinter took great pains to remove the specific references from the text during revision (156). His alterations made the play more ironic and abstract, a modern day *Everyman* of torture and victimization.

Reading the play so specifically, moreover, overlooks the relationship between language and abuse, and the incredible power language can have over oppression. Ultimately the play illustrates that the pen is mightier than the sword. Furthermore, by examining the play in the light of language and power, the masochistic readings of Rebecca are no longer feasible.

The play clearly draws our attention to narrative from the very beginning. Devlin asks Rebecca for more information on the story that she is in the middle of telling. As she tells the story of her sadomasochistic relationship, Devlin demands more specific information, particularly concerning the lover:

> DEVLIN: Look. It would mean a great deal to me if you could define him more clearly.
> REBECCA: Define him?   What do you mean define him? (11)

On the one hand, Devlin is clearly becoming simultaneously aroused and jealous as she tells the story, as many have concluded. But, on the other hand, the scene suggests that Rebecca is creating a character who may or may not be real. Perhaps, as some have argued, she is a repository for all oppressed people, a psychic "channel" for victims everywhere, so the request to define abusers is difficult, given this Jungian collective unconscious of political oppression (Brantley, 1999). I would like to suggest yet another reading: Devlin is not removed from the sadomasochistic relationship; he is not merely a viewer who becomes caught up in the narrative. He is, in fact, the abuser, and the events of the play are not a unique occurrence; they are part of the torture. In this way, the play underscores the complicity of viewers to crimes. They are not merely innocent bystanders; they participate in the oppression. As I have argued elsewhere, Pinter's work is extremely metatheatrical. In *The Birthday Party*, for example, the entire strategy of speculation is exposed and indicted as oppressive. The stage, the act of spectacle, of watching, all have consequences; they are not innocent activities (Hall, 1996, 54-90; 1996, 48-56). Devlin could very well be describing the audience in the following speech from *Ashes to Ashes*:

> There are so many things I don't know. I know nothing . . . about any of this. Nothing. I'm in the dark. I need light. Or do you think my questions are illegitimate?

Rebecca, however, will not answer the questions, and rather than using explicit disobedience, she distracts him by the comment, "No one has ever called me darling. Apart from my lover" (13). Again, this comment could be taken literally, or it could indicate that Devlin is, in fact, her lover, the only person to call her "darling."

Whatever the case, the play solidifies Devlin's position as interrogator. He is frequently standing over Rebecca, and he attempts to direct the conversation at all times. As the play progresses, he becomes more abusive, moving from questions about the physical characteristics of Rebecca's lover to requiring and subsequently offering explanations for the existence of God, or at least humanity's need for God:

> If you turn away from God it means that the great and noble game of soccer will fall into permanent oblivion. No score for extra time after extra time after extra time, no score for time everlasting, for time without end. Absence. Stalemate. Paralysis. A world without a winner. (39)

Nowhere could a better illustration of patriarchal control be given--"a world without a winner." Devlin needs the competition, power, and dialectical means of oppression. For some postmodernists, this is the human condition, the very nature of language, history and culture, with no way out.[5]

Devlin continues to question Rebecca in a manner reminiscent of Goldberg and McCann pummeling Stanley with meaningless references. When Rebecca, for example, begins to tell the story of a child being torn from its mother's arms, Devlin asks, "What authority do you think you yourself possess which would give you the right to discuss such an atrocity?" (41). The use of the word "authority" is significant in the context of this discussion, because it not only indicates power but it also indicates authorship, the specific power over words, language, and narrative. At this point in the play, Rebecca succumbs to his linguistic brutality: "I have no such authority. Nothing has ever happened to me. Nothing has ever happened to any of my friends. I have never suffered. Nor have my friends" (41). In true Pintereque fashion, Devlin responds, "Good." And he proceeds to harangue Rebecca further: "Let's talk about more intimate things, let's talk about something more personal . . ." (41). For some, this exchange indicates that Rebecca has not suffered; she is merely channeling the oppression of historical and present-day beings. But it is equally likely that she deflects Devlin's rage by temporary submission. Furthermore, the fact that he responds so violently to her story suggests that by the very act of telling the story Rebecca assumes a position of power.

Rebecca is not without an arsenal of linguistic defenses. Earlier, she avoids describing the lover to Devlin by distracting him about the world "darling," and later a song title. When Devlin decides that the lover wanted to murder her, to suffocate her, Rebecca will not allow such conclusions. She tells him that this man "had compassion" for her (45). As the play continues, Rebecca continues to evade Devlin's desires, through stories of her sister, a movie, and people along a beach escorted into the sea by the menacing "travel guides." In the hopes of regaining control, Devlin says:

> Now look, let's start again. We live here. You don't live . . . in Dorset . . . or *anywhere else.* You live here with me. This is our house. You have a very nice sister. She lives close to you. She has two lovely kids. You're their aunt. You like that. (65)

Because Rebecca has been digressing from the focus of the narration, her relationship with her lover/abuser, Devlin's demands are more than just requests for a shift in conversation. He defines her, and he hopes to define her imagination. Like Martha in Albee's *Who's Afraid of Virginia Woolf*, Rebecca has brought up the "bundle"; she has violated the rules of the linguistic game. Consequently, Devlin wishes to "start again," but Deborah corrects him, saying, "I don't think we can start again . . . We can end again" (67). In the speech, she repeats the fact that they have ended "again and again and again" (67). Such semantic quibbling is important. Not only does the repetition suggest that the couple has played these scenes before, but it also demonstrates that Rebecca is no longer willing to play the game according to Devlin's rules. She gains control of the narrative.

Rebecca continues with the story of her baby being taken away as she is about to board the train, and because the play concludes with this story, as well as the silence of Devlin throughout, it suggests that Rebecca has, in fact, achieved the upper hand. She may be telling a story of her own victimhood or the victimization of millions of women throughout centuries, but she is, finally, able to tell it. She will not succumb to Devlin's verbal intimidation, and though the story is incredibly painful, it, like the siren earlier, is something that she can claim as her own.

That Pinter believes in the power of language is clearly demonstrated in his works from *The Birthday Party* to *Mountain Language*. Language is powerful, both politically and personally. The loss of narrative is the ultimate oppression, and as in *Mountain Language* Pinter uses a voice-over or echo in this play to illustrate or underscore its importance. Speaking, Rebecca is finally in power. She does have the last word.

Such a reading does not suggest that by her triumphant narrative the play diminishes her pain. Rather, in the context of growing revisionist history that claims that there was no Holocaust or other atrocities, the play illustrates that the stories of these crimes must be told "again and again and again." There is power in the telling. Through these recent plays and Pinter's own political comments, Pinter may have lost faith in the future of humankind and may have his doubts about the afterlife, but he has not lost faith in language. Stories are important, and we must continue to tell them.

NOTES

1. See, for example, Gussow (69), as well as "A Play and its Politics," an interview between Nicholas Hern and Pinter during which Pinter says that there was a "political metaphor" in *The Birthday Party*, and political considerations "were alive in" his "mind over those years, 1957-60 or so" (7-8). Robert Cushman says "that Pinter came out politically late in life--because he was outraged by specific inhumanities--is to his credit. I trust him more than I would a writer who chose a cause in youth as he might choose a football team and went on supporting it just as automatically" (1996, 18).

2. See, for example, Margo Jefferson, Vincent Canby, and Michael Billington, who called the London production a "postmodern Lear raging against the fear of death." Raymond Armstrong offers the most comprehensive analysis of the father-son relations in *Moonlight* (115-171).

3. When asked about the younger son, Pinter says, "I don't think he is literally dying, but he makes it quite clear that he doesn't want to get out of that bed. So that's another kind of death. I think the fellow's just having a kind of nervous breakdown. I think it's a common condition for a lot of young men . . ." (Gussow 1994, 99).

4. Pinter notes that Bridget in his mind is dead; "she was the embodiment" of the "dead being present." Pinter also notes "there are no grandchildren. . . . To anyone who cares to listen to the play that is pretty evident" (Gussow 1994, 99).

5. See, for example, Derrida's *Writing and Difference*.

WORKS CITED

Armstrong, Raymond. *Kafka and Pinter: Shadow-Boxing: The Struggle Between Father and Son*. New York: St. Martin's Press, 1999.

Billington, Michael. *The Life and Work of Harold Pinter*. London: Faber and Faber, 1996.

———. The Triumph: Poet of Darkness. *The Guardian*. 21 September 1996. 7.

Brantley, Ben. No Refuge from Terror for a Sphinx in Pinter Land. *The New York Times*. 8 February 1999. Sec. E1.

Canby, Vincent. Taking Dysfunctional to New Depths in a Pinter Work. *The New York Times*. 18 October 1995. Sec. C15.

Cushman, Robert. Playing Pinter. *The Independent*. 15 September 1996. 18.

Derrida, Jacques. *Writing and Difference*. Edited and translated by Alan Bass. Chicago: University of Chicago Press, 1978.

Esslin, Martin. *The Theatre of the Absurd.* New York: Doubleday, 1961.

Gussow, Mel. *Conversations with Harold Pinter.* London: Nick Hern Books, 1994.

Hall, Ann C. *"A Kind of Alaska":* Women in the Plays of O'Neill, Pinter, and Shepard. Carbondale: Southern Illinois University Press, 1993.

————. Looking for Mr. Goldberg: Spectacle and Speculation in Harold Pinter's *The Birthday Party.* *The Pinter Review: Collected Essays 1997 and 1998.* Edited by Francis Gillen and Steven Gale. Tampa: University of Tampa Press, 1999: 48-56.

Hern, Nicholas. A Play and Its Politics: A Conversation between Harold Pinter and Nicholas Hern: *One For the Road* by Harold Pinter. London: Methuen, 1984: 5-23.

Jefferson, Margo. Despite Pinter, *Moonlight* Falls into Eclipse. *The New York Times.* 29 October 1995. Sec. 2. 4.

Merritt, Susan Hollis. Rev. of *Ashes to Ashes.* *The Pinter Review: Collected Essays 1997 and 1998.* Edited by Francis Gillen and Steven Gale. Tampa: University of Tampa Press, 1999: 156-159.

Pinter, Harold. *Moonlight.* London: Faber and Faber, 1993.

————. *Ashes to Ashes.* New York: Grove, 1996.

CELEBRATING PINTER

Michael Billington

No doubt about it. The highlight of the Pinter in London Conference, organised by the Harold Pinter Society at the Hotel Russell in June 2000, was the author's own reading of *Celebration.* Clad in a sober black suit, he stood before us at a lectern. Briefly, he explained the physical staging of the play in his production at the Almeida Theatre. The setting was a restaurant and the audience was confronted by two groups of diners at adjacent tables: as the lights came up on the group that was speaking, they would dim on the silent partners. In the reading Pinter indicated the switches from Table One to Table Two with a peremptory snap of his fingers. Pinter went all out for--and certainly got--a lot of laughs arising from the collision between the diners' coarse banter and the restaurant owner's emollient smoothness. But what was striking was Pinter's joyful characterisation of the play's nine speakers: in particular, he seemed to relish playing the female roles lending the banker's wife, Suki, a mocking flirtiness. This, I felt, was what it must have been like seeing Dickens embodying his own characters in his famous public readings. The highest drama, however, was reserved for the end. As the diners all departed, Pinter thwacked the side of the lectern with his right hand to indicate a closing door and launched into the Waiter's resonant, poetic, and mysterious final speech. As Pinter admitted afterwards, he was hardly the right age to play the Waiter. But what he successfully reproduced was the violent and dramatic change of tone that occurs in the play's final seconds.

Since so much of *Celebration*'s power resides in the character of the Waiter, it might be worth touching on the play's element of recollected experience. In my biography of

Pinter, I suggest there is a pattern to his work: that his plays are consistently triggered by some event in his own life but that, in the process of writing, the event is totally transfigured by his imagination. I believe something similar happened in the case of *Celebration*. At a lunch in London in April--where Pinter received the annual Lifetime Achievement award donated by the Critics' Circle--he talked quite openly about his own experiences as a young waiter. As an out-of-work actor in the early 1950s, he worked for a spell at the National Liberal Club. One evening he overheard two members discussing the date of publication of the first English version of Kafka's *The Trial*. The members got it wrong. Pinter, being a Kafka buff, knew that the Edwin and Willa Muir translation first appeared in 1930 and said so. The members were impressed and engaged this far-from-dumb waiter in animated conversation. But the moment Pinter returned to the club kitchens, he was dismissed on the spot and given his cards. In those days waiters did not fraternise with members.

This incident doesn't explain *Celebration*. What it does do is confirm the retentive nature of Pinter's memory and show his ability to filter his own experience through a transformative imagination. Pinter's sacking was the product of a rigid, class-structured 1950s world. But *Celebration* is very much a play for today. The restaurant diners divide into two groups. At Table One are two couples--Lambert and Julie, Matt and Prue--who are brothers and sisters who have intermarried and who are celebrating the first couple's wedding-anniversary with raucous abandon. At Table Two are Russell and Suki: a young banker and his wife whom he treats with insulting derision. When Lambert realises he knows Suki--whom he claims to have fucked when she was eighteen--the two parties come together. Collectively, the diners represent the vulgar materialism that was a direct product of Thatcher's Britain in the 1980s and that still persists today, though Pinter draws a clear distinction between the bumptiously egotistic males and their more self-aware and quietly mocking wives.

But it is the restaurant staff who intrigue Pinter as much as the diners. Richard, the owner, is a deft and faintly oleaginous restaurant diplomat who deflects obscene complaints and sexual overtures with the same unwavering imperturbability: he prides himself on running a "happy" restaurant. Sonia, the maitresse d'hotel, who hails from Bethnal Green (close to Pinter's own Hackney birthplace), expresses a patronising attitude to the sundry foreigners who pass through the restaurant ("I've often said 'You don't have to speak English to enjoy good food'") and has had an unhappy love life which she is only too ready to impart to the customers. Most complex of all is the Waiter, who eavesdrops on the clients' conversations and who uses them as a starting point for his own obsessive fantasies, all involving his grandfather. In one, the grandfather was an intimate of all Modernism's literary giants, even achieving the role of James Joyce's godmother. In another the grandfather was a close chum of the Hollywood immortals. And in a third he becomes an idealised Christ-figure who has offered salvation to a motley collection of twentieth-century greats. Only in the final speech, when the diners have departed, does the Waiter talk about his real grandfather in a manner that implicitly contradicts everything he has said before.

On one level, *Celebration* is a comic satire on the nerdy nouveau-riche. They are coarse, greedy, loud, and raffish. But, if that were all Pinter were saying about them, the play would be as snobbish as one or two London critics superficially assumed. As in *Party Time*, Pinter goes far beyond that to suggest that materialistic individualism breeds moral vacancy and that there is an umbilical connection between male chauvinism and political brutality. In *Party Time*, while round-ups of dissidents are taking place in the streets, the partygoers prattle on about the wonderful recreational facilities of the club of which they are almost all members. In *Celebration* the restaurant ("the best caff in town," in Lambert's phrase) operates as a similar refuge from reality. Again in *Party Time* the male fascistic instinct is expressed through sexual coarseness: in

Celebration there is also an implied equation between the ribald sexual bullying of Lambert and Matt and their profession as "strategic consultants," which sounds like a euphemism for arms dealers. Pinter is not just taking the piss out of a group of walking wallets or writing a comedy of grotesquely bad manners: he is writing a quasi-political play in which wealth, greed, vanity, and sexual loutishness symbolise both moral emptiness and hermetic isolation from the real world of pain and suffering.

But what fascinates me most about *Celebration*--particularly when seen, as it was at the Almeida, in conjunction with Pinter's first play, *The Room*--is its use of the theme that pervades all Pinter's work: memory. Remembrance of things past has always seemed to me the key to Pinter; and what one notices is how the exploration of memory grows in subtlety and depth with the years. In early plays, such as *The Room* and *The Birthday Party*, a real or romanticised past is often used to buttress the insecure present. One thinks of Mr. Kidd in *The Room*, wistfully recalling the heyday of his property--"Floors. Ah, we had a good few of them in the old days"--or McCann in *The Birthday Party* woozily summoning up all-night drinking sessions at Mother Nolan's in Roscrea (a direct reference to Pinter's own years as a touring actor with Anew McMaster in Ireland). By the period of *Old Times*, first seen in 1971, Pinter's use of memory has become infinitely more complex: what we see is three characters creating the past according to the tactical and psychological needs of the moment and in the process giving that past a tangible reality. And in *Ashes to Ashes*, the immediate predecessor of *Celebration*, something even more remarkable happens: Rebecca, by an act of imaginative transference, at the climax embodies the collective memory of persecuted refugees in the blood-stained twentieth century. In Pinter's early work memory is used largely for comic or terrifying effect. By the time of *Ashes to Ashes* it has become an active force and a symbol of the female gift for historical empathy.

Underneath the social satire, *Celebration* is also clearly a work about memory. It takes place during a wedding anniversary: nominally an occasion for sentimental recollection but, in theatrical terms, more often an excuse for recrimination. One of the most powerful postwar British plays, David Storey's *In Celebration*, shows how a family reunion for a parental wedding anniversary reveals all the unhealed wounds of the past. Pinter's similarly-titled play is somewhat different: it sets up a deliberate counterpoint between the fitful, spasmodic, and largely sexual memories of the diners and those of the staff themselves which are variously rose-tinted, rebarbative, fantastic, and spellbindingly real. But the restaurant itself becomes a memory chamber in which everyone present is engaged in an act of recollection.

Sex is the dominating experience for the diners who all exist in a world of sensual gratification. The tone is set by Russell and Suki at Table Two. He is clearly atoning for an act of infidelity with his secretary: something that provokes Suki into recalling that she, too, was once a plump young secretary who existed in a state of seemingly permanent sexual arousal. "Sometimes," she remembers, "I could hardly walk from one cabinet to another I was so excited"--lines which Lia Williams delivered at the Almeida with a breathy ecstasy that sent the audience into paroxysms of delight.

But sex is also the door to the past for the fractious siblings and partners at the adjacent table. They engage in a confused, drunken, Freudian argument about the proposition that "all mothers want to be fucked by their sons." Lambert reminisces about a girl he loved whom he used to take for walks by the river: palpably not his wife, Julie, who recalls that Lambert fell in love with her on top of a bus ("It was a short journey. Fulham Broadway to Shepherd's Bush, but it was enough"). With even greater insensitivity, Lambert recalls how on his wedding day he was all ready to have sex at the altar until stopped by Matt, his fraternal best man; though quite whether Lambert was in heat for his intended wife or his future sister-in-law is left deliberately equivocal. And when Lambert spots Suki at the adjoining table it is because he recalls "I fucked her when she was eighteen."

Memory for these characters is largely a form of sexual twitch: a recollection of who had whom and when. Even when they engage in the Pinteresque game of competitive memory, it is only to reveal more sharply than ever the banality of their thinking and the mutual suspicions that lurk behind the supposed marital celebration. Suki, when invited to join the party, remembers Lambert as obsessed with gardening, which prompts the following exchange:

JULIE:	Funny that when you knew my husband you thought he was obsessed with gardening. I always thought he was obsessed with girls' bums.
SUKI:	Really?
PRUE:	Oh yes, he was always a keen wobbler.
MATT:	What do you mean? How do you know?
PRUE:	Oh don't get excited. It's all in the past.
MATT:	What is?
SUKI:	I sometimes feel that the past is never past.
RUSSELL:	What do you mean?
JULIE:	You mean that yesterday is today?
SUKI:	That's right. You feel the same, do you?
JULIE:	I do.
MATT:	Bollocks.
JULIE:	I wouldn't like to live again though, would you? Once is more than enough.
LAMBERT:	I'd like to live again. In fact I'm going to make it my job to live again. I'm going to come back as a better person, a more civilized person, a gentler person, a nicer person.
JULIE:	Impossible. (52-53)

Lightly, glancingly, and comically, Pinter exposes the hollowness of these marriages and the spiritual coarseness of the diners. Lambert on his wedding anniversary invites a former sexual conquest to his table. Prue lets slip that she had a fling with her brother-in-law. And Julie, by her concluding line, reveals the depth of her contempt for her husband: significantly, in Pinter's production, she was seated as far from him as possible at the opposite end of the banquette. But, reviewing that production, one critic, Benedict Nightingale in *The Times*, posed a very interesting question: "The crudeness gets so extreme, the mockery so weird that you wonder if you aren't witnessing a waking nightmare in which emotional flashers are indecently exposing their hidden angers and anxieties about sex, power, mothers, children, everything." I suspect Pinter's play is closer to observed truth than we suspect: it triggered my own memory, on a Sunday night journey from Paris to London in a first-class Eurostar compartment, of overhearing a drunken mother boasting to her friends, in front of her teenage daughter, of a hotel holiday where she and her husband had been admonished by the proprietor for their disturbingly noisy coupling. One felt an acute sense of pained embarrassment for the child listening to her mother broadcasting her sexual exploits to the whole compartment.

Children, of course, are conspicuously absent from Pinter's anniversary celebration: a fact on which Julie herself comments. And when the characters do talk of their children it is as if they were once pawns in marital power games and are now strangers with whom they have lost all real contact:

PRUE:	They always loved me much more than they loved him.
JULIE:	Me too. They loved me to distraction. I was their mother.
PRUE:	Yes, I was too. I was my children's mother.
MATT:	They have no memory.

LAMBERT: Who?
MATT: Children. They have no memory.
            They remember nothing. They don't
            remember who their father was or
            who their mother was. It's all a hole
            in the wall for them. They don't
            remember their own life. (41-42)

There is sadness and bitterness behind these remarks; but
also an acute irony. Children are rebuked for having no
memory. Yet the adult diners themselves have a single-
track memory that is almost entirely concerned with their
sexual exploits. And the irony is compounded by the fact
that the play's profoundest memory is articulated by the
young Waiter and is based on familial connection. Pinter is
juxtaposing two worlds in *Celebration*--one in which
memory is highly selective and crudely foreshortened, and
another in which it is capable of infinite, mysterious
perspectives.

      The Waiter offers an emotional counterpoise to the
diners. But he is not the only member of the restaurant staff
with a keen memory. Richard, the owner, lapses into a rosy
nostalgia that is both comic and politic: you feel it is there
to offer the guests the kind of nannying comfort and
reassurance they desperately crave. Russell, the merchant
banker (which, of course, is Cockney rhyming slang for
"wanker"), admits that the restaurant smothers his inherent
psychopathic tendencies and that normally he feels "malice
and hatred towards everyone within spitting distance." If
the restaurant has a soothing effect, its owner attributes it to
his attempt to recreate the atmosphere of the village pub he
was taken to as a child. Indeed, Richard recalls "Old men
smoking pipes, no music of course, cheese rolls, gherkins,
happiness. I think this restaurant--which you so kindly
patronise--was inspired by that pub in my childhood. I do
hope you notice that you have complimentary gherkins as
soon as you take your seat." The idea that an elitist,
expensive London restaurant bears any resemblance to an
oak-beamed English village pub is, of course, laughable:

what Pinter is doing is showing memory as a mixture of skilled professional tactic and sentimental self-delusion. In Pinter's own production, the joke was enhanced by the striking resemblance of the actor playing Richard, Thomas Wheatley, to a notoriously unctious London restaurateur. If Richard soothes and flatters his guests, Sonia, the grand-sounding maitresse d'hotel, offers instant identification: between them they go to work like a pair of counsellors, turning this high-class caff into a therapy centre. Richard is the benign host who is socially superior to his guests. Sonia is an East End working-class girl made good: even her patronising xenophobia ("I've known one or two Belgian people who love sex and they don't speak a word of English") echoes that of the diners. And, if their marriages are a bit of a mess, her own fraught emotional memories provide consolation. As she refers to a Moroccan lover, she starts to break down. And when Prue enquires about his fate, Sonia retorts: "He's dead. He died in another woman's arms. He was on the job. Can you see how tragic my life has been?" It may all be true; or it may be another example of a skilled professional using memory as a form of cathartic reassurance.

The dramatic impact of *Celebration*, however, depends on the contrast between the Waiter and the guests. In the first instance, the Waiter is a classic example of a familiar Pinter figure: the intruder who unnerves people by occupying their clearly-defined space. Straight after one had seen *The Room*, it was difficult not to compare him with the invasive Riley who enters Rose's drab sanctuary and alarms her with his invocations to return home; and Pinter's own production emphasised the Waiter's territorial sense by at one point having him sit down on the banquette next to Suki and Russell.

But the Waiter is not simply a space-invader. For one thing, he himself refers to the restaurant as "my womb" and says that he prefers to stay inside it rather than be born; so, in a curious way, he takes on a dual Pinter role of both invasive intruder and immured victim. But the Waiter's fantasising memories of his mythic grandfather are also

used by Pinter to represent everything that is absent in or
has been lost from the world of the celebratory diners.
Each of his comic arias is also carefully pointed and placed.
His first discourse on his grandfather's supposed literary
chums is addressed to Suki and Russell: the latter is a
banker, as famously was T.S. Eliot who triggers the whole
speech, but the litany of great names that follows only
serves to emphasise the gulf in modern life between
commerce and literature. The Waiter's second memory trip
about the intimate connection between movie stars and
gangsters is directed toward the wedding anniversary
celebrants who, on the male side, at least, talk like flash
hoodlums. And his third speech, portraying his grandfather
as an altruistic saint ("He was tall, dark and handsome. He
was full of good will. He'd even give a cripple with no legs
crawling on his belly through the slush and mud of a
country lane a helping hand") is addressed to both sets of
diners for whom, you deduce, Christian charity towards
one's fellow men is not exactly high on the agenda. Indeed
Lambert cuts the Waiter short as he's reaching his climax,
as if the speech has simply bounced off him.

But both Pinter's staging and his solo reading
showed that the meaning of the play turns on the Waiter's
final speech after the diners have departed. What
immediately strikes one is its direct, honest, personal tone.
"When I was a boy," the Waiter begins, "my grandfather
used to take me to the edge of the cliffs and we'd look out
to sea." This sets up several resonances. Not just of the
mutual love that exists within families and between
different generations (something signally absent from the
play so far). It also reminds one of the way Pinter
throughout his work uses the memory of sea and cliffs as an
emotional touchstone: it's an idea that occurs in *A Slight
Ache*, *Landscape*, *Old Times*, *Moonlight*, and *Ashes to
Ashes* and that originates, I suspect, in Pinter's own
experience as a wartime evacuee when he would go for
long walks along the Cornish coast.

The Waiter's speech continues with his memory of
his grandfather's gift of a telescope. "I don't think," he

says, "they have telescopes any more": not a literal truth but an evocation of a vanished world, pre-computer games and video toys, when children were delighted with simple gifts. But a telescope is also an optical instrument that changes perspectives and that brings distant objects into focus. I don't think it's too fanciful to see this as a poetic contrast with the prosaic fixity of the restaurant world with its hermetic self-display, its limited horizons, its bankruptcy of thought and feeling. Through the telescope the boy also saw people on a boat: "A man, sometimes, and a woman, or sometimes two men. The sea glistened." Contrast this with the world he now inhabits, where the Waiter sees people in relentless closeup and overhears the jangled discord of their ugly lives. The final sentences are the strangest of all:

> My grandfather introduced me to the mystery of life and I'm still in the middle of it. I can't find the door to get out. My grandfather got out of it. He got right out. He left it behind him and he didn't look back. He got that absolutely right. And I'd like to make one further interjection. (66-67)

What, a student asked me recently, does this mean? I answered that it is dangerous sometimes with Pinter to parse every sentence or pin too exact a meaning on each line. But what it clearly conveys is a sense of entrapment, enclosure, and confinement that comes with the passage from boyhood and adolescence into adulthood. The Waiter is in the middle of the mystery of life. The grandfather "got out of it": either, one assumes, by death or, more probably, by escaping from the restrictions of social conformity and imposed responsibility. The Waiter himself, played in Pinter's production by a young actor in his twenties, is left standing still in a fading light and offering another interjection to nonexistent hearers.

You can, broadly speaking, intepret Pinter's plays in either Freudian or sociopolitical terms. But the two approaches are not mutually exclusive and *Celebration* is susceptible to both lines of enquiry. One should say that, on the evidence of the Almeida performance, it is the funniest play Pinter has written in years and is borne along by a wave of constant laughter. At the same time, it is full of serious undertones. On one level, it is about what Freud called "the phantasy of intra-uterine existence" and the attempt to recreate in adult terms an experience of womblike safety and comfort: it is an idea that has obsessed Pinter from *The Dwarfs* onwards and here applies to all the characters but, most specifically, to the Waiter who discovers in the restaurant a world in which he can operate by imposing himself on the customers and who is terrified of external banishment. On a social and political level, the play also strongly resembles *Party Time* in its condemnation of a materialistic individualism that leads to a moral indifference and to a narrow focus on the gratification of personal appetites: in this case, those of sex and food.

But the means Pinter uses to explore these ideas is that of memory. The people in *Celebration* live fiercely in the present. But they deploy memory for a variety of motives, out of sexual triumphalism, reflex professionalism, nostalgic sentimentality, or simply in order to take the piss. It is only with the Waiter's climactic memory of his grandfather, however, that Pinter's purpose becomes clear: the final speech admits us to the true voice of feeling and, by its evocation of a world of familial closeness and natural beauty, offers a retrospective rebuke to the hollow social rituals we have previously witnessed. Memory is the key to Pinter; and in *Celebration*, performed in his seventieth year, he both explores the dialectic of memory and plays on our own accumulated memories of his astonishingly consistent lifetime's work.

SELECTED BIBLIOGRAPHY

Primary Works

I. PLAYS

Ashes to Ashes. Staged London, 1996; New York, 1999. London: Faber and Faber, 1996; New York: Grove, 1997. Video: New York Roundabout Theatre production, 1999, New York Public Library #NCOV 2296.

The Basement. Televised London, 1967; staged New York (with *Tea Party*), 1968. In *Tea Party and Other Plays.* London: Methuen, 1967; *The Lover, Tea Party, The Basement.* New York: Grove, 1967.

Betrayal. Staged London, 1978; New York, 1980. London: Eyre Methuen, 1978; New York: Grove, 1979.

The Birthday Party. Staged Cambridge and London, 1958; New York, 1967. London: Encore, 1959; Methuen, 1960; *The Birthday Party and The Room.* New York: Grove, 1961. Educational text, edited by Margaret Rose. London and Boston: Faber and Faber, 1993.

The Black and White. Staged London, 1959. In *One to Another*, by John Mortimer, N. F. Simpson, Pinter. London: Samuel French, 1960.

The Caretaker. Staged London, 1960; New York, 1961. London: Methuen, 1960; *The Caretaker and The Dumb Waiter.* New York: Grove, 1961.

Educational text, edited by Margaret Rose. London
and Boston: Faber and Faber, 1993.

Celebration. Staged (with *The Room*) London, 2000.
London: Faber and Faber, 2000; New York: Grove,
2000.

The Collection. Televised London, 1961; staged London
and New York, 1962. London: Samuel French,
1962; in *Three Plays: A Slight Ache, The
Collection, The Dwarfs.* New York: Grove, 1962.

The Collection, The Dwarfs. New York: Grove, 1962; *A
Slight Ache and Other Plays.* London: Methuen,
1964.

Dialogue for Three, *Stand* (Newcastle upon Tyne) 6, no. 3,
1963.

The Dumb Waiter. Staged Frankfurt-am-Main, 1959;
London (with *The Room*), 1960; New York (with
The Collection), 1962. In *The Birthday Party and
Other Plays.* London: Methuen, 1960; *The
Caretaker and The Dumb Waiter.* New York:
Grove, 1961.

The Dwarfs. Broadcast London, 1960; staged (with *The
Lover*) London, 1963; Boston, 1967. In *Three
Plays: A Slight Ache, and Other Plays, 1962.*

The Dwarfs and Eight Revue Sketches (includes *Trouble in
the Works, The Black and White, Request Stop, Last
to Go, Applicant, Interview, That's All, That's Your
Trouble.* New York: Dramatists Play Service, 1965.

Family Voices. Broadcast and staged in Cambridge, Mass.,
and London, 1981. London: Next Editions, 1981;
New York: Grove, 1981.

The Homecoming. Staged Cardiff, 1965; London, 1967; New York, 1967. London: Methuen, 1965; New York: Grove, 1966. Sound recording, Caedmon (original production).

The Hothouse. Staged London, 1980; Providence, Rhode Island, 1982. New York: Grove, 1980; London: Eyre Methuen, 1980.

A Kind of Alaska. Staged with *Victoria Station* and *Family Voices*, London, 1982; New York, 1984. In *Other Voices* (with *Family Voices* and *Victoria Station*), London: Methuen, 1982; New York: Grove, 1983.

Landscape. Broadcast London, 1968; staged (with *Silence*) London, 1969; New York, 1970. London: Pendragon Press, 1968; in *Landscape and Silence.* New York: Grove, 1970.

Last to Go. Staged London, 1959. In *A Slight Ache and Other Plays*, Methuen, 1961; New York: Dramatists Play Service, 1965.

The Lover. Televised London, 1963; staged (with *The Dwarfs*) London, 1963; New York, 1964. In *The Collection and The Lover.* London: Methuen, 1963; *The Lover, Tea Party, The Basement.* New York: Grove, 1967.

Moonlight. Staged London 1993; New York, 1995. Boston and London: Faber and Faber, 1993; New York, Grove, 1994.

Monologue. Televised London, 1973. London: Covent Garden Press, 1973.

Mountain Language. Televised and staged London, 1988; New York, 1989. In *Times Literary Supplement*

7-13, October 1988, pp. 1110-11; London and Boston: Faber and Faber, 1988.

The New World Order. Staged with Ariel Dorfman's *Death of the Maiden*, London, 1991. London and Boston: Faber and Faber, 1993.

Night, in *Mixed Doubles.* Staged London, 1969. In *Silence and Landscape.* London: Methuen, 1969; New York: Grove, 1970.

A Night Out. Broadcast London, 1960; staged London, 1961; New York, 1971. London: Samuel French, 1961; New York: Grove, 1968.

Night School. Televised 1960. Included in *Tea Party and Other Plays.* London: Methuen, 1967; New York: Grove, 1968.

No Man's Land. Staged London, 1975; New York, 1976. London: Eyre Methuen and New York: Grove, 1975.

Old Times. Staged London and New York, 1971. London: Methuen, 1971; New York: Grove, 1971.

One for the Road. Televised London, 1985. London: Methuen, 1984; New York: Dramatists Play Service, 1984.

Other Places [*A Kind of Alaska, Victoria Station, Family Voices*]. Staged London, 1982. London: Methuen, 1982; New York: Grove, 1983. Revised version (substituting *One for the Road* for *Family Voices*), staged London and New York, 1984.

Party Time. Staged Columbus, Ohio, 1991; with *Mountain Language*, directed by Harold Pinter, London, 1991; London and Boston: Faber and Faber, 1991; *Party*

Time and The New World Order: Two Plays by Harold Pinter, New York: Grove, 1993.

Precisely. Staged London, 1983. *Harper's*, May 1985, 37.

Request Stop, Last to Go, Special Offer, Getting Acquainted, in *Pieces of Eight* (review). Staged London, 1959. In *Complete Works*. New York: Grove, 1977-1981.

The Room. Staged Bristol, 1957; London (with *The Dumb Waiter*), 1960; New York (with *A Slight Ache*), 1964. In *The Birthday Party and Other Plays*. London: Methuen, 1960; *The Birthday Party and The Room*. New York: Grove, 1961.

Silence. Staged (with *Landscape*) London, 1969; New York, 1970. In *Landscape and Silence*. London: Methuen, 1969; New York: Grove, 1970.

Sketches, in *"One to Another."* Staged London, 1959. London: French: 1960.

A Slight Ache. Broadcast London, 1959; staged, 1961; New York (with *The Room*), 1964. In *A Slight Ache and Other Plays*. London: Methuen, 1961; *Three Plays: A Slight Ache, The Collection, The Dwarfs*. New York: Grove, 1962.

Tea Party. Televised London, 1965: staged (with *The Basement*) New York, 1968; London, 1970. London: Methuen, 1965; New York: Grove, 1966.

Trouble in the Works. Staged London, 1959. In *A Slight Ache and Other Plays*. London: Methuen, 1961; New York: Dramatists Play Service, 1965.

II.   OTHER WORKS

Collected Poems and Prose. London: Faber and Faber, 1991; New York: Grove, 1996.

Collected Screenplays 1-3. London: Faber and Faber, 2000.

Complete Works 1-4. New York: Grove, 1977-1981; *Plays 1-4.* London: Methuen, 1977-81, rev. 1998.

The Comfort of Strangers and Other Screenplays. London and Boston: Faber and Faber, 1990 (includes *Reunion, Turtle Diary,* and *Victory*).

The Dwarfs: A Novel. New York: Grove Weidenfeld, 1990; London: Faber and Faber, 1990.

Five Screenplays. London: Methuen, 1971; New York: Grove, 1973 (Includes *Accident, The Go-Between, The Pumpkin Eater, The Quiller Memorandum,* and *The Servant.*)

The French Lieutenant's Woman: A Screenplay. London: Cape, 1981; Boston: Little, Brown, 1981; *The French Lieutenant's Woman and Other Screenplays.* London: Methuen, 1982 (Includes *Langrishe, Go Down* and *The Last Tycoon.*)

Girls [short story]. *Granta* 51 (autumn 1995): 25-55.

The Handmaid's Tale: A Screenplay. Video and film: Conecom Entertainment Group, 1990.

The Heat of the Day. London and Boston: Faber and Faber, 1989.

I Know the Place: Poems. Warwick: Grenville Press, 1979.

Jimmy. London: Pendragon Press, 1984.

Mac. London: Pendragon Press, 1968.

New Poems 1967: A PEN Anthology. Edited with John Fuller and Peter Redgrove. London: Hutchinson, 1968.

Ninety Poems in Translation: An Anthology. Edited with Anthony Astbury and Geoffrey Godbert. London: Faber and Faber, 1994; New York: Grove/Atlantic, 1994.

100 Poems by 100 Poets. Edited with Geoffrey Godbert and Anthony Astbury. London: Methuen, 1986; New York: Grove, 1987.

Party Time: A Screenplay. London and Boston: Faber and Faber, 1991.

Poems. London: Enitharmon, 1968.

Poems and Prose 1949-1977. New York: Grove, 1978; London: Eyre Methuen, 1978.

The Proust Screenplay: à la recherche du temps perdu. Broadcast by BBC, 1995. New York: Grove, 1978; London: Eyre Methuen/Chatto & Windus, 1978.

Rememberance of Things Past. By Pinter and Di Trevis, based on Pinter's screenplay. London: Faber and Faber, 2000.

Selections. Collected Poems and Prose. New York: Grove, 1996.

Ten Early Poems. Warwick, Eng.: Grenville Press, 1992. *The Trial: Adapted from a Novel by Franz Kafka.* London and Boston: Faber and Faber, 1993.

Various Voices: Prose, Poetry, Politics. London: Faber and
    Faber; New York: Grove, 1998.

Interviews, Biographical Articles, and Public Statements*

"Mr. Harold Pinter--Avant Garde Playwright," *The Times*,
    16 November, 1959, 4.

"Pinter's Reply to Open Letter by Leonard Russell,"
    Sunday Times, 14 August 1960, 21.

Harry Thompson. "Harold Pinter Replies," *New Theatre
    Magazine* 11 (January 1961): 8-10.

"*Caretaker*'s Caretaker," *Time*, 10 November 1961, 76.

"Writing for Myself," *Twentieth Century*, 168 (February
    1961): 172-175.

"People Are Talking About . . . ," *Vogue*, 139 (15 January
    1962): 38-49.

"Pinter Between the Lines," *Sunday Times*, 4 March 1962,
    25.

"Pinterview," *Newsweek*, 23 July 1962, 69.

Kenneth Cavander. "Filming *The Caretaker*: Harold Pinter
    and Clive Donner," *Transatlantic Review* 13
    (summer 1963): 17-26.

"Writing for the Theatre," *Evergreen Review* 8 (August-
    September 1964): 80-82.

*Interviews and essays published in *The Pinter Review* are
listed at the end of the bibliography.

"Accident," *Sight and Sound*, August, 1966, 179-84.

Lawrence Bensky. "Harold Pinter: An Interview," *Paris Review* 10 (fall 1966): 13-37.

Alain Schifres. "Harold Pinter: Caretaker of Britain's New Theater," *Réalités* 193 (December 1966): n.p.

"Two People in a Room: Playwriting," *New Yorker*, 25 February 1967, 34-36.

"Probing Pinter's Plays," *Saturday Review*, 8 April 1967, 56, 58, 96.

William Packard. "An Interview with Harold Pinter," *First Stage* 6 (summer 1967): 82.

Charles Marowitz. "Harold Pinter," *New York Times*, 1 October 1967, II, 36-37, 89-90, 92, 94.

Kathleen Tynan. "In Search of Harold Pinter," *Evening Standard*, 25 April 1968, 7.

Judith Crist. "A Mystery: Pinter on Pinter," *Look*, 24 December 1968, 77-78.

"Harold Pinter Talks to Michael Dean," *Listener*, 6 March 1969, 312.

Joan Bakewell. "In an Empty Bandstand," *Listener*, 6 November 1969, 630-31.

Harold Hobson. "'I Am Not Concerned with Making General Statements,'" *Christian Science Monitor*, 16 March 1971.

"Speech: Hamburg 1970," *Theatre Quarterly* 1 (July-Sept. 1971): 3-4.

Mel Gussow. "A Conversation [Pause] with Harold Pinter," *New York Times*, 5 December 1971, 42-43, 126-29, 131-36.

"Public and Private: Notes by Harold Pinter," *Manitoba Theatre Centre Newsletter*, 1 January 1972, 1-2.

"Master of Silence," *Observer*, 27 April 1975, 11.

Jack Kroll. "The Puzzle of Pinter," *Newsweek*, 29 November 1976, 75-78, 81.

Sidney Edwards. "To Hell and Back with Pinter," *Evening Standard*, 18 May 1979, 28-29.

Mel Gussow. "I Started with two People in a Pub," *New York Times*, 30 December 1979, II, 5, 7.

"A Rare Interview with Harold Pinter," *San Francisco Chronicle*, 2 January 1980, 48.

Mel Gussow. "London to Broadway: How a Culture Shapes a Show," *New York Times*, 3 February 1980, II, 1, 35.

Miriam Gross. "Pinter on Pinter," *Observer*, 5 October 1980, 25, 27.

"A Letter to Peter Wood (1958)," *Drama* 142 (winter 1981): 4-5.

Howard Kissell. "The Man in the Ironic Mask," *Women's Wear Daily*, 23 February 1983, 40.

"A Play and its Politics: A Conversation between Harold Pinter and Nicholas Hern." In *One for the Road*. London: Methuen, 1986, 5-24.

Stephen Farber. "Topical Relevance," *New York Times*, 10 May 1987, II, 25.

"Togetherness," *New York Times*, 22 January 1988, C6.

"Growth of an Angry Playwright," *Observer*, 16 October 1988, 13.

"Radical Departures, Harold Pinter and Anna Ford," *Listener*, 27 October 1988, 4-6.

"Reunion: Harold Pinter Visually Speaking," *Film Comment* 25 (May-June 1989): 20-22.

Mel Gussow. "Pinter's Plays Following Him Out of Enigma and into Politics," *New York Times*, 6 December 1988, C17, 22.

Lawrence Van Gelder. "Pinteresque Pinter," *New York Times*, 28 July 1989, B4.

Lois Gordon. "Harold Pinter in New York" (an interview with Mel Gussow, following Pinter's reading of *One for the Road* and an extract from *The Hothouse*), *The Pinter Review: Annual Essays 1989:* 48-52.

Stephen Schiff. "Pinter's Passions," *Vanity Fair* (September 1990): 219-22, 300-303.

Polly Toynbee. "The Master of Strident Silences," *Guardian Weekly*, 14 October 1990, 24.

Alan Frank. "After the Silence: The New Pinter: The Unmellowing of Harold Pinter, [London] *Times*, 19 October 1991, 4-6.

Barry Davis. "*The Jewish Quarterly* Interview: The 22 from Hackney to Chelsea: A Conversation with Harold Pinter." *Jewish Quarterly*. 38 (winter 1991-92): 9-17.

John Gross. "Genius Revived--Profile: Harold Pinter," *Sunday Telegraph*, 8 November 1992, 33.

Edward T. Jones. "Harold Pinter: A Conversation," *Literature/Film Quarterly* 21 (1993): 2-9.

Fintan O'Toole. "An Unflinching Gaze," *Irish Times*, 30 April 1994, Living Sec., 3.

John Casey. "The Master's Hand," *Daily Telegraph*, 7 January 1995, 158.

Harold Pinter. "A War on Words [speech at the University of Sofia when awarded honorary degree]," *Red Pepper* 12 (May 1995): 24-25.

Kate Saunders. "Pause for Thought," *Sunday Times*, 9 July 1995, Sec. 10: 4-5.

Harold Pinter. "Literature Matters [David Cohen prize acceptance speech]," *Newsletter of the British Council* (September 1995): 4-5.

Mel Gussow. "Humor and Mysticism: Pinter Improvises Pinter," *International Herald Tribune*, 17 October 1995.

Austin Quigley, "The Art of Drama," *Columbia University Record* 6 (December 1996): 27.

"Harold Pinter" in *Playwrights at Work*, ed. George Plimpton, New York: Modern Library, 2000 (*Paris Review* Interviews).

Recent Letters Authored by Pinter, by Pinter and Others

"The US Elephant Must Be Stopped," *Guardian*, 5 December 1987, 10.

"Yanquis Go Home! *Independent*, 27 May 1990, 10-11, 15.

"Bush's Comic Talent," *Independent*, 24 May 1991, 22.

"America's $17bn Debt to Nicaragua," *Independent*, 18 June 1991, 16.

[On Abbas Cheblak] *Independent*, 29 June 1991, 16.

"Mordecai Vanunu: More in Help Than Ever," *Independent*, 29 September 1991: 21.

"Why Harold Hates Christopher," *Independent* 4 July 1992, 8.

"Travel Ban on Mikhail Gorbachev Condemned as Abuse of Power," *Guardian*, 13 October 1992, 18.

"Reprisal Murders of Journalists in Turkey," *Independent*, 18 January 1993, 16.

"U.S. Should Admit Role in El Salvador," *Ottawa Citizen*, 29 March 1993, A11.

"Turkish Responsibility for Kurdish Fears. . . ," *Independent*, 28 April 1993, 21.

"How the Law Lies in Russia," *Guardian*, 12 October 1993, 91.

[On *Schindler's List* and U.S. moral turpitude] *New York Review of Books*, 9 June 1994, 60.

"U.S. Troops' Ambiguous Role," *Guardian*, 17 September 1994, 21.

[On Vanunu] *Independent*, 30 September 1994, 18.

"Playwrights at the Palace," *Guardian*, 13 January 1995, 25.

"Vanunu and Israel's Secrets," *Sunday Telegraph*, 22 January 1995, 26.

"Europe Sells Its Soul for a Euro," *Observer*, 17 December 1995, 14.

"Hollow Reforms in Turkey," *Independent*, 1 January 1996, 10.

"First Person: Picking a Fight with Uncle Sam," *Guardian*, 4 December 1996, 4.

"Picking a Fight with the Bully of the West," *Mail and Guardian*, 16 December 1996.

[On the U.S. and Nicaragua] *Independent*, 18 June 1997, 18.

"A Cry from a People Too Long Ignored," *Sydney Morning Herald*, 23 February 1999.

"Playwright Harold Pinter Presents a Powerful Case in Opposition to NATO Bombardment of Serbia," *World Socialist Web Site*, 7 May 1999, wsws.org.

[In *Various Voices: Prose, Poetry, Politics 1948-1998*: "The US Elephant Must be Stopped"; "Eroding the Language of Freedom" (*Sanity*, March 1989); "Oh Superman," from *Opinion*, Channel 4, 31 May 1990); "Blowing Up the Media," *Index on Censorship*, May 1992; "The US and El Salvador," *Observer*, 28 March 1993; "Caribbean Cold War," *Red Pepper*, May 1996; "A Pinter Drama in Stoke Newington," *Guardian* 9 July 1996; "It Never Happened," *Guardian*, 4 December 1996; "Scenario for the Bugging of a Home," *The Times*, 8 January 1997; "An Open Letter to the Prime Minister," *Guardian*, 17 February 1998.]

Major Criticism

I. BIBLIOGRAPHY

Susan Hollis Merritt has prepared an exhaustive Harold Pinter Bibliography for the *Pinter Review*, since its inception in 1987.

Carpenter, Charles A. *Modern Drama: Scholarship and Criticism 1966-1980. International Bibliography.* Toronto: University of Toronto Press, 1986, 112-17.

Gale, Steven H. *Harold Pinter: An Annotated Bibliography.* Boston: G. K. Hall, 1978.

King, Kimball. *Twenty Modern British Playwrights: A Bibliography 1956 to 1976.* New York and London: Garland, 1977, 125-92.

Rüdiger, Imhof, ed. *Pinter: A Bibliography.* London and Los Angeles: TQ Publications Ltd., 1976.

Schroll, Herman T. *Harold Pinter: A Study of His Reputation (1958-1969) and a Checklist.* Metuchen, New Jersey: Scarecrow Press, 1971.

David S. Palmer. "A Harold Pinter Checklist," *Twentieth Century Literature* 16 (1970): 287-96.

Gordon, Lois G. "Pigeonholing Pinter: A Bibliography," *Theatre Documentation* I (fall 1968): 3-20.

II. BOOKS

Armstrong, Raymond. *Kafka and Pinter.* New York: St. Martin's, 1998.

Baker, William and Stephen Ely Tabachnick. *Harold Pinter*. Edinburgh: Oliver & Boyd, 1973.

Batty, Mark. *Harold Pinter.* Plymouth: England: Northcote House, 2000.

Billington, Michael. *The Life and Work of Harold Pinter.* London: Faber and Faber, 1996.

Burkman, Katherine H. *The Dramatic World of Harold Pinter: Its Basis in Ritual.* Columbus: Ohio State University Press, 1971.

———. *All in the Family.* New York: Grove, 1995.

Burton, Deirdre. *Dialogue and Discourse: A Sociolinguistic Approach to Modern Drama Dialogue and Naturally Occurring Conversation.* London: Routledge and Kegan Paul, 1980.

Cahn, Victor L. *Gender and Power in the Plays of Harold Pinter.* New York: St. Martin's, 1993.

Diamond, Elin. *Pinter's Comic Play.* Lewisburg: Bucknell University Press, 1985.

Dukore, Bernard. *Harold Pinter.* Basingstoke: Macmillan, 1988. 2nd ed.

Esslin, Martin. *Pinter: The Playwright.* London: Methuen, 2000 (revised edition of *The Peopled Wound*, 1970).

Gabbard, Lucina Paquet. *The Dream Structure of Harold Pinter's Plays: A Psychoanalytic Approach.* Rutherford, New Jersey: Fairleigh Dickinson University Press, 1976.

Gale, Steven H. *Butter's Going Up: A Critical Analysis of Harold Pinter's Work.* Durham: Duke University Press, 1977.

Gordon, Lois. *Stratagems to Uncover Nakedness: The Dramas of Harold Pinter.* Columbia, Missouri: University of Missouri Press, 1969.

Gussow, Mel. *Conversations with Pinter.* London: Nick Hern, 1994.

Hall, Ann C. *"A Kind of Alaska": Women in the Plays of O'Neill, Pinter, and Shepard.* Carbondale: Southern Illinois University Press, 1993.

Hinchliffe, Arnold P. *Harold Pinter.* Boston: Twayne, 1967. Rev. 1981.

Hollis, James R. *Harold Pinter: The Poetics of Silence.* Carbondale: Southern Illinois University Press, 1970.

Homan, Sidney, with S. Dugan, S. Langsner, and T. Pender. *Pinter's Odd Man Out: Staging and Filming "Old Times."* Lewisburg: Bucknell University Press, 1993.

Kahn, Victor L. *Gender and Power in the Plays of Harold Pinter.* New York: St. Martin's Press, 1995.

Klein, Joanne. *Making Pictures: The Pinter Screenplays.* Columbus: Ohio State University Press, 1985.

Knowles, Ronald. *"The Birthday Party" and "The Caretaker": Text and Performance.* London: Macmillan, 1988.

_____. *Understanding Pinter.* Columbia, S.C.: University of South Carolina Press, 1995.

Malkin, Jeanette. *Verbal Violence in Contemporary Drama: From Handke to Shepard.* New York: Cambridge University Press, 1992.

Mengel, Ewald. *Harold Pinters Dramen im Spiegel der Soziologischen Rollentheorie.* Frankfurt: Lang, 1978.

Merritt, Susan Hollis. *Pinter in Play.* Durham: Duke University Press, 1990.

Milman, Yoseph. *Opacity in the Writings of Robbe-Grillet, Pinter, and Zach.* Lewiston, N.Y.: E. Mellen Press, 1991.

Morrison, Kristin. *Canters and Chronicles.* Chicago: University of Chicago Press, 1983.

Naismith, Bill. *Harold Pinter: The Caretaker, The Birthday Party, The Homecoming.* London: Faber, 2000.

Orr, John. *Tragicomedy and Contemporary Culture.* Houndmills: Macmillan, 1991.

Page, Malcolm, compiler. *File on Pinter.* London: Methuen, 1993.

Peacock, D. Keith. *Harold Pinter and the New British Theatre.* Westport: Greenwood Press, 1997.

Prentice, Penelope. *Harold Pinter: Life, Work, and Criticism.* Fredericton, New Brunswick: York Press, 1991.

_____. *The Erotic Aesthetic.* New York: Garland Publishing, 1993.

Quigley, Austin E. *The Pinter Problem.* Princeton: Princeton University Press, 1975.

Regal, Martin. *Harold Pinter: A Question of Timing.* New York: St. Martin's, 1995.

Sakellaridou, Elizabeth. *Pinter's Female Portraits: A Study of Female Characters in the Plays of Harold Pinter.* Basingstoke: Macmillan, 1988.

Silverstone, Marc. *Harold Pinter and the Language of Cultural Power.* Lewisburg: Bucknell University Press, 1993.

Strunk, Volker. *Harold Pinter: Toward a Poetics of His Plays.* New York: Peter Lang, 1989.

Sykes, Altrene. *Harold Pinter.* New York: Humanities Press, 1970.

Taylor, John Russell, *Harold Pinter.* London: Longmans, Green, 1969. Rev. 1973.

Thompson, David T. *Pinter: The Player's Playwright.* New York: Schocken Books, 1985.

Trussler, Simon. *The Plays of Harold Pinter: An Assessment.* London, Gollancz, 1973.

Zarhy-Levo, Yael. *The Theatrical Critic as Cultural Agent: Constructing Pinter, Ortin and Stoppard as Absurdist Playwrights.* New York: Peter Lang, 2000.

III.   ARTICLES, ESSAYS, CHAPTERS

The *Pinter Review*, after its first two issues, became a collection of essays, and its contributors are listed below, under "Collections."

Adler, Thomas P. "From Flux to Fixity: Art and Death in Pinter's *No Man's Land*," *Arizona Quarterly* 35 (1979): 197-204.

———. "Notes toward the Archetypal Pinter Woman," *Theatre Journal* 33 (1981): 377-85.

Alexander, Nigel. "Past, Present and Pinter," *Essays and Studies* 27 (1974): 1-17.

Almond, Ian. "Absorbed into the Other: A Neoplatonic Reading of *The Birthday Party*," *Literature and Theology* 14 (2000): 174-88.

Back, Lillian. "The Double in Harold Pinter's *A Slight Ache*," *Michigan Academician* 15 (1983): 383-90.

Ben-Zvi, Linda. "Harold Pinter's *Betrayal*: The Patterns of Banality," *Modern Drama* 23 (1980): 227-37.

Berkowitz, Gerald M. "The Destruction of Identity in Pinter's Early Plays," *Ariel* 9 (1978): 83-92.

Bernhard, F. J. "Beyond Realism: The Plays of Harold Pinter," *Modern Drama* VIII (September 1954): 185-91.

Bogumil, Mary L. "Gamesplaying: Conventional and Narrative Games in Pinter's *The Birthday Party*." *Massachusetts Studies in English* 11 (summer 1992): 72-83.

Brater, Enoch. "Cinematic Fidelity and the Forms of Pinter's *Betrayal*," *Modern Drama* 24 (1981): 503-13.

Braunmiller, Albert R. "A World of Words in Pinter's *Old Times*," *Modern Language Quarterly* 40 (1979): 53-74.

———. "Harold Pinter: The Metamorphosis of Memory," in *Essays on Contemporary British Drama*, ed. Hedwig Boch and Albert Wertheim. Munich: Hueber, 1981, 155-70.

Brigg, Peter. "Old Times: Beyond Pinter's Naturalism, *English Studies in Canada* 1 (winter 1975): 466-74.

Brody, Alan. "The Gift of Realism: Hitchcock and Pinter," *Journal of Modern Literature* 3 (1973): 149-72.

Brown, John Russell. "Dialogue in Pinter and Others," *Critical Quarterly* VII (autumn 1965): 225-43.

_____. "Mr. Pinter's Shakespeare," *Critical Quarterly* V (autumn 1963): 251-65.

Burkman, Kathryn H. "And Who's Godot When He's At Home?" "Godot Arrives: *The Homecoming*," in *The Arrival of Godot: Ritual Patterns in Modern Drama*. Rutherford, N.J.: Fairleigh Dickinson University Press, 1986, 117-48.

_____. "Harold Pinter's *Betrayal*: Life before Death--And After," *Theatre Journal* 34 (December 1982): 505-18.

_____. "Hirst as Godot: Pinter in Beckett's Land," *Arizona Quarterly* 39 (spring 1983): 5-14.

Cardullo, Bert. "Comedy and Meaning in the Work of Harold Pinter," *Notes on Contemporary Literature* 16 (May 1986): 9-12.

Carpenter, Charles A. "'Victims of Duty'? The Critics, Absurdity, and *The Homecoming*," *Modern Drama* 25 (1982): 489-95.

Chesterman, Andrew. "The Need of Power or the Power of Need? An Analysis of Pinter's *Last to Go*," *English Language Studies* 74 (August 1993): 359-68.

Cleary, Michael. "Opposing Images in Pinter's 'Plays of Menace,'" *Theatre Annual* 35 (1980): 45-56.

Coe, Richard. "Logic, Paradox and Pinter's *Homecoming*," *Educational Theatre Journal* 27 (1975): 489-97.

Cohn, Ruby. "The Absurdly Absurd: Avatars of Godot," *Comparative Literature Studies* 2 (1965): 233-40.

———. "Phrasal Energies: Harold Pinter and David Mamet." *Anglo-American Interplay in Recent Drama* (Cambridge: Cambridge University Press, 1995): 58-93.

———. "Words Working Overtime: *Endgame* and *No Man's Land*," *Yearbook of English Studies* 9 (1979): 188-203.

Collins, R. G. "Pinter and the End of Endings," *Queen's Quarterly* 85 (spring 1978): 114-21.

Cooper, Marilyn. "Shared Knowledge and *Betrayal*," *Semiotica* 64 (1987): 99-117.

Coppa, Francesca. "Coming Out of the Room: Joe Orton's Epigrammatic Re/Vision of Harold Pinter's Menace," *Modern Drama* 40 (1997): 11-22.

Dodson, Mary Lynn. "*The French Lieutenant's Woman:* Pinter and Reisz's Adaptation of Fowles's Adaptation," *Literature/Film Quarterly* 26 (1998): 296-303.

Dawick, John. "'Punctuation' and Patterning in *The Homecoming*," *Modern Drama* 14 (1971): 37-46.

Deer, Harriet and Irving. "Pinter's *The Birthday Party*: The Film and the Play," *South Atlantic Bulletin* 45 (1980): 26-30.

Dobrez, L. A. C. "Pinter and the Problem of Verification," in *The Existential and Its Exits: Literary and Philosophical Perspectives in the Works of Beckett,*

Ionesco, Genet and Pinter. London: Athlone, 1986, 311-70.

Dodson, Mary-Lynn, "*The French Lieutenant's Woman:* Pinter and Reisz's Adaptation of Fowles's Adaptation," *Literature-Film Quarterly* 26 (1998): 296-303.

Dohmen, William F. "Approach and Avoidance: Pinter's Recent Antagonists," *South Atlantic Bulletin* 45 (1980): 33-42.

Dukore, Bernard F. "What's in a Name?: An Approach to *The Homecoming*," *Theatre Journal* 33 (1981): 173-81.

_____. "Pinter's Staged *Monologue*," *Theatre Journal* 32 (December 1980): 499-504.

_____. "Violent Families: A Whistle in the Dark and *The Homecoming*, *Twentieth-Century Literature* 35 (spring 1990): 23-32.

Dutton, Richard. "*The Birthday Party*," "*The Caretaker*," "*The Homecoming*," "*Old Times*," "*No Man's Land*," in *Modern Tragicomedy and the British Tradition*. Brighton: Harvester, 1986, 90-112, 125-34, 162-71, 196-208.

Fendt, Gene, "A Medieval Reading of Pinter's *Homecoming*," *Literature and Theology* 8 (1994): 47-63.

Fletcher, John. "Pinter and the Pinteresque," in *British and Irish Drama Since 1960*. New York: St. Martin's, 1993: 18-31.

Gale, Steven H. "Character and Motivation in Harold Pinter's *The Homecoming*," *Journal of Evolutionary Psychology* 8 (August 1987): 278-88.

————. "Nature Half Created, Half Perceived: Time and Reality in Harold Pinter's Later Plays," *Journal of Evolutionary Psychology* 5 (1984): 196-204.

————. "The Variable Nature of Reality: Harold Pinter's Plays in the 1970's," *Kansas Quarterly* 12 (fall 1980): 17-24.

Gaggi, Silvio. "Pinter's *Betrayal*: Problems of Language or Grand Metatheatre?" *Theatre Journal* 33 (1981): 504-16.

Gillan, Francis. "'Nowhere to Go': Society and the Individual and Harold Pinter's *The Hothouse*," *Twentieth Century Literature* 29 (spring 1983): 86-96.

Gordon, Lois. "*The Go-Between*--Hartley by Pinter," *Kansas Quarterly*, 4 (spring 1972): 81-92.

————. "Harold Pinter--Past and Present [*Silence* and *Landscape*]," *Kansas Quarterly* 3 (spring 1971): 89-99.

Gray, Simon. *An Unnatural Pursuit.* London: Faber & Faber, 1985, 29-34, 57-84, 147-55, 161-62.

Gregory, Stephen. "Ariel Dorfman and Harold Pinter: "Politics of the Periphery and Theater of the Metropolis," *Comparative Drama* 30 (1996); 325-45.

Gussow, Mel. "The Prime of Harold Pinter," *American Theatre* 11 (March 1994): 21.

Hall, Peter. "Directing Pinter," *Theater Quarterly* 4 (1974-75): 4-17.

Hammond, B. S. "Beckett and Pinter: Towards a Grammar of the Absurd," *Journal of Beckett Studies* 4 (1979): 35-42.

Hays, Peter L. and Stephanie Tucker. "No Sanctuary: Hemingway's 'The Killers' and Pinter's *The Birthday Party*," *Papers on Language and Literature* 21 (1985): 417-24.

Hinden, Michael. "To Verify a Proposition in *The Homecoming*," *Theatre Journal* 34 (1982): 27-39.

Hudgins, Christopher. "*The Basement*: Harold Pinter on BBC-TV," *Modern Drama* 28 (1985): 71-82.

_____. "Dance to a Cut-Throat Temper: Harold Pinter's Poetry as an Index to Intended Audience Response," *Comparative Drama* 12 (1978): 214-32.

_____. "*The Last Tycoon*: Elia Kazan's and Harold Pinter's Unsentimental Hollywood Romance," in *Hollywood on Stage: Playwrights Evaluate the Culture Industry*, ed. Kimball King. New York: Garland Publishing, 1997, 157-83.

Hurrell, Barbara. "The Menace of the Commonplace: Pinter and Magritte," *Centennial Review* 27 (spring 1983): 75-95.

Hyman, Joseph. "Pinter and Morality," *Virginia Quarterly Review* 68 (fall 1992): 140-52.

Hynes, Joseph. "Pinter and Morality." *Virginia Quarterly Review* 68 (1992): 740-52.

Imhof, Rüdiger. "Pinter's *Silence*: The Impossibility of Communication," *Modern Drama* 17 (1974): 449-60.

Innes, Christopher. "Harold Pinter: Power Plays and the Trap of Comedy," in *Modern British Drama, 1890-1990*. Cambridge: Cambridge University Press, 1992, 279-97.

Kennedy, Andrew. "Natural, Mannered, and Parodic Dialogue," *Yearbook of English Studies* 9 (1979): 28-54.

_____. "Pinter," in *Six Dramatists in Search of a Language: Shaw, Eliot, Beckett, Pinter, Osborne, Arden*. Cambridge: Cambridge University Press, 1975, 165-91.

King, Noel. "Pinter's Progress," *Modern Drama* 23 (1980): 246-57.

Kishi, Tetsuo, "They Don't Make Them Like That Any More: Intertextuality in *Old Times*, in *Reading Plays: Interpretation and Reception*, ed. Peter Holland. Cambridge: Cambridge University Press, 1991, 227-35,

Knowles, Ronald. "*The Caretaker* and the 'Point' of Laughter," *Journal of Beckett Studies* 5 (1979): 83-97.

_____. "'The Hothouse' and the Epiphany of Harold Pinter," *Journal of Beckett Studies* 10 (1985): 134-44.

_____. "*A Kind of Alaska:* Pinter and Pygmalion." *Classical and Modern Literature* 16 (1996): 231-40.

Kreps, Barbara. "Time and Harold Pinter's Possible Realities: Art as Life, and Vice Versa," *Modern Drama* 22 (March 1979): 47-60.

Lamont, Rosette. "Pinter's *The Homecoming*: The Contest of the Gods," *Far-Western Forum* 1 (1974): 47-73.

Lutterbie, John. "Subjects of Silence," *Theatre Journal* 40 (1988): 468-81.

Malkin, Heanette R. *Verbal Violence in Contemporary Drama: From Handke to Shepard.* New York: Cambridge: Cambridge University Press, 1992.

Matterson, Stephen. "A Life in Pictures: Harold Pinter's *The Last Tycoon,*" *Literature-Film-Quarterly* 27 (1991): 50-54.

Mayberry, Bob. "Still Life: Pinter's *Landscape* and *Silence,*" in *Theatre of Discord.* Rutherford, N.J.: Fairleigh Dickinson University Press, 1989, 52-68.

Melrose, Susan. "Theatre, Linguistics and Two Productions of *No Man's Land,*" *New Theatre Quarterly* 1 (1985): 213-24.

Mengel, Ewald. "Pinter's Politics of Violence," *Gramma* 2 (1994): 119-25.

Merritt, Susan Hollis. "Pinter's 'Semantic Uncertainty' and Critically 'Inescapable' Certainties,'" *Journal of Dramatic Theory and Criticism* 1 (fall 1986): 49-76.

Nightingale, Benedict. "Harold Pinter/Politics," in *Around the Absurd: Essays on Modern and Postmodern Drama.* ed. Enoch Brater and Ruby Cohn. Ann Arbor: University of Michigan Press, 1990, 129-154.

Norrington, Neal R. and William Baker. "Metalingual Humor in the Early Plays." *English Studies* 76 (1995): 253-63.

Orr, John. "Pinter and the English Tradition" and "Pinter: The Game of Shared Experience from Beckett to Shepard," in *Theory/Text/Performance*, ed. Enoch

Brater. Ann Arbor, Michigan: University of Michigan Press, 1991, 129-154.

Pearse, Howard. "Harold Pinter's 'The Black and White': Mimesis and Vision." *Contemporary Literature* 33 (1992): 688-711.

_____. *"The Doll's House* in Pinter's *Betrayal,"* Journal of *Comparative Literature* 17 (1996): 46-52.

Postlewait, Thomas. "Pinter's *The Homecoming*: Displacing and Repeating Ibsen," *Comparative Drama* 15 (fall 1981): 195-212.

Powlick, Leonard. "A Phenomenological Approach to Harold Pinter's *A Slight Ache*," *Quarterly Journal of Speech* 60 (1974): 25-32.

_____. "Temporality in Pinter's *The Dwarfs*," *Modern Drama* 20 (March 1977): 67-75.

Prentice, Penelope. "Love and Survival: The Quintessence of Harold Pinter's Plays," *Cithara* 27 (May 1988): 30-39.

_____. "Ruth: Pinter's *The Homecoming* Revisited," *Twentieth Century Literature* 26 (1980): 458-78.

Quigley, Austin E. *"Betrayal,"* in *The Modern Stage and Other Worlds*, New York: Methuen, 1985, 221-52.

_____. *"The Dumb Waiter*: Undermining the Tacit Dimension," *Modern Drama* 21 (1978): 1-11.

Rabey, David Ian. "Violation and Implication," in *Violence in Drama.* Cambridge: Cambridge University Press, 1991.

Rayner, A. "Harold Pinter: Narrative and Presence," *Theatre Journal* 40 (December 1988): 482-97.

Rabillard, Sheila. "Destabilizing Plot, Displacing the Status of Narrative Local Order in the Plays of Pinter and Shepard," *Theatre Journal* 43 (1991): 41-58.

Richardson, Brian. "Pinter's *Landscape* and the Boundaries of Narrative," *Essays in Literature* 18 (spring 1991): 37-45.

Rose, Brian, "The City Beyond the Door: Effects of the Urban Milieu in Pinter's Early Plays," *Theatre Studies* 37 (1992): 57-65.

Roberts, Patrick. "Pinter: The Roots of the Relationship," in *The Psychology of Tragic Drama.* London: Routledge & K. Paul, 1975, 69-103.

Roland, Alan. "Pinter's *Homecoming*: Imagoes in Dramatic Action," *Psychoanalytic Review* 61 (1974): 415-28.

Rosador, Kurt T. "Pinter's Dramatic Method: *Kullus, The Examination, The Basement,*" *Modern Drama* 14 (1971): 195-205.

Rowe, M.W. "Pinter's Freudian Homecoming." *Essays in Criticism* 41 (July 1991): 189-207.

Sakellaridou, Elizabeth. "Audience Control, British Political Theatre and the Pinter Method," *Gramma* 2 (1994): 159-70.

_____. "Harold Pinter and the Gender of the Text," *Journal of Gender Studies* 2 (1993): 27-44.

Salem, Daniel. "The Impact of Pinter's Work," *Ariel* 17 (January 1986): 71-83.

Salmon, Eric. "Harold Pinter's Ear," *Modern Drama* 17 (1974): 367-75.

Salz, David Z. "Radical Mimesis: The Pinter Problem Revisited," *Comparative Drama* 26 (fall 1992): 218-36.

Savran, David. "The Gitardian Economy of Desire: *Old Times* Recaptured," *Theatre Journal* 34 (1982): 40-52.

Schechner, Richard. "Puzzling Pinter," *Tulane Drama Review* 11 (winter 1966): 176-84.

Silverstein, Marc. "One for the Road: *Mountain Language* and the Impasse of Politics," *Modern Drama* 34 (1991): 422-40.

Smith, Leslie. "Pinter the Player," *Modern Drama* 22 (1979): 349-63.

States, Bert O. "Pinter's *Homecoming*: The Shock of Nonrecognition," *Hudson Review* 21 (1968): 474-86.

Stamm, Rudolf. "*The Hothouse*: Harold Pinter's Tribute to Anger," *English Studies* 62 (1981): 290-98.

Tanner, Deborah. "Silence as Conflict Management in Fiction and Drama: Pinter's *Betrayal* and a Short Story 'Great Wits,'" in *Conflict Talk: Sociolinguistic Investigations of Arguments in Conversations*, ed. Allen D. Grimshaw. Cambridge: Cambridge University Press, 1990, 260-79.

———. "Ordinary Conversation and Literary Discourse: Coherence and the Poetics of Repetition," in *The Uses of Linguistics*. ed. Edward H. Bender. *Annals of the New York Academy of Sciences*. 1990, 15-32.

Van Laan, Thomas F. "*The Dumb Waiter*: Pinter's Play with the Audience," *Modern Drama*, 24 (1981): 494-502.

Warner, John M. "The Epistemological Quest in Pinter's *The Homecoming*," *Contemporary Literature* 2 (1970): 340-53.

Wells, Linda S. "A Discourse on Failed Love: Harold Pinter's *Betrayal*," *Modern Language Studies* 13 (winter 1983): 22-30.

Whitaker, Thomas R. "Playing Hell," *Yearbook of English Studies* 9 (1979): 167-87.

Woodroffe, Graham. "Taking Care of the 'Coloureds': The Political Metaphor of Harold Pinter's *The Caretaker*," *Theatre Journal* 40 (1988): 498-508.

Worth, Katharine. "Harold Pinter," in *Revolution in Modern English Drama*. London: G. Bell & Sons, 1972, 86-100.

Wright, D. G. "Joyce's Debt to Pinter," *Journal of Modern Literature* 14 (spring 1988): 517-26.

Zeifman, Hersh. "Ghost Trio: Pinter's *Family Voices*," *Modern Drama* 27 (1984): 486-93.

Zarhy-Levo, Yael. "The Riddling Map of Harold Pinter's *Ashes to Ashes*," *Journal of Theatre and Drama* 4 (1998): 133-46.

IV. COLLECTED ESSAYS, CASEBOOKS

Bloom, Harold, ed. *Harold Pinter*. New York: Chelsea House, 1987.

This is a series of reprinted essays by Bert O. States, Raymond Williams, John Russell Brown, Enoch Brater, James Eigo, Austin E. Quigley, Barbara Kreps, Guido Almansi, Martin Esslin, Elin Diamond, and Thomas F. Van Laan.

Bold, Alan, ed. *Harold Pinter: You Never Heard Such Silence*. Totowa, N.J.: Barnes and Noble, 1985.
   Bold includes "Directing Pinter," Peter Hall; "Harold Pinter--Innovator?" Randall Stevenson; "Harold Pinter as Screenwriter," Jennifer L. Randisi; "Pinter's Stagecraft: Meeting People is Wrong," Stanley Eveling; "What Have I Seen, the Scum or the Essence? 'Symbolic Fallout' in Pinter's *The Birthday Party*," Charles A. Carpenter; "Names and Naming in the Plays of Harold Pinter," Ronald Knowles; "Death and the Double in Three Plays by Harold Pinter," Katherine H. Burkman; "Harold Pinter's *Family Voices* and the Concept of Family," Steven Gale; and "Alaskan Perspectives," Bernard Dukore.

Burkman, Katherine H. and John L. Kundert-Gibbs, eds. *Pinter at Sixty*. Bloomington: Indiana University Press, 1993. [Papers presented at the Pinter Festival, 19-21 April, 1991, at Ohio State University]
   The volume includes "Pinter in Rehearsal: from *The Birthday Party* to *Mountain Language*," Carey Perloff; "Producing Pinter," Louis Marks; "Harold Pinter's Theatre of Cruelty," Martin Esslin; "Harold Pinter's *The Hothouse:* A Parable of the Holocaust," Rosette C. Lamont; "Disjuncture as Theatrical and Postmodern Practice in Griselda Gambaro's *The Camp* and Harold Pinter's *Mountain Language*," Jeanne Colleran; "The Outsider in Pinter and Havel," Susan Hollis Merritt; "The Betrayal of Facts: Pinter and Duras beyond

Adaptation," Judith Roof; "Image and Attention in Harold Pinter," Alice Rayner; "Pinter and the Ethos of Minimalism," Jon Erickson; "Chekhov, Beckett Pinter: The St[r]ain upon the Silence," Alice N. Benston; "That first last look . . . ," Martha Fehsenfeld; "A Rose by Any Other Name: Pinter and Shakespeare," Hersh Zeifman; "From Novel to Film: Harold Pinter's Adaptation of *The Trial*," Francis Gillen; "I am powerful . . . and I am only the lowest doorkeeper: Power Play in Kafka's *The Trial* and Pinter's *Victoria Station*," John L. Kundert-Gibbs; "Art Objects as Metaphors in the Filmscripts of Harold Pinter," Steven H. Gale; "Pinter and Bowen: The Heat of the Day," Phyllis R. Randall; "Portrait of Deborah: *A Kind of Alaska*," Moonyoung C. Ham; "Deborah's Homecoming in *A Kind of Alaska:* An Afterword," Katherine H. Burkman.

Eyre, Richard, ed. *Harold Pinter: A Celebration*. London: Faber and Faber, 2000.
   Untitled essays are by Edna O'Brien, Alan Bates, Ronald Harwood, Eileen Diss, David Hare, Douglas Hodge, Penelope Wilton, Patrick Marber, Janet Whitaker, Louis Marks, Simon Gray, John Pilger, Hilary Wainwright, Robert Winder, Lindsay Duncan, Ian McDiarmid and Jonathan Kent, Peggy Paterson, and Henry Wolf.

Gale, Steven H., ed. *Harold Pinter: Critical Approaches*. Rutherford, N.J.: Fairleigh Dickinson University Press, 1986.
   This contains "My, How We've Changed," Bernard F. Dukore; "'What the Hell is *That* All About?' A Peek at Pinter's Dramaturgy," Leonard Powlick; "Harold Pinter's *The Birthday Party*: Menace Reconsidered," Francis Gillen; "Harold Pinter's Work for Radio," Martin Esslin; "Tearing of

Souls: Harold Pinter's *A Slight Ache* on Radio and Stage," Albert Wertheim; "Toying with *The Dwarfs*: The Textual Problems with Pinter's 'Corrections,'" Scott Giantvalley; "Design and Discovery in Pinter's *The Lover*," Austin E. Quigley; "Intended Audience Response, *The Homecoming*, and the 'Ironic Mode of Identification,'" Christopher C. Hudgins; "Pinter's *Silence*: Experience without Character," A. R. Braunmuller; "Pinter/Proust/ Pinter," Thomas P. Adler; "*The French Lieutenant's Woman*: Screenplay and Adaptation," Enoch Brater; "After *No Man's Land*: A Progress Report," Arnold P. Hinchliffe; "*Family Voices* and the Voice of the Family in Pinter's Plays," Katherine H. Burkman; "The Pinter Surprise," Lucina Paquet Gabbard; "Time after Time: Pinter's Plays with Disjunctive Chronologies," William F. Dohmen; "The Uncertainty Principle and Pinter's Modern Drama," John Fuegi; and "A Chronological Index to Harold Pinter: An Annotated Biography, Steven H. Gale.

————. *Critical Essays on Harold Pinter.* Boston: G.K. Hall, 1990.

The reprinted essays are by Harold Hobson, Mel Gussow, John Barber, Miriam Gross, Elin Diamond, Alrene Sykes, Christopher C. Hudgins, Vera M. Jiji, Thomas P. Adler, Katherine H. Burkman, Hersh Zeifman, Francis Gillen, Elayne P. Feldstein, Foster Hirsch, Beverle Houston and Marsha Kinder, Stephanie Tucker, Ronald Knowles, David T. Thompson, Leslie Smith, Gay Gibson Cima, Katharine Worth, John Russell Taylor, Austin E. Quigley, and Martin Esslin; the bibliographic essay by Susan Hollis Merritt, "Major Critics, Strategies, and Trends in Pinter Criticism," is a new essay, as is Linda Ben-Zvi's "*Monologue:* The Play of Words" and Gale's "Deadly Mind Games: Harold Pinter's *Old Times.*"

Ganz, Arthur, ed. *Pinter: A Collection of Critical Essays.*
Englewood Cliffs: Prentice Hall, 1972.
Ganz includes excerpts and reprints of earlier
work by Lawrence Bensky, Martin Esslin, John
Lahr, Valerie Minogue, Ruby Cohn, James T.
Boulton, John Russell Taylor, John Pesta, R. F.
Storch, Bert O. States, and Ganz.

Lahr, John, ed. *A Casebook on Harold Pinter's The
Homecoming.* New York: Grove, 1971.
This includes interviews and essays: "A
Director's Approach," Peter Hall; "An Actor's
Approach," John Normington," "A Designer's
Approach," John Bury; "An Actor's Approach," Paul
Rogers; "The Homecoming: An Interpretation,"
Martin Esslin; "The Territorial Struggle," Irving
Wardle; "Pinter's Game of Happy Families," John
Russell Taylor; "Pinter's 'Family' and Blood
Knowledge," Steven M. L. Aronson; "Plotting
Pinter's Progress," Rolf Fjelde; "A Woman's Place,"
Bernard F. Dukore; "Why the Lady Does It,"
Augusta Walker, and "Pinter's Language" and
"Pinter the Spaceman," both by John Lahr.

Scott, Michael, ed. *Harold Pinter: The Birthday Party,
The Caretaker, The Homecoming: A Casebook.*
London: Macmillan, 1986.
Scott reprints essays and reviews published
between 1958 and 1982. This includes work by
Nigel Alexander, John Russell Brown, Ruby Cohn,
John Elsom, Andrew Kennedy, Charles Marowitz,
Austin E. Quigley, Martin Esslin, Clive Donner,
Peter Hall, Bernard F. Dukore, Ronald Knowles,
Simon Trussler, T. C. Worsley, Philip Hope-
Wallace.

See also *Modern Drama* 17 (December 1974), a Pinter
issue, which includes "Pinteresque," Frederick J.
Marker, ed.; "Harold Pinter's Ear," Eric Salmon;

"Game Playing in Three by Pinter," Lorraine Hall Burghardt; "Symbolic Fallout in Pinter's *Birthday Party*," Charles A. Carpenter; "Pinter as a Radio Dramatist," Mary Jane Miller; "*The Dwarfs:* A Study in Linguistic Dwarfism," Austin E. Quigley; "Mother and Whore: The Role of Woman in *The Homecoming*," Anita R. Osherow; "Pinter's Four-Dimensional House: *The Homecoming*," Vera J. Jiji; "Pinter's *Homecoming* on Celluloid," Enoch Brater; "Pinter's Silence: The Impossiblity of Communication," Rüdiger Imhof; "Pinter's *Night*": A Stroll Down Memory Lane," Thomas P. Adler; "Myth and Memory in *Old Times*," Alan Hughes; "All These Bits and Pieces: Fragmentation and Choice in Pinter's Plays," Francis Gillen.

Cycnos [Nice, France], 3 (1997), ed. Geneviève Chevallier, is another Pinter issue and it contains "Pinter (a dialogue)," David Z, Saltz; "*The Birthday Party:* its origins, reception, themes and relevance for today," John Somers; "Quine's Field Linguist and Pinter's Dialogue," Sheila Rabillard; "Revisiting the Game: One More Look at Structure in *The Caretaker*," Richard Hansen; *"The Caretaker:* Cain and Abel Replayed," Lois Gordon; "Exiles in *No Man's Land* and *The Caretaker:* A Comparison of Two of Pinter's Tramps," Kathleen M. McGeever; *Old times . . .* and older times," Elizabeth Gennarelli; "*Old Times:* Pinter's Meditation on *Sweeney Agonistes*," Natalie Crohn Schmitt; "*No Man's Land* as Dream Play," Prapassaree T. Kramer; "Pinter's game of betrayal," Hanna Scolnicov; "History as a Single Act: Pinter's *Ashes to Ashes*," Francis Gillen; "'You can only end once': Time in *Ashes to Ashes*," Martin S. Regal; "Pinter as Novelist, or, Cobbler, Stick to Thy Last," Toby Silverman Zinman; "'Opening Out': Harold Pinter's *The Caretaker* from Stage to Screen," Steven H. Gale; "Harold Pinter's *The Go-Between;* The Courage To

Be," Christopher C. Hudgins; "Peopling the Wound: Harold Pinter's Screenplay for Kafka's *The Trial*," Leslie Kane; "Whydunnit?: Pinter's revival of *Twelve Angry Men*," Steven T. Price.

The Pinter Review: vols. 1 (1987) and 2 (1988) became *The Pinter Review: Annual Essays* (1989-   ), ed. Francis Gillen and Steven H. Gale. See in each, Susan Hollis Merritt, "*Harold Pinter Bibliography*" and Ronald Knowles, "From London."

1987: "From *The Dwarfs*," Harold Pinter; "Introduction to Harold Pinter's Unpublished Novel, *The Dwarfs*," Francis Gillen; "The Temporality of Structure in Pinter's Plays," Austin E. Quigley; "The Multiple Levels of Action in Harold Pinter's *Victoria Station*," Katherine H. Burkman; "Pinter's Scenic Imagery," Katharine Worth; "Observations on Two Productions of Harold Pinter's *Old Times*, Steven H. Gale; "For Harold Pinter (Poem)," Alan Bold; "Recent Developments in Pinter Criticism," Susan Hollis Merritt.

1988: "From *The Dwarfs* (unpublished novel)," Harold Pinter; "From Chapter Ten of *The Dwarfs* to *Mountain Language:* The Continuity of Harold Pinter," Francis Gillen; "Staging the Ideology Behind the Power: Pinter's *One for the Road* and Beckett's *Catastrophe*," Judith Roof; "The Weasel Under the Cocktail Cabinet: Rite and Ritual in Pinter's Plays," Leslie Kane; "Pinter's *Turtle Diary: Text into Subtext*," Katherine H. Burkman; "The Medieval Roots of Pinter's *A Slight Ache:* The Matchseller as Fool," Kelly Bellanger; "The Beat Goes On: Sexual Politics in Harold Pinter's *The Lover*," Ann C. Hall.

1989: "Correcting the Space: Scenic Negotiations in *No Man's Land*," Stanton B. Garner, Jr.; "Ambiguity,

Identity, and the Violent Struggle for Dominance in *The Birthday Party*," Penelope Prentice; "Harold Pinter, Citizen," Ronald Knowles; "'I Decided She Was': Representation of Women in *The Homecoming*," Debra A. Sarbin.

1990: "Pinter: A Culture of Absence," Carlos Fuentes; "Harold Pinter's Film Version of The *Servant:* Adapting Robin Maugham's Novel for the Screen," Steven H. Gale; "Light and Shadow in *No Man's Land*," Ayako Kuwahara; "Time Passages," Leslie Kane; "Between Fluidity and Fixity: Harold Pinter's Novel *The Dwarfs*," Francis Gillen; "Melodramatic Problematics in Pinter's Film of *Betrayal*," Harriet A. Deer; "Antonia Fraser Presents 'No Man's Homecoming,' a newish play by Harold Pinter," Antonia Fraser.

1991: *The New World Order*, Harold Pinter; "The Embrace of Silence: Pinter, Miller and the Response to Power," Thomas Adler; "Pinter's Spy Movie," Bernard F. Dukore; "Voices in the Dark: The Disembodied Voice in Harold Pinter's *Mountain Language*," Ann C. Hall; "*Victory:* A Pinter Screenplay Based on the Conrad Novel," Christopher C. Hudgins; "An Italian Kind of Alaska," Margaret Rose; "American Football," Harold Pinter.

1992-93: "Keeping the Other in Its Place: Language and Difference in *The Room* and *The Birthday Party*," Marc Silverstein; "Two Kinds of Alaska: Pinter and Kopit Journey Through 'Another Realm,'" Norman J. Meyers; "*Old Times* and *Betrayal* as a Rorschach Test," Robert Conklin; "'. . . Whatever Light is Left in the Dark': Harold Pinter's *Moonlight*," Francis Gillen; "Harold Pinter's Death in Venice: *The Comfort of Strangers*," Katharine H. Burkman; "Cold Comfort: Harold Pinter's *The Comfort of Strangers*," Stephanie Tucker; "Nothing to Fight for: Repression of the Romance Plot in Harold Pinter's Screenplay of *The Handmaid's Tale*," Grace Epstein; Harold Pinter on *The Trial.*

1994:   Early Draft, *The Homecoming*, Harold Pinter; "The Pinter Archive: Description of the Archive in the British Library," Susan Hollis Merritt; "Echo[es] in *Moonlight*," Katharine H. Burkman; "Violence and Festivity in Harold Pinter's *The Birthday Party*, *One for the Road*, and *Party Time*," Robert Baker-White; "Comments on Harold Pinter's Adaptation of Franz Kafka's *The Trial*," Frederick R. Karl; "*The Trial*," Jeanne Connolly; "Pinter, Trevor, and Quiller 'in the Gap,'" Mark Auburn.

1995-96:   "Harold Pinter: A Speech of Thanks"; "Early Typed Draft, *The Homecoming*," Harold Pinter; "Spatialized Time in Harold Pinter's *Silence*," C. Clausius; "Pinter in Russia," Charles Evans; "Harold Pinter's *The Comfort of Strangers:* Fathers and Sons and Other Victims," Christopher C. Hudgins; "Pinter Playing Pinter: *The Hothouse*," Susan Hollis Merritt; "Notes on a Lecture-Workshop on Pinter's *Monologue*," Margaret Rose; "Charting Pinter's Itinerary: Literary Allusion in *A Kind of Alaska*," Lisa Tyler; "The Harold Pinter Archives II: A Description of the Filmscript Materials in the Archive in the British Library," Steven H. Gale and Christopher C. Hudgins; "Expanding upon Nothing: *A Slight Ache* and *King Lear*," Robert Cooperman.

1997-98:   "First Draft, *The Homecoming*," Harold Pinter; "Pinter at Work: An Introduction to the First Draft of *The Homecoming* and Its Relationship to the Completed Drama," Francis Gillen; "Looking for Mr. Goldberg: Spectacle and Speculation in Harold Pinter's *The Birthday Party*," Ann C. Hall; "'Voiceless Presence': Desire, Deceit and Harold

Pinter's *The Collection*," Christopher Wixon; "'Talking About Some Kind of Atrocity': *Ashes to Ashes* in Barcelona," Marc Silverstein; "Harold Pinter's *Ashes to Ashes:* Rebecca and Devlin as Albert Speer," Katherine H. Burkman; "From real to Real: Pinter and the Object of Desire in *Party Time* and *The Remains of the Day*," Linda Renton; "'My Dark House': Harold Pinter's Political Vision in His Screen Adaptation of Karen Blixen's 'The Dreaming Child,'" Francis Gillen.

1999-2000: "Pinter at School," Henry Grinberg; "Pinteresque," Margaret Atwood; "Body and Soul: Poetics and Politics in the Work of Harold Pinter," Donald Freed; "Harold Pinter and the Case of the Guilty Pen," Katherine H. Burkman; "Harold Pinter: from *Moonlight* to *Celebration*," Martin Esslin; "Harold Pinter's Achievement and Modern Drama," Kimball King, with the assistance of Marti Greene; "An Experience of Pinter: Address to the International Conference on Harold Pinter," Michael Billington; "A Comment on a Holograph Fragment Found Among the Drafts of *No Man's Land*: A Feminine Voice," Francis Gillen; "Holograph Draft Fragment: *No Man's Land*," Harold Pinter; "Vision and Desire in Harold Pinter's Unpublished Poem: 'August Becomes,'" Linda Renton; "*Celebration* in Performance: The Drama of Environment," Robert Gordon; "Harold Pinter's *Ashes to Ashes:* Political/Personal Echoes of the Holocaust," Susan Hollis Merritt; "Harold Pinter's Screenwriting: The Creative/Collaborative Process," Steven H. Gale; "An Interview with Harold Pinter," Elizabeth Sakellaridou; "Aristotle University of Thessaloniki. Degree Speech, April 18, 2000," Harold Pinter; "Harold Pinter and T.S. Eliot," Ronald Knowles; "Living in the Present: Pinter and O'Neill, Parallels and Affinities," Robert Combs; "Finding Pinter's Subtext: Directing *The*

Lover," Sidney Homan; "Political and Personal Worlds of Play: Women at Play Perform *Ashes to Ashes*," Robert Conklin; "Shaping Ambiguity: The Chemistry between Silence, Ghosting, and Framing Devices within a Production of Harold Pinter's *Ashes to Ashes*, Christy Stanlake; "Finding Themselves: The Mandrake Theatre Company's Production of Harold Pinter's *The Dwarfs*," Ann C. Hall; "Harold Pinter's *The Dwarfs* in London: A Playwright's Perspective," Penelope Prentice; "*No Man's Land* in Athens," Elizabeth Sakellaridou; Program of the International Pinter Conference, London, England.

INDEX

333